G. T. EMERY
GRONINGEN
19 JULI 1986

SAGE

SAGE

A Life of J. D. Bernal

Maurice Goldsmith

HUTCHINSON
London Melbourne Sydney Auckland Johannesburg

Hutchinson & Co. (Publishers) Ltd

An imprint of the Hutchinson Publishing Group

3 Fitzroy Square, London WIP 6JD

Hutchinson Group (Australia) Pty Ltd
30–32 Cremorne Street, Richmond South, Victoria 3121
PO Box 151, Broadway, New South Wales 2007

Hutchinson Group (NZ) Ltd
32–34 View Road, PO Box 40–086, Glenfield, Auckland 10

Hutchinson Group (SA) (Pty) Ltd
PO Box 337, Bergvlei 2012, South Africa

First published 1980
© Maurice Goldsmith 1980

Set in Monotype Baskerville

Printed in Great Britain by The Anchor Press Ltd
and bound by Wm Brendon & Son Ltd, both of Tiptree, Essex

ISBN 0 09 139550 X

To Anna and David

Here shall be all; what has been lived through
And that by which I live yet,
My aspirations and principles,
And what has been seen in reality.

PASTERNAK

Contents

Illustrations

In Moscow with Dorothy Hodgkin and A. V. Shubnikov

Physics department outing on the Thames about 1957. The
   group includes, from left: Anita Rimel, Herman Mendel,
   Wolfie Traub, Lisl Weissmann (Heller), Marianne
   Ehrenberg, E. Michaelis, W. Ehrenberg, Elena
   Scoloudi, Amina abdel Relim, Chi-shi Lang, A. D. Booth,
   K. Booth, Stan Ward, David Brett, J. W. Jeffrey,
   Laurie Miller, A. Prahani, Jock Bowles, Joc Franks,
   F. Ansbacher, Nina Clayton, Joan Ferguson, R. Furth,
   M. Rosemeyer, S. Lenli

The Bernal goniometer

Bernal left, Ms Dornberger looking at him, Isadore
   Fankuchen standing

July 1968, with Anita Rimel

Acknowledgements

I am grateful, in particular, to: Joseph Needham, Nora and Peter Wooster, Bill Pirie, Ned Warner, Jim Crowther, Reinet and John Fremlin, John Kendrew, Charles Goodeve, Max Perutz, Aaron Klug, Marcus Brumwell, Harry Carlisle, Stan Lenton, and Hugh Faulkner. And to Kevin Bernal for photographs.

I owe much to the late Earl Mountbatten of Burma and Lord Zuckerman for providing me with some special insights.

I am thankful, also, to Kay McLeod and to Gary Werskey for making available to me their unpublished PhD theses.

Before the order came to pull down the curtain on me, Anita Rimel, Eileen Bernal, Margot Heinemann, and Brenda Swann gave me their friendly warmth. I miss Anita: her withdrawal of personal friendship is still a cause of distress.

Above all, my thanks to Alan Mackay: without him I would have been lost.

The Author to Desmond Bernal

I began to prepare for this book some time in 1952, when I
narrowly avoided killing you. Now, almost thirty years later,
I am again involved in an attempt on your life.

In Paris in the early 50s, I was working at UNESCO, and you
came to have lunch with me and my wife. As we consumed
food and ideas, you asked suddenly, 'Is it half-past two yet?'
My wife said it was 'nearer half-three'. 'Oh, my goodness,'
you exclaimed, 'I should have been at Chatillon by three to
give a talk.'

I offered to take you, and as I accelerated up one of those
boulevards in the then speed-limitless Paris, a *deux-chevaux*
darted out from a side road. I said in near panic, 'We'll be
lucky if we miss that car. . . .' You replied, 'Well, if you put
on your brakes . . .' which I intended, 'and go into a skid . . .'
which I succeeded in doing, thus narrowly avoiding killing us
all. I believe that experience contributed to building up some
kind of attachment between us. However, I have always
looked back on that moment with horror.

And it is with horror and bewilderment that I view the
question of your biography. Puzzlingly, those to whom you
have entrusted your future have deep objections to my writing
about you. They seem to me to wish to perpetrate, and
perpetuate, a portrait of you as a hero of our time, a portrait
painted by them alone, in the socialist-realist style, before
which we must stand and suspend judgement. I am sure you
would have none of such nonsense. That way lies perpetual
death for you, and a spurious immortality for them. I tell
your story as I know it, and I do not seek to invent you,
endowing you with qualities you would repudiate.

I was told by Eileen, your wife, that you conceived of your

biography as in three main sections, each printed in different coloured paper, so that the reader might take up just the section he was interested in: white paper for science, yellow for the arts, and purple for the personal. I would have wished to be so detailed. If you feel I have failed, that I am too general in my approach, my excuse is that your 'death perpetuators' have laid such obstacles in my way as to ensure that some essential layers of documentation have been withheld from me. Their incredible behaviour included the despatch of a warning letter to individuals who they know I would need to speak to, denying me access to the Bernal papers stored in the main university library in Cambridge; and persuading C. P. Snow to urge me, at the very least, not to discuss your love life. Perhaps they fear that I may cause others different from them to sing about you.

Certainly, in blowing the dust off your shrine a decade after your death, I have assumed a great responsibility. The pages that follow are my justification. Another decade gone, I could not have written them.

I

Beginnings

. . . We declare ourselves subversives or conservatives
for reasons we carry in ourselves, often in very vague
terms. Before we choose, we are chosen, without
knowing it.

IGNAZIO SILONE[1]

What, the six-year-old Desmond Bernal asked himself, was the connection between the shadows of the bones he
saw outlined in his hand when he held it up in the strong
sunlight and the mysterious X-rays in the machine used to
examine his sister's knee in the hospital at Limerick? Geraldine
had begun to crawl, a needle entered her knee; a clumsy
attempt to extract it left half somewhere under the skin. The
new machine, said the doctor, should determine its where-
abouts, because it made rays which could see through human
flesh.

Desmond, his parents insisted, was too young to go with
them to the hospital, but from determined questioning he
learned later how a special kind of photograph had been taken
to reveal the shadow of the needle, which the doctor had then
been able to pull out. How did that remarkable machine
work? He would find out for himself.

In that year, 1907, in his home town of Nenagh, some 13
miles from Limerick, there was no electricity. Candles were
in general use. But Desmond was privileged. As he was a
voracious reader, his parents had agreed to allow him a
paraffin lamp when he read in bed – to ease the strain on his
eyes, and for safety. He decided he would use the lamp in an

experiment to determine whether the X-rays were 'some very, very, very strong kind of light',† which he imagined they must be.

He got all the whitest books he could find (because 'white' and 'light' must go together), and placed them around the paraffin lamp on a table so that only a small opening was left across which he could put his hand; the light should then shine through and show the bones, as the sunlight did. Unfortunately, he could not entice the angel of success; when he placed his hand against the opening the books came tumbling down, the lamp went crashing to the floor, and the oil spilled as the glass broke – but did not catch fire.

For a moment he was alone, amid the uncertainty. Then came his father, rushing up the stairs, and in his relief at finding the boy and the house unharmed gave him a most severe beating. Desmond forgave his father, but he was still left with the endless 'whys' and 'hows' which tormented him. The effect of the fearful hiding, too deep to be sounded then, remained with Desmond even when the passions of that moment were as faded as an old photograph: the hiding served not to kill, but to touch off a determination to know more about the X-rays, and science, and everything.*

Desmond was fascinated by what he was told was 'science', about which his parents knew nothing. It was clear that their first child had a call: no one had any doubts that he would grow up to be involved in scientific activity, to become a man of science. But no one could foresee that with this would be welded a passion for the use of reason in social behaviour. And that that combination of science and of reason would produce an originality of mind unique in his generation, embodied in a personality which could not be ignored.

Desmond Bernal was born on 10 May 1901 in the farm

---

† Here and in the following text this sign indicates quotations from Bernal's 'How I became a scientist', sent to Boris Polevoi, USSR, in 1954 for inclusion in a series entitled *Real Men of the Western World*.

* I am reminded that vivid memories are linked with sharp moments of pain or pleasure. When Benvenuto Cellini was about five years old, his father saw a little creature like a lizard in the midst of the fire. He called him to look at it, and gave him a great box on the ears, which made him cry bitterly, to make sure he would remember that 'the lizard' he had seen was a salamander.[2]

called Brook Watson (in which the Bernal family lives still) in Nenagh, a market town in Co. Tipperary, 96 miles south-west of Dublin by train, almost at the centre of Ireland. His birth increased the population of the town to 4705. He was the first child of Samuel George Bernal, described variously as 'a land agent' and 'a farmer', and Elizabeth Miller, who had him christened John Desmond and brought up a Catholic.

The Bernal family came originally from Spain. They were of Sephardic Jewish origin, and settled down as small farmers in Ireland in 1644, during an uneasy period of local truce before Cromwell's invasion of 1649. A story, which has not been authenticated, is that a Bernal – not necessarily a relative, for Bernal is a common name – was ship's doctor to Columbus in the historic voyage across the Atlantic.

Samuel Bernal was a Catholic; Elizabeth Miller was an American, brought up as a Protestant, who converted to Catholicism. She had met the young Samuel in California where he had been living with some cousins during a five-year stay in the USA, following a period of two or three years of sheepfarming in Australia. She was one of the first graduates of Stanford University, had a feel for languages (she spoke four), and had turned to journalism. As an American she was horrified at the class-ridden nature of Irish society, at the general poverty and backwardness of the mass of the people. The fragility of poverty and the fatality of privilege were made much sharper by added distinctions of nationality and religion.

The rulers of the country were the ascendancy or gentry, who owned most of the land and dominated all forms of government: as officers in the army and police, as magistrates and judges in interpreting the law, as controllers of all higher education. They were the settled English, whose families had lived in the country for centuries, but who had kept themselves to themselves, feudal overlords loyal to the English Crown. They knew themselves to be the conquerors, the descendants of the Normans, the Elizabethans, the Cromwellians, the Orangemen who imposed English rule and put down rebellions with great ruthlessness. These rulers were Protestants: those whom they ruled were Catholics. The Catholics were the people, the original Irish, driven from their land and turned into tenants and workers. For them their religion was their last badge of independence, their inheritance, their right to manhood and to survival. In Ireland, you were either a Protestant or a Catholic. A common Bernal family story was of an official who, on finding a person had completed a form by describing his religion as 'atheist', demanded to know whether he was 'a Catholic atheist' or 'a Protestant atheist'.

The sensitive young boy could not take the divisions for granted, and his family did not really belong to either side politically. There was a confusion of neutrality to which he found it impossible to be reconciled. What he was taught and what existed seemed to have no relation to each other. In Church, he heard that all men were brothers, that there was the same divine law for the rich as for the poor. But he observed how the gentry lived well, spending their time largely 'on the pleasures of the field, on hunting, fishing, and shooting'. By contrast, the people 'were held down to one long round of work'.† The worker on the land existed only whilst he was working, and went to Heaven without glory. 'The gentry occupied the great eighteenth-century mansions, often with a hundred rooms, with magnificent staircases and halls, while around them were the thatched huts with earthen floors in which the people were still living, eating potatoes and poor American bacon.'†

All this the boy saw, and he asked questions. 'I was told by priests and nuns that these differences were decreed by God, and they were something to be accepted. The poor had to be with us always to encourage charity.'† But he came to know that was not the only doctrine. There were many around who were setting fire to life. There had been riots in April 1900 when Queen Victoria, as part of her diamond jubilee celebrations, made a ceremonial visit to Ireland. Excitement was swelling again in the centuries-old struggle for Irish independence.

In Nenagh, the four most imposing buildings were the law court, the gaol, and the military and police barracks. The young boy would often linger at the old gaol, now occupied by the nuns. He would look up at the statue of the Virgin which stood over the porch. It marked the spot where two innocent men were hanged many years gone in the last public hanging in the town. 'The story was that ruin came to every member of the jury, who had been stupefied by drink into condemning the innocent men: some went mad, some died in drink and poverty, some of horrible diseases. When the authorities put up a lamp outside the gaol at the place of the hanging, it went out and always did. But since the nuns came the lamp has begun to burn bright, that is the spirits of the dead are gone.'[3]

Desmond was bright. A gifted child, he chose his own entertainment, began to read very early, and had an outstanding memory. He was greatly attached to his mother and remained so until her death at eighty. She was a lively intelligent person, who read widely and in depth. She was not devoted exclusively to the welfare of her children – Desmond had a brother and two sisters* – but had outside interests. At the age of eight, he was sent to the local Protestant school, where he learned to intone:

> I thank the goodness and the grace
> That on my birth have smiled,
> And made me on these Christian days
> A happy English child.

This sentiment was taught also in the Catholic schools, many of which were in great disrepair. Robert Lynd had described how at that time in schools in Tipperary 'holes had been worn in the floors by the drip of rain through corresponding holes in the roof, and where the ivy had pushed its way through numberless cracks, and was climbing in ease and disease over the walls and ceilings'.[4] Desmond came to understand the role of the National schools in seeking 'to make children forget there was any such country as Ireland'.‡

As a schoolboy, it appeared to Desmond that the injustices

* Brother, Kevin O'Carroll Diaz, born 22 January 1903; sisters, Catherine Elizabeth Geraldine, born 26 March 1906, and Fiona Letitia Evangeline, born 16 January 1908.

‡ Here and in the following text, this sign indicates quotations from Elga Kern (ed.) *Wegweiser in der Zeitwendaer*, Munchen/Basel, 1955, to which Bernal contributed an autobiographical essay, 'Verantwortung und Verpflichtung der Wissenschaft'.

were mainly political and national, and 'that all the troubles would be ended if only the English could be driven out'.‡ Yet, he mixed with those English, who 'in many ways were as Irish as anyone could be. They had assimilated the attitudes of the Irish – a most kindly, generous, open-hearted people. They enjoyed talking to the real Irish, though marriage between them was almost unthinkable. In fact, as long as everybody knew their place, they had the warmest feelings towards them.

'It was not, I sensed even as a small child, the individuals who were responsible for the injustices and the struggle, it lay deeper in the whole system of society. It was that same system that those who gained by it said was natural and just, and those who had the harder time of it said must be destroyed.

'I interpreted it as a boy in terms of history. Before I even read the history of Ireland I had seen it written in the country itself – written in the simplest language, the language of ruins and legends. The country is full of ruins, as no one bothered to clear them away. They were the ruins of the ancient Irish, of the graves, halls, and the forts of the clans even before the arrival of Christianity. There were ruins of castles, abbeys, and churches. And, most of all, because they were newer and more widespread, there were ruins of houses, cabins of the small people who had been evicted by the landlords in the famine of sixty years before, when more than half the country had died or emigrated. And all these ruins, old and new, had accumulated legends of battles and executions of a people who had suffered but never forgotten their wrongs, legends not written but preserved in story and song, preserved in the very names of the people who still lived where their ancestors did a thousand years before.' ‡

That was the past, which spoke in silence. And in the present there spoke social and political activities aimed at the restoration of bygone beauties in the green spring of a golden future. With this was linked throughout his childhood 'another strain turned towards the future – to science and machinery'.

Ireland was untouched by the industrial revolution. Those industries that had come into existence found development very difficult. Between the censuses of 1881 and 1901, the principal industries in manufacturing had decreased by 17

per cent (and the population by only 13·8 per cent). In the
flax and linen industry, the number of persons employed
decreased in those twenty years from 92,650 to 75,100; in the
leather trades, from 30,766 to 19,891.[5]

The new machines filled the young boy with wonder. He
felt that where they lived, everything men touched would
grow. In later years he recalled the excitement of seeing a
motorcar for the first time. The whole family was called out to
watch a procession of cars racing through the streets of his
little town. He remembered, also, the thrill of being taken to
Limerick, and pressing the switch that put on the electric light.

'I realized that something was moving in the world, something that depended on a special knowledge of things, on
science – and it seemed to me, even before I was ten years old,
that these two things, the relief of the sufferings of the country
and the possibilities of science, could in some sense be united.
Science had offered the means, perhaps the only means, by
which the people of Ireland could liberate themselves. I saw
it narrowly in a purely nationalist sense, but it led me to an
interest in science which grew to be a dominating interest in
my life.'‡

But science was never to be for him solely 'a pure interest'.‡
Perhaps, he would suggest, it never was for anybody. Of course,
he liked science for its own sake – to know all about the different animals, plants, birds, and fishes he found around him;
about the rocks and other natural forms; about chemistry and
electricity. 'They were all exciting and interesting things, but
they – and even the abstractions of mathematics to which I
became devoted – seemed to me to be skills I learned for a
purpose. This was to help the people, and to deliver them
from oppressions, miseries, and ignorance.'‡ There is something rather salvationist in the way he put this. But that belief
and purpose came very early in his life, and it never faded
even when it was illumined by wider perception.

He was about seven when he chanced upon some understanding of what 'science' might be. In a book at home he
found a reprint of a lecture given by a man of science named
Faraday, at a place called The Royal Institution. It was the
title of the lecture that excited him: 'The chemistry of the

candle'. He was very familiar with the candle, an object of everyday use. And even if he did not know any chemistry, he thought this was how he might find out. 'Well, I read through this lecture and it fascinated me: the shape of the candle flame, and the black part in the middle where there was the burnt gas – you could show that by putting out the candle, and you could see the smoke, and smell the kind of smoke it was that was in that space. But what excited me still more were all those strange words of "oxygen" and "hydrogen", things I had never heard of before. Not only that, it told you how to make them!' †

That was the exciting challenge he took up. But what to make first? He decided not to make oxygen, because the lecturer referred to retorts and other apparatus he had never seen and knew nothing about, and there were no illustrations in his copy of the lecture. He chose hydrogen because it seemed safer, and read it up: 'take some diluted sulphuric acid, and mix it in a Florence flask with granulated zinc'. † He did not know what these were, but he thought the local chemist might be of help. He copied down the words very carefully, and asked his mother to write a letter to the chemist asking for these things. 'My mother, who knew less science than I did, because she had not read Faraday on "The chemistry of the candle", obediently wrote it all down, and the chemist handed the stuff over to me, which, of course, if he had had any sense he would not have done, because what he gave me, in fact, was a small bottle of concentrated sulphuric acid (oil of vitriol), with which I could have done myself and the house very much damage.

'However, the word "diluted" saved me. I knew that this meant adding water. So I poured some water into the sulphuric acid. And then I got my first surprise. I thought there must be something in this science, because the most amazing thing happened: it suddenly became very hot and started to boil. It rather frightened me at first, but nothing else seemed to happen, and it cooled down, so I thought it was all right.' †

What of the Florence flask? He remembered that in a cupboard there was 'an old bottle which had been wrapped up in straw, and which had a label on it saying it contained wine, and that it had come from Florence. So I thought this was the nearest I could get to a Florence flask.'† (And that child was right, because the original of the flasks used by chemists was the wine bottle that the Florentines began to make long ago.)

Now for the experiment. His mother had a rule that there were to be no experiments in the house. 'So the only thing to do was to take it out, outside the back door, where there was an old stump of a tree. There I thought I could set up my Florence flask. By this time, with all the preparations, it was getting towards evening. It was winter time, and beginning to get dark. However, I thought I dare do the experiment, and, greatly frightened, I put the granulated zinc inside the Florence flask and then poured on the sulphuric acid – and nothing whatever happened! Absolutely nothing!'†

Desmond waited, but still nothing was happening. 'The zinc sat in the bottom of the flask, and the acid was above it. There was no action of any kind. I thought, "Well, this is after all what I should have expected. We have all kinds of stories in the reading book, some are fairy stories and some are jokes, and this must be one of the fairy stories or one of the jokes. There is nothing in it: I thought this science was a fake!" '†

He was bitterly disappointed. He went off to have his supper, and then decided to have a final look before going to bed. 'So I slipped out of the back door, and then, of course, I could not see it because by that time it was quite dark. But I knew roughly where it was, and I went somewhere near it, but still could not see it. Well, I thought, I must have a look at it, so I took a box of matches out of my pocket and lit a match. As I brought the match near it there was a most magnificent explosion, and everything went to blazes.'†

He was more frightened than hurt, because he received only a few little splashes of sulphuric acid on his right hand. 'But I was absolutely convinced of the truth of science.'†

His parents, following the dominant middle-class tradition, sent him at the age of ten to Stonyhurst College, a boarding school in Lancashire in England run by the Jesuits. 'There he founded, until it was stopped by sensible priests, a Society for Perpetual Adoration. He had been reading the life of St

Aloisius Gonzaga, the patron boy saint of the Jesuits. Having accepted that adoration was desirable, he followed St Aloisius, decided with characteristic wholehogging logic, that it must never stop: and, with characteristic power of leadership, he got his contemporaries in the dormitory out of bed one by one throughout the night for hourly spells, so that there was always a solitary praying figure. And, foreshadowing his life, he took more than his share himself.'[6]

But at Stonyhurst there was no science taught until the sixth form, so at thirteen he moved to Bedford School, a minor English public school, which he found extremely unpleasant. For almost five years, from 1914 to 1919, he felt himself in a foreign and hostile country with stupidities and cruelties he regarded as essential elements in any army-type – as he described it – English institution. Most of his fellow students bored him, although there was some consolation in that his younger brother Kevin was there at the same time.

With the outbreak of war, the universal profession had become that of soldiering. The younger masters began to disappear into military service, and the sixth form was made up of boys awaiting their call for service at the front. He was just too young to be called up, but he saw boys, some of them friends, going out to the trenches and not coming back. He longed for an end to the slaughter, and felt its purposelessness all the more because he could not identify with it as did his fellow students. It was not possible for him as an Irishman to give his support to a government that was still oppressing his own people. But he did not regard the enemies of England as the friends of Ireland.

On a visit home during the Easter 1916 holidays, he had his first experience of the physical destruction which was becoming normal twentieth-century behaviour, and which he was to see at first hand in different parts of the world throughout his life. He saw Dublin with some of its finest streets in flames after the rebellion of 1916. One night in the following year, he saw all around his home in Nenagh, leaping from the earth, flames of the big country houses that had been put to the devouring torch. And he came to see the destruction in the battle of liberation that led to the creation of the Irish Free

State, with the violence of death that accompanied ambushes, burnings, and shootings. The violence was not new to Nenagh which had spat blood so often in the past.

He found it difficult to take the flow of burning violence from every house, a shock in a world where a war to end all wars had left only ghosts waltzing in empty halls. But he sided with those in rebellion, and accepted their argument that without violence nothing good would come. He had seen that constitutional methods of liberation were not at all successful. He understood that violence, or the threat of it, showed that the people cared enough about liberty to die for it – and that was how they won an independence in the end.

Bedford School had a bias towards the classics, but he was repelled by Greek and Latin, and disgusted by the chauvinism of the History course. He found some consolation in English, and all the time he was learning as much science and mathematics as he could. These came easily to him, because he found them interesting in themselves, and because he had a purpose in learning them – to put them at the service of the people. Before he left Bedford, he had mastered the classical nineteenth-century ideas of physics, chemistry, and biology that were taught, and he had become a tolerable amateur astronomer.

He was influenced, too, by the major writers of the day, such as Bernard Shaw and H. G. Wells. Their impact was to be expressed most obviously in his first published work a decade later. Although Shaw wrote much about scientific topics that were not acceptable to the established men of science, Bernal did not place him among the cranks and mystics. He found in Shaw 'a natural, almost effortless grasp of the commonsense scepticism which is the lifeblood of scientific advance: a refusal to have pompous platitudes put over him in any form or backed by any authority: a determination to accept only what seems to him, simple, straightforward and fundamentally right'.[7]

He was excited by the early works of Wells, such as the volume of essays *Anticipations*, published in 1900, described by the author himself as a first attempt to forecast the human future, and providing 'new data of quite primary importance for rationalized social, political, and economic effort. I was writing the human prospectus,'[8] which is what all Bernal's writings were to be concerned with.

In his last year at Bedford, an advanced mathematics master introduced him to Einstein's first papers on general relativity. They were a revelation: the first hint that the science he had learned thus far was already being superseded. But the fuller knowledge of the great revolution that had occurred in science as he was growing up was not made clear until he went to Cambridge University in 1919, with a mathematical scholarship to Emmanuel College: there to find the formula which would transform his private aspirations into a whirlwind of truths to deal with the ills and toils of society.

2
Development

The which observ'd, a man may prophesy
With a near aim, of the main chance of things
As yet not come to life, which in their seeds
And weak beginnings lie intreasured

SHAKESPEARE[9]

Cambridge

As an undergraduate, Bernal enjoyed life at Cambridge. He was interested in everything, and in his capacious mind he could take hold of any field of learning and assimilate it speedily to produce a fresh and illuminating synthesis. He was to be seen regularly laden with books covering a great variety of subjects: Wells's *Outline of History* (which he thought quite interesting), Tawney's *Acquisitive Society* (which did not interest him much), Whitehead's *Science in the Modern World* (of which he was very critical), and oddities such as the history of church architecture in Romania in the sixth century. He was truly learned: he could plunge his mind through hundreds of years of human behaviour to provide the most imaginative links between yesterday and today, and he was a hypnotizing talker. 'He always talked as if he were in love, and that perhaps explains why women, even more than men, found his conversation and personality so irresistible.'[10] He came to be known as 'Sage', a nickname given to him by a girl working at Ogden's Bookshop at the corner of Bridge Street in about 1920. He recalled that he was embarrassed by this, but in time he came to accept it, although he would say, seemingly apologetically, 'I've been trying to live it down ever since.'[11]*

Life at the university immediately after the war had a sense of reality greater than it was to have for many years afterwards because of the hundreds of returning soldiers, grown men who brought with them a sense of their survival of death, and, for many, a savage expectancy of a better world to come. Although Bernal knew a great deal of science and mathematics,** he could not relate them to the social and economic forces that were causing great changes – in Europe, in particular. The meaning of the word 'socialism' had never been explained to him, and the Russian revolution had come only as news of inexplicable violence arising from political extremism.***

In the early 1920s Bernal was introduced to the works of Marx and Lenin by Allen Hutt, later a distinguished newspaper typographer and trade union historian, who became chief sub-editor of the Communist *Daily Worker* throughout its existence. Then he was to be seen reading such classics as *The Communist Manifesto*, Engels's *Origin of the Family*, Lenin's *Materialism and Empirio-Criticism*, and Marx's *Capital*. He became a dedicated Marxist as he came to understand Marxism's all-embracing freshness: here was 'the formula' he was seeking in which socialism and science were linked. Socialism could

* 'When I was a student I wanted to solve a great problem in biochemistry. One day I set out from Vienna, my home town, to find the Great Sage of Cambridge. . . . The Sage was Desmond Bernal. . . . We really did call him Sage, because he knew everything, and I became his disciple.'
    M. F. Perutz, *Scientific American*, December 1978, vol. 239, No. 6.
** G. H. Hardy, the distinguished mathematician, used to say that Bernal could have been a *real* mathematician, which from Hardy was high praise.[12]
*** Compare Christopher Isherwood a few years later – in 1924 – stating that in the year of 'Hitler's Munich *Putsch*, of Mussolini's final campaign against the democrats, of the first English Labour Government, of Lenin's death', the name of Hitler was hardly known to a dozen people in all Cambridge. 'Mussolini was enjoying a certain popularity . . . the Labour Government and all its works were, for ourselves, comprehended in the withering word "politics" and therefore automatically dismissed as boring and vile. As for Lenin, he was a vaguely exotic figure, labelled, along with Trotsky, in our hazy minds as an "anarchist", and therefore worthy of mild benevolence.'[13]
    And W. H. Auden remembered, 'We were far too insular and preoccupied with ourselves to know or care what was going on across the Channel. Revolution in Russia, inflation in Germany and Austria, Fascism in Italy, whatever fears or hopes they may have aroused in our elders, went unnoticed by us. Before 1930 I never opened a newspaper.'[14]

provide an alternative system to that which he had been brought up to believe was the natural order, and with it went a commitment to science as the key to human progress and survival. His socialism and his science could walk together to provide fruits for all, especially the obscure and underprivileged. He found that many who despised socialism also despised science. He was convinced that science, applied wisely, could benefit society. In place of the acquisitive society in which people took what they could, a co-operative society of common endeavour and sharing could be built.

And he became an atheist. He saw that religion in practice was more than a set of beliefs or a way of life: it was an organization grouped under churches which were firmly on the side of the existing order and always at the service of reaction.

When, inevitably, he broke with Catholicism he gave up Christianity completely. Disillusion overtook him in three stages. 'First of all I lost my faith in the Church as an organization, but this didn't trouble me because being man-made, clearly it could be fallible. Then I lost my faith in God as creator, but since I was a scientist, I accepted that too. Finally, I lost my faith in the Virgin, and that was a real deprivation. My family in Ireland, much concerned, sent a Jesuit to reason with me, and we talked through the whole night.' The friend to whom he was telling this asked, 'Did this shake your belief?' 'Not at all', was his answer, 'but six weeks later the priest himself left the Church.'[15]

Pirie, a life-long friend, has another story. Bernal told him that he left the Church finally because he found he had committed inadvertently a mortal sin: bicycling with friends to see Ely Cathedral on a Sunday on which he had not been to mass. Some, such as C. P. Snow, insist the essential traits of a Catholic upbringing remained always with him, recognizable to those who could see, in a turn of phrase ('all men are equal in the love of mankind') and a twist of the head, rather as the traits remain with the rabbinical Talmudist turned scientist/atheist.

Cambridge in the 1920's was not the radical centre it was to become a decade later. It was, with Oxford, 'essentially the place where the young man was on his own, tasted freedom, had to support himself morally by his own wings'.[16] Most undergraduates were products of the public school system; they sought to continue, and to impose, their adolescent uniformity of discipline. To such hearties ,'the Irish Catholic, atheist Marxist' Bernal was a symbol of that which had to be fought and destroyed. A group of young naval officers – benefiting from a post-war arrangement to attend a university – 'didn't approve of eccentric leaders of thought. They decided to break up his rooms and toss him into the pond. They – how many varied according to the teller, but the accepted number was five or six – duly loomed into his room, at the top of the staircase. They had noticed that he was undesirable; but they hadn't noticed that he was quick-witted, fearless, and physically tough. He demonstrated the first quality by switching off the lights; his adversaries were smoking cigarettes, so that he could see them and they couldn't see him. The second and third qualities came in when he plunged into the mêlée and got his arms around various necks, so that they were hitting out at each other, not at him. He duly slipped out of the room and returned with reinforcements from the college.'[17]*

There was intense discrimination against women. Cambridge, like Oxford, was a centre of male chauvinism, and of a degree of homosexuality. But Bernal was utterly hetero-sexual, but he was not . . . he was not a frequent user of 'The Flying Fornicator', as the 10.20 p.m. train from London's Liverpool Street Station to Cambridge (arriving before college gates were locked at midnight) was known. He liked women, and very many women were attracted by him. This was so throughout his life. He led a determined Bohemian life, through which he expressed his rejection of the rapacious and religious attitudes which he believed barred honest and natural relations between men and women.

Allied to this was his earnest search for a new world picture based on science and reason, which he saw expressed in the

* C. P. Snow adds that there was a pleasant coda: Bernal met some of the principal parties, twenty-two years later, in the wardroom of a cruiser off the French coast.

newly forming Soviet Union. His continuing interest in Communist politics was unusual for his generation of university
students. It was not until the early 1930s that contemporary
politics became the main subject of discussion. Until then it
was usually poetry.*

Bernal was introduced to socialism by Henry Douglas
Dickinson, whose father was curator at the Science Museum
in London and who revealed to him the significance of the
history of science. Through Henry Dickinson he became
familiar with the working-class movement. In 1918, the
Labour Party for the first time had fought an election as an
independent party with an independent policy. Although the
word 'socialism' did not appear in the Labour Party's new
constitution, one of the stated aims was 'to secure for the
producers by hand and by brain the full fruits of their industry
. . . the basis of the common ownership of the means of
production'. In that 1918 election Labour won 63 seats. In
the 1922 election that was increased to 142, and, in the
following year, when it won 191 seats, the first Labour (albeit
minority) government took office.

In 1923, Bernal became an active, card-holding member of
the Communist Party of Great Britain, which had been formed
in 1920 by the British Socialist Party, the Socialist Labour
Party, the Workers Socialist Federation, and others from
among the Shop Stewards and Workers' Committee Movement. He was also a member of the Cambridge University
Labour Club. (In those days, there was no ban to prevent C P
members from being L P members.) He lost his C P card in
1933 or 1934, and never rejoined: this made no difference in
his practice. Others concerned intimately with Communism
at Cambridge were Allen Hutt, Philip Spratt (one of the
defendants in the Meerut conspiracy case), historian A. L.

*'For MacNeice and his contemporaries newly arrived at Oxford, the most
significant choice presented to them was between brain and brawn, between
homo- and hetero-sexuality, rather than the need to choose between the miners,
who remained on strike and were starved back to work, and all that Stanley
Baldwin's government stood for. Cambridge was little different. Julian Bell wrote
that, "In the Cambridge that I first knew, in 1929 and 1930, the central subject
of ordinary conversation was poetry. As far as I can remember we hardly ever
talked or thought about politics. . . ." '[18]

Morton, biochemist B. (Woggy) Woolf, and Ivor Montagu.* The group adopted the suggestion made by Montagu to call themselves 'the Spillikins'. They were not really Communists, because they did not discuss Communism or know properly what it was. They formed, essentially, a ginger group within the university Labour Club.

Bernal was a fringe member, not a regular participant, because he was involved increasingly in researches into the nature of geometric beauty made possible by the insight given by the new knowledge of the atom. He saw that the enormous revolution that had occurred in science as he was growing up – the revolution of relativity and the quantum theory, the great extension of knowledge of biochemistry – was filled with the promise of a revelatory advance into the future. 'I threw myself into it; I found that my own particular interest, in form and geometry, was best expressed in the new atomic knowledge of the structure of matter. I started to work on the structure of crystals.' He was aware of the influence of geometry, in the older Greek sense with the emphasis on measure (*metron*) rather than in the more modern sense as topology (pure form and position), on the study of crystalline matter. From the beginnings of crystallography Euclidean geometry had been 'a guiding light which extended to the interpretation of atomic position'.[20]

Overall in the Tripos he got a second class: in 1920, Mathematics Part I, Class II; in 1922, Natural Sciences Part I, Class I; in 1923, Natural Sciences, Part II, Class II. He was awarded a BA degree on 20 June 1922, and on the following day – aged just twenty-one – he married, in the local Registry Office, the attractive, twenty-three-year-old secretary Agnes Eileen Sprague, with whom he had been living. He was fortunate enough to be taken into the Davy-Faraday laboratory directed by Sir William Bragg, one of the pioneers of crystal structure, at the Royal Institution in London. This arose because whilst still an undergraduate he had written, in

* Montagu recalled that they met in the rooms of M. H. Dobb, 'then a recent graduate at Pembroke; since, an economist don at Trinity; all his life a student of Marxism with a deserved worldwide respect and reputation for commonsense analysis and clear unjargonized exposition.'[19]

1922, a remarkable scientific paper, a derivation of the 230 space groups using Hamiltonian quaternions. It was a study of the symmetries of crystals, done without any diagrams, and purely algebraic in form. For this, he was awarded in 1923 the college's Sudbury-Hardyman prize. Because of the expense involved, the paper remains unpublished, although accepted by the Cambridge Philosophical Society. Almost the only man who read it with complete comprehension was Carl Hermann, who came back the next day with a list of minor corrections. It may be this paper which Bernal concluded with the arrogance of youth, 'I have included no references, as none is necessary'.

Royal Institution days

Mindful of his boyish experiment with a candle based on Faraday's classic lecture given at the Royal Institution, Bernal was amused – and flattered – to be working, as Faraday had, as an assistant, and in the very same cellar. When he began his researches in 1923, the science of crystal analysis by means of X-rays was but ten years old: Sir William Bragg and his son Lawrence (knighted in 1940), eleven years older than Bernal, were its founders. They had followed up brilliantly, and speedily, a discovery made in 1912 by Max von Laue in Munich that the atoms within a crystal diffract X-rays, as ordinary light is diffracted by a grating. It was a little more complicated; since the atoms are arranged regularly and periodically in space – that is, the pattern is repeated like the pattern in wallpaper, but in three dimensions – the X-rays could be used to provide a direct insight into the crystal structure, and could be received on a fluorescent screen or recorded on a photographic plate. Von Laue's work confirmed that X-rays were electromagnetic waves like light. Here, then, was a powerful new tool to reveal the internal structure of crystals. The diffraction of X-rays by crystals in many ways was central in the great chain of experimental discoveries in physics that accompanied the basic theories of Einstein and Planck.

This was a key period in the development of crystallography

B

as a recognized science within the British academic scene.
New techniques were developed to lighten the boredom involved in looking indirectly at the inside from the outside
through laborious experimental work, and involved geometrical conceptions. In 1923, Bernal was happy amongst the
happiest of people: scientists echoed Rutherford's booming
pronouncement, 'We are living in the heroic age of physics.'*
That exuberance was the pervading humour of science.

The crystallographers were part of an open intimacy under
the guidance of Sir William Bragg at the Davy-Faraday
Laboratory, and Lawrence Bragg at Manchester University:
these were the two world centres of study. 'All of those who
worked at the Royal Institution or in Manchester carried
away for the rest of their lives recollection of the atmosphere
of active and exciting research which grew up around the
Braggs, and the fact that they were father and son helped
enormously to unify the whole subject.'[21]

The problems of crystallography divided themselves naturally into the determination of the inner atomic structure of
the crystals of a pure substance, and of the mutual arrangements of small crystals in aggregates and mixtures. To these
was added something extra – crystallography, the determination of the wavelengths of X-rays from different sources. At
the Royal Institution, research was concentrated on organic
crystals (except for the crystalline forms of silica): in Manchester, on minerals and metals.

The researchers in the excitement of those days were like
'a flock of crazy prophets, that by staring at a crystal can fill
it with more fancies than there are herrings in the sea'.[22]

In all, they numbered twelve in the Davy-Faraday laboratory, and they shared a privileged enthusiasm in discovery.
The field was big enough for all their individual efforts: there
was no real rivalry: it was a very happy time. 'They were
effectively and actually a band of research workers, dropping
into each other's rooms, discussing informally over lunch and
ping-pong, and formally in Bragg's colloquia every week.'[23]
These colloquia were begun about 1925, and were held in the

* Made at the 1923 annual meeting of the British Association for the Advancement of Science.

study of Sir William's flat on the top floor of the R I. They sat in easy chairs and discussed each other's work with continual comments and interruptions. There was Bernal himself with his 'shock of fairish hair gone wild and humorous hazel eyes',[24] armed with the transcendental span of his great fund of knowledge, who 'used to agitate us rather because he was so very pale in face and so red in outlook';[25] Kathleen Yardley (afterwards Mrs Lonsdale), who, despite her unobtrusive ways, had such an underlying strength of character that she became from the outset presiding genius of the place;[26] and Bill Astbury, who worked with her in preparing the first British (Astbury Yardley) tables of space groups: he was 'slapdash and imaginative with unflagging enthusiasm which kept us going'.[27] Bernal remembered 'how exciting it was: the change from the large to the small metal ions, the ideas of packing, the break into organic chemistry' – and how Sir William 'planned the attack and was as excited himself as the youngest of us'.[28]

Crazy experiments were always being done. Bernal took an X-ray photograph of the leg of a live frog stimulated by an induction motor to see whether the contraction made any difference to the X-ray pattern. The experiment is only now within the technical capabilities of science using the X-rays from a synchrotron. The frog was released, seemingly unharmed, and the patterns were quite indistinguishable. Everyone was left free to choose his own problems. That was the style of Bill Bragg (as Sir William was called behind his back). When, infrequently, he looked in on a researcher it was to seek information or help in preparing some photograph or material for a lecture he was to give. This was not too popular, because it took time off work; the preparation of the successful children's lecture usually occupied the whole of the autumn term. Later, Bernal and his colleagues came to understand that it often proved the most valuable and instructive part of their research training: it was one of Sir William's 'most subtle ways of directing research – because less of a director you could hardly imagine.'[29] Or, meeting a colleague on the stairs, Sir William would say, 'Hello! How's the family?' He would avoid talking shop, especially at the communal tea each day, which he would try hard to be present at. Bernal came to recognize that Sir William was 'in a way, scientifically, my father, too. He took me up and helped me through all the critical stages of my career.' Bernal was proud of having worked with him, had meant always to tell him how grateful he was, 'but somehow one never does and then it is too late'.[30]

There were really two experimental schools at the RI. Those old hands such as Astbury and Yardley, who followed the Bragg method using the ionization spectrometer, and those, such as Bernal, who were pioneers in X-ray photographic analysis. Yardley began to instruct Bernal on the spectrometer, but he found it an incredibly tedious method of working. It was not for him, he decided after a few days. He recognized it as a very precise method which, the Braggs had shown, was effective in determining simple structures in the mineral field. But he saw that it was useless for complicated organic structures where it was necessary to have only relatively accurate measurements on a large number of planes.

Bernal did not have green fingers for experimental work. That was made clear once again when he was asked to make a certain apparatus from scratch. In his small room,* he was left with some pieces of glass, some miners' lamp glasses, a little aluminium foil, and plenty of sealing wax with which to stick things together. He was given, also, some glass tubing and a little mercury to make a diffusion pump, some copper and iron wires for the transformer, and, as an essential ingredient, an aluminium hot-water bottle, and a small piece of platinum to make the interrupter.[31] Everything went wrong; the Winchester bottle in which the back vacuum was kept broke with a loud explosion, he burned himself and broke things endlessly.

After three months, when he had not been able to get a trace of an X-ray out of his apparatus, he went to see Sir William. He pleaded, 'I want to give up experimental physics, it is not for me. May I go back to the theory of crystallography?' At this encounter, the first with the director since

---

* Space was always a problem at the R I. When A. L. Patterson arrived from Canada, Bernal remembered him trying to settle down between the glass cases containing the historic apparatus used by Bragg's predecessors.

beginning at the RI, Sir William revealed that he had not read Bernal's spectacular undergraduate paper which had given him the job. His forthright spontaneity, 'My God, man, you don't think I've read it!' so cheered Bernal that he went back to his unpalatable task, determined to finish it and to get out the structure of graphite and have it printed by the end of the year. 'To do that I had to make my own cylindrical camera which I did in the most amateur way out of a piece of brass tubing which I had cut with a hacksaw, bored a hole in it, stuck in with sealing wax a smaller piece of brass tubing with two bits of lead with pin holes through them for the aperture. The film was held together in place with bicycle clips and I used an old alarm clock and a nail to mount and turn the crystal.' He was delighted that it worked, and it became a prototype of all cylindrical cameras.* [32]

But it was not only Bernal's awkwardness as an experimenter that provided him with problems, there were also 'environmental hazards' in the laboratory. Thus, after much persuasion, he had managed to obtain a grudging few flakes of graphite from the Natural History Museum. 'I made a selection under the microscope, and put them out on a piece of paper by the window, and then went down to eat my sandwich lunch with the ping-pong players. When I came back the graphite crystals had completely disappeared!' Puzzled, he asked Mrs Duke, the charwoman, noted for an extreme and quite unnecessary interest in laboratory cleanliness, whether she had seen them. She said, 'Them smuts?' (There were quite a lot which used to come through the window.) 'I swep 'em up.' So he had to start all over again.

(Shortly after that episode, the same charwoman tried to clean the X-ray apparatus while it was going. The terminals always collected much dust. She said, 'It jumped at me, like.' Bernal confessed he was not entirely upset, for she was lucky to escape injury.)

Another hazard occurred among the chimney pots. A device in use was the Shearer gas tube for X-rays, which had a hand-adjustable leak. Bernal could not get his to work without his active nursing presence. Now and again, the interrupters

* A replica made by John Mason is in the Science Museum, London.

would develop leaks causing them to fill up with explosive gas and go off with a loud bang. The noise was unbearable, so the gas tubes were put up on the roof. That meant he could not maintain a continuing, watchful eye. He had to wait for his bottle to 'pop off', and then hunt it out among the chimney pots.

Despite these difficulties, the variety of the crystal was a challenge: as an explorer, but never leaving his laboratory, Bernal began to penetrate the mists and cavities of crystal structure to reveal new knowledge as a basis for understanding the nature of solid matter and its applications in chemistry, metallurgy, and geology, and in the definition of life. His first published scientific paper on the structure of graphite appeared in the *Proceedings of the Royal Society* in 1924. In this he proved successfully the planarity of the layers in graphite (that is, that the crystal of graphite breaks into thin flakes because the atoms are arranged in layers). He did very little more experimental work at the R I – he was more interested in 'developing methods of analysis'. This led him to prepare charts for flat and cylindrical cameras. A lot of calculation was involved, and he asked Sir William for £20 to hire an adding machine. The answer was obvious: he spent two months doing the whole thing by hand and eye, using seven-figure logarithm tables. His charts for the interpretation of X-ray, single crystal, rotation photographs were published in 1926.

In the following year he had published in the *Journal of Scientific Instruments* the first part of a lengthy study on a universal X-ray photogoniometer; part II appeared in 1928, and III and IV in 1929. (The goniometer is an instrument used for measuring angles.) Bernal concerned himself with the problem when he realized that the applications of X-ray diffraction were of 'such large dimensions that it becomes profitable at this stage to treat of instruments made for this specific purpose rather than to leave to each investigator the burden of creating special apparatus for his own needs'. He saw no reason why universal instruments 'should not be used, for all but very special problems, to give results as reliable and easily obtainable as those, say, of the spectroscope'. His four papers described the general problems of the requirements and

capabilities of apparatus for the diffraction of X-ray crystallography, and then one particular universal instrument in detail
with an account of its adjustment and operation.

He remembered almost the last experiment he did at the
RI: it featured his weakness as an experimenter. The experiment concerned the structure of alloys. There he was in
Faraday's own cellar in the basement, surrounded by flasks
full of Dewar's rare gases. It was a fine low-temperature place
where things could be crystallized slowly. 'I was trying, by a
flotation method, to measure to several points of decimals the
density of a very small single crystal of a delta bronze. It involved a very great number of weighings and measurings, and
in the very last weighing on which all the rest depended, the
little crystal slipped out of my fingers and disappeared.' He
looked around, appalled. He never found it again; he found,
instead, that 'an eighteenth-century cellar is not the best place
to look for a crystal of less than half a millimetre in size'.[33] It
proved also 'a most joyous recollection' for Kathleen Yardley,
of Bernal on his knees looking for his one and only crystal.

Although Bernal agreed with Kathleen that the Davy-
Faraday Laboratory enveloped them in warmth so embracing
that they had to be 'kicked out' into the wider world, he had
applied for a new post as a lecturer in structural crystallography in Cambridge. In 1927 he was interviewed together
with W. A. (Peter) Wooster, and his Royal Institution colleague, Astbury. The chairman of the selection committee was
Arthur Hutchinson, Master of Pembroke and Professor of
Mineralogy in the university, who had taught crystal physics
to all three as undergraduates. Astbury, typically, declared
abruptly when asked his view on collaboration, 'I am not
prepared to be anybody's lackey.'

Wooster made a competent impression. He had been
appointed to the vacant demonstratorship in mineralogy by
Hutchinson himself, who had also had him take over the
teaching of crystal physics, and introduce X-ray crystallography into this.

But both were outclassed by Bernal who, according to
C. P. Snow, appeared at first ill at ease and sullen, just replying 'yes' or 'no' to questions. In despair, Hutchinson asked

him what he would do with the proposed crystallographic laboratory. 'Bernal threw back his head, hair streaming like an oriflamme, began with the word No (as he usually began his best speeches), and gave an address, eloquent, passionate, masterly, prophetic, which lasted forty-five minutes. There was nothing for it but to elect him: said Hutchinson. . . .'[34]

3
Future Perfect

Now I have come to reason
And cast my schoolboy clout,
Disorder I see is without,
And the mind must sweat a poison
Keener than Thessaly's brew;
A pus that, discharged not thence,
Gangrenes the vital sense
And makes disorder true.
It is certain we shall attain
No life till we stamp on all
Life the tetragonal
Pure symmetry of brain.

DAY LEWIS[35]

Despite his intense scientific involvement, Bernal remained politically alert, concerned with safeguarding the Soviet Union as the first socialist state, and basing on this the activity to avert a premature clash of swords with the capitalist world which many regarded as inevitable. The General Strike of 1926 was a great scab adventure for many in the academic world: for undergraduates it was a lark. Established heads of departments made it clear in 'a Kitchener tradition' that they expected their young researchers 'to do their duty'. Sir William Bragg asked Bernal to help to drive trains. He refused; most of his colleagues did not. He welcomed Britain's first Labour Government, but resented its timidity and ineffectiveness. As a Communist, he saw the collapse of the strike as 'a betrayal, and a defeat of the united working class'.

His involvement with the working-class movement burned

into him, and he submitted his being to its firing embrace with a total intensity. 'Indeed, if it had not been for that activity and the real contact it brought me with the people, I, as an intellectual, would have found existence intolerable.'‡ Without such action he felt that he would be helping to betray mankind and to abet the destruction of the advances made as a result of the scientific and industrial revolutions and the enlightenment that went with them. Action gave him hope, especially as in action he felt he was not alone, but linked with 'the people', with their 'immense fund of goodwill, courage, and endurance'.

There was no retreat from those thoughts. They underlay his behaviour for the rest of his days. They were the sweet contentment arising from awareness of class-consciousness. As an intellectual, he was to be always on the outside of the working-class movement. As a Communist, he had a passport to involvement. To do what? To find satisfaction 'in taking part in the struggle against the destructive tendencies of our time, and by contributing, however little, to the movements against them'.

Bernal's passion for the introduction of reason into the conduct and organization of social behaviour was undiminished. The gods, not only God, were the enemies of human advance; their heavens were ripe for invasion and takeover by the devices created by men's minds and hands. He was concerned with drawing a new world picture based on science to replace that given by religion. All this he expressed in his first book *The World, the Flesh, and the Devil*, published in 1929.* A brave, striking title, and with a sub-title that made clear his basic wish 'An enquiry into the future of the three enemies of the rational soul'. It was essentially a demand for a planned society in which scientific method could be introduced into all areas of human activity. Given that, he believed there could

---

* Compare the priest's words in the baptism of those of riper years. 'Grant that they may have power and strength to have victory, and to triumph, against the devil, the world, and the flesh.' It is typical that on the strength of being an author for the first time he gave a party which cost him five pounds more than he was paid for the MS. He could not have done otherwise as the leader of 'the petty', the 'third Bloomsbury' of the 1920s. The other two were 'the high' and 'the mezzo'.

be a tremendous acceleration in man's understanding of himself and his universe, and release from war, famine, and disease. The three enemies of the rational soul would retreat in defeat; these were the World (the forces of nature), the Flesh (man's body and its physical limitations), and the Devil (man's passions, stupidity and ignorance).

The book is a vision of the future. In this regard, he was returning to the early days of modern science, when such speculations were common. Newton, for example, at the end of his *Opticks*, had many queries which were, in effect, speculations. The twentieth-century scientists would not normally engage in such speculation. They have been trained not to say anything for which they have no evidence, and certainly not to make their presentation personal. Bernal was, as always, an exception.

There are six chapters in the book. The first is entitled 'The Future'. Its opening sentence reads, 'There are two futures, the future of desire and the future of fate, and man's reason has never learnt to separate them.' Bernal argued that as religion gave place to science we could demand our chosen future in the world of men. But how could we reconcile desire and fate? Could we do that by examining the future scientifically? The initial difficulty in the general prediction of the future was its enormous complexity, and the interdependence of all its parts. But the events out of which so complicated a thing as the general state of the universe was built consisted of complexes (nebulae, planet, sea, animal, society) of which the components were themselves complex parts. This hierarchy of complexes was an expression of the modes of human thought, a convenient simplification which made science possible. Inside each complex, development proceeded according to its own rules.

In human affairs, he went on, the immediate future revealed itself in following tendencies visible in the present. But beyond that must come the application and development of present knowledge. He was directly concerned with that, and the secondary results that flared from them. He cautioned that we could not predict the rates of development in different fields, so the resultant future became more and more uncertain the further we looked forward. 'The only way to deal with the complexity is by separating the variables as best we can, by arbitrarily considering developments as proceeding in one field without any developments in any of the others, and then combining the results attained by applying this method in different fields. At the same time we must keep in mind that the state of development at any one period must be a self-consistent whole.'

Chapter II deals with 'The World'. The prognostications are remarkably accurate. But Bernal himself admitted that in the material world prediction was on its surest ground, 'almost a business of mathematics', in the first stages.

The discoveries of the early and mid-nineteenth century gave a macro-mechanical age of power and metal. But this century's discoveries, particularly quantum theory, which touched on the nature of matter itself, were more fundamental, and must produce more important results: in, for example, new materials and processes in which physics, chemistry, and mechanics would be fused. Thus, materials would be made to specifications of molecular architecture. He foresaw the passing of the age of metals (and with that mines, furnaces, and engines of massive construction), and the beginning of a world of light and elastic fabric materials, 'a world which will imitate the balanced perfection of a living body'.

Food and clothing would be made with much less expenditure of energy in manufacture and transport. The development of mechanism should lead to the efficient transmission of energy by low frequency (wireless) waves, and the direct utilization of the high frequency (light) waves of the sun. It should be possible to produce food under controlled conditions, bio-chemical and ultimately chemical. The great variety of available combinations should enable gastronomy to rank with the other arts.

Bernal then made a remarkable forecast: the conquest of space, reinforced by necessity. 'Ultimately it would seem impossible that it should not be solved. Our opponent is here simply the curvature of space-time – a mere matter of acquiring sufficient acceleration on our own part.' He proposed the use of the rocket, and saw that the first space vessels would be cramped and uncomfortable. However, 'the travellers, if they return to earth at all, will have to abandon their machine and descend in parachutes'. He envisaged a form of space sailing which used the repulsive effect of the sun's rays instead of wind.

Then, in space, the possibilities of the spread of humanity would be multiplied, for there would be the idea of building a permanent home in space. He then went on to describe in some detail a three-dimensional, gravitationless way of living in space in a spherical shell, ten miles or so in diameter, made up in the main of the substance of one or more smaller asteroids, rings of Saturn, or other planetary detritus. 'A globe interior eight miles across would contain as much effective space as a countryside 150 miles square, even if one gave a liberal allowance of air, say fifty feet above the ground.' (In the 1970s, some astronomers conceived of a large spherical settlement, with 50,000 people, orbiting the Earth: they called it the Bernal Sphere.)

'In time, competitive pressures, or the knowledge of imminent failure of the sun, would initiate a venture beyond the solar system. A space vessel would then have to be a comet. And, by then, men would have ceased to be parasitic on the stars, those essentially immense reservoirs of energy, but would organize them into, say, efficient heat engines. So by intelligent organization, the life of the universe could probably be prolonged to many millions of millions of times what it would be without organization.'

In his Chapter III 'The Flesh', Bernal was striving for some such tool of understanding as the double helix, whereby man would not be bound to the very limited range of methods of change which nature adopted. He argued that the physical nature of man would have to be altered radically, because the modern mechanical and chemical discoveries to a large extent had made the skeletal and metabolic functions of the body useless. 'In a civilized worker the limbs are mere parasites, demanding nine-tenths of the energy of the food and even a kind of blackmail in the exercise they need to prevent disease, while the body organs wear themselves out in supplying their requirements.' But the increasing complexity of man's existence demanded a much more complex sensory and motor organization, and a better organized cerebral mechanism. 'Sooner or later the useless parts of the body must be given more modern functions or dispensed with altogether.'

For him, 'to have a brain suffused by fresh and correctly prescribed blood is to be alive – to think.' The man of the future would probably have a great number of typical forms, each specialized in certain directions. It was beyond his imagination to predict the shapes men would adopt if they made of themselves a harmony of form and sensation. Normal man was an evolutionary dead end; mechanical man, apparently a break in organic evolution, was more in the true tradition of a further evolution.

Bernal then considered the possibility of 'the permanent compound brain', the linking together of several individual brains. What would be the effect if this were to come into existence? Death would become different. It would still exist, but to be postponed for 300 or 1000 years. Not for ever, only for as long as the brain cells could be persuaded to live in the most favourable environment. But the multiple individual would be immortal, the older components being replaced by newer ones, and the continuity of the self would be maintained. And, Bernal went on, if this seems only a way of cheating death, 'we must realize that the individual brain will feel itself part of the whole in a way that completely transcends the devotion of the most fanatical member of a religious sect'.

He admitted that it would be difficult to imagine this state of affairs effectively. Literally, he saw it as a state of ecstasy. It was the second change made possible by the compound mind. The limitations of human individuality would be overcome, but not the identity and continuity of individual development. With barriers down, feeling would truly communicate itself, memories would be held in common. Division of labour would set in, and there would grow up a hierarchy of minds which could extend their perceptions and understanding and their actions far beyond those of the individual. 'Sense organs would tend to be less and less attached to bodies, and the host of subsidiary, purely mechanical agents and perceptors would be capable of penetrating those regions where organic bodies cannot enter or hope to survive. The interior of the earth and the stars, the inmost cells of living things themselves, would be open to consciousness through these angels, and through these angels also the motion of stars and living things would be directed.'

And he went on to further possibilities: men would not be content to manufacture life, they would want to improve on it. Men will make 'living material' which would come to substitute for inferior functions, such as memory, reflex actions, etc. The brain would become separated into different groups of cells, and probably occupy considerable space. The loss of motility would be compensated by the extension of sense faculties.

The flesh would be conquered finally, as 'bit by bit the heritage in the direct line of mankind – the heritage of the original life emerging on the face of the world – would dwindle, and in the end disappear effectively, being preserved perhaps as some curious relic, while the new life which conserves none of the substance and all the spirit of the old would take its place and continue its development. . . . Finally, consciousness itself may end or vanish in a humanity that has become completely etherealized, losing the close-knit organism, becoming masses of atoms in space communicating by radiation, and ultimately perhaps resolving itself entirely into light. That may be an end or a beginning, but from here it is out of sight.'

'The Devil' (Chapter IV), was another matter. He was powerful. Only when he was expelled could the world be abandoned, and the flesh subdued. But he was most difficult to deal with for he was unseen, within ourselves. For him, the progress of the future no longer depended on physiological evolution, but on the reaction of intelligence on a material universe. Intellectual work must be organized for definite ends. This involved a fundamental change, analogous to the change from a food-gathering to a food-producing society. The modern scientist was a primitive savage. For his success he was dependent not only on his skill and tradition, but also on the richness of nature and the paucity of his companions. Bernal saw that researchers would have to be planned and directed. That would mean the risk of loss of independence and originality. These would be overcome, and the dangers of pedantry and bureaucracy, symptoms of an unintelligent respect for the past, would be caused to go.

He then pointed out how the very wideness of the field of science had introduced specialization, but as they penetrated more deeply into nature ordinary modes of thinking became inadequate. They might not be able to produce sufficient minds to deal with the deeper problems, although nature was never so complicated as it looked. The chief danger to progress could arise because people would turn from physics to metaphysics as the hope that what physics held out was seen to be vain. The ideals of the super-ego should be brought in line with external reality, using and rendering innocuous the power of the Id, and leading to a life where a full adult sexuality would be balanced with objective activity.

Where had Bernal's analysis led him thus far? Chapter V is concerned with 'Synthesis'. The beings he has described, 'nuclearly resident in a relatively small set of mental units, each utilizing the bare minimum of energy, connected together by a complex of ethereal intercommunication, and spreading themselves over immense areas and periods of time by means of inert sense organs which, like the field of their active operations, would be, in general, at a great distance from themselves'. The scene of life would then be the cold emptiness of space, so there would be advantage in beings without organic material. As our descendants might be more occupied with scientific research than with satisfying primary physiological and psychological needs, machinery would be organized for discovery, and the necessity for production of food, etc., would disappear with the process of de-humanization.

What this amounted to was an understanding that the cardinal tendency of progress was the replacement of an indifferent chance environment by one deliberately created. As time passed, the understanding of nature would be replaced by the need to determine the desirable form of humanly controlled universe – and that was art. What was to be the nature of feeling? Were the mechanical or corporate men of the

future to be emotional or rational? The psychology of the
mechanized organism was a mystery.

Finally, Chapter VI dealt with 'Possibility'. Bernal recognized that the total result of what he had written might seem
unbelievable. But, he argued, that scheme was more than a
bare possibility. Permanent plenty was no longer a utopian
dream: it awaited permanent peace. Through rationalized
capitalism, or Soviet state planning, uniform and intelligent
method was being used to deal with the production and distribution of necessaries. The aristocracy of scientific intelligence
might give rise to new developments. 'More and more, the
world may be run by scientific experts. . . . The scientists
would then have a dual function: to keep the world going as
an efficient food and comfort machine, and to worry out the
secrets of nature for themselves. A happy, prosperous humanity
enjoying their bodies, exercising the arts, patronizing the
religions, may well be content to leave the machine, by which
their desires are satisfied, in other and more efficient hands.
Psychological and physiological discoveries will give the ruling
powers the means of directing the masses in harmless occupations and of maintaining a perfect docility under the appearance of perfect freedom. But this cannot happen unless the
ruling powers are the scientists themselves . . .

'Even a scientific state could only maintain itself by per-
petually increasing its power over the non-living and living
environment. . . . The separation of the scientists and those
who thought like them – a class of technicians and experts
would perhaps form 10 per cent or so of the world's population
– from the rest of humanity, would save the struggle and
difficulty which would be bound to ensue if there were any
attempt to change the whole bulk of the population.' Mankind
then lulled would let matters go on until it would be too late
for them to do anything, even if they wished to: 'Even if a
wave of primitive obscurantism then swept the world clear of
the heresy of science, science would already be on its way to
the stars.'

However, scientists were not masters of the destiny of science.
They might be forced into positions which they never might
have chosen, as a result of the changes they had brought about.

Their curiosity and its effect might be stronger than their humanity. He considered the problem of whether a permanent human dimorphism might arise, or be prevented. In a Soviet state, scientific institutions would become the government, and scientists would identify themselves with the progress of science, while the rest of the population, because of an education with scientific values, would not be opposed. Either scientists would emerge as a new species and leave humanity behind, or humanity as a whole might change, leaving behind those too stupid or too stubborn to change. Assuming colonization of space, the old mankind might be left on earth, and 'the world might be transformed into a human zoo, so intelligently managed that its inhabitants are not aware they are merely for observation and experiment'.

Bernal ended this speculation: 'Have we not here the criterion which will decide the direction of human development? We are on the point of being able to see the effects of our actions and their probable consequences in the future; we hold the future still timidly, but perceive it for the first time, as a function of our own action. Having seen it, are we to turn away from something that offends the very nature of our earliest desires, or is the recognition of our new powers sufficient to change those desires into the service of the future which they will have to bring about?'

In after years, Bernal modified his views. He rejected, for instance, 'science rule' although 'an enlightened technocracy' was implicit in most of his construction plans. We shall see how, during the war, he had a chance to join such a technocracy and see plans realized physically. But he confirmed forty years later that the book, which contained many of the ideas he had been elaborating throughout his scientific life, still had validity in its own right.

To read it now is to recognize how brilliantly he stated the thoughts and aspirations of the first three decades of this century.* The emphasis was on the rational, and on a science

* He may have been present at a meeting of The Heretics, in Cambridge on 4 February 1923, when J. B. S. Haldane read a paper, *Daedalus, or Science and the Future* to which *The World, the Flesh, and the Devil* owes a great deal of its inspiration. If he were not present, he read the book published in the same series *Today*

capable of saving mankind if scientists were given an opportunity to take part in managing society. The opponents of this
viewpoint identified science with Soviet Communism. This
was a key part of the ideological battle waged in the pre World
War II years. Bernal was at the centre of it. And the battle
still continues.

Typical of the reaction of the popular press to the book was
the following which appeared in the *Daily Herald* (the newspaper of the Labour movement) on 19 February 1929:

MEN WITH EARS UNDER LUNGS

WHAT HUMANS MAY BE LIKE ANOTHER DAY

PEEP INTO FUTURE

Are we slowly passing out of the age of metals, mines, furnaces and
engines into a new age in which we shall use fabrics as light and
elastic as chewing gum? And, if we are, that is nothing to what is
in store for us.

The astounding things that may happen to humanity in the time
to come are discussed in a fascinating manner by Mr J. D. Bernal,
M A, lecturer in structural crystallography at the University of
Cambridge in *The World, the Flesh and the Devil*, published today
by Kegan Paul as part of the Today and Tomorrow Series.

Mr Bernal says we – meaning our posterity – will one day take
to travelling about space so that we shall become as familiar with
the Milky Way as we now are with the morning milk. He foretells
'joyrides on asteroids' – those tiny little worlds, some of them only

---

and Tomorrow by Kegan Paul, Trench, Trubner & Co., 1 November 1923, and
which ran to nine impressions in the next seven years. (The Heretics was founded
in 1904 to promote the scientific-rationalist viewpoint among students.)

Haldane wrote, 'We must regard science, then, from three points of view.
First, it is the free activity of man's divine faculties of reason and imagination.
Secondly, it is the answer of the few to the demands of the many for wealth,
comfort and victory, for "noson t aspeirois Kai makraionas biois" gifts which it
will grant only in exchange for peace, security, and stagnation. Finally, it is man's
gradual conquest, first of space and time, then of matter as such, then of his own
body and those of other living beings, and finally the subjugation of the dark
and evil elements in his own soul.' Here is the text of Bernal's own book.

a few miles across, which move in their appointed orbits around the sun.

But there is more to come. 'Sooner or later some eminent physiologist will have his neck broken in a supercivilized accident, or find his body cells worn beyond capacity for repair. *He will then be forced to decide whether to abandon his body or his life.* (The italics are mine; the decision will be the physiologist's.)

NO MORE SEX!

In other words, man will become merely a detached headpiece. Even that is a substantial, recognizable something compared with him (or *her*, for sex will have vanished) when he is 'in shape rather a short cylinder' with his ears (probably tucked up under his lungs) as efficient as a 40-valve wireless set.

More than that. We shall live to be a thousand years old, much more. In fact, '. . . the multiple individual would be, barring cataclysmic accidents, immortal. . . .'

In a way, although the writer does not say so, he has reversed every idea of God that man has ever had, for he hints that creation is creating the creator. . . .

What Mr Bernal would say if he really let himself go I leave you to imagine. His contribution to this singularly daring series makes me think that Mr H. G. Wells is but a timid prentice prophet.

GSS

Talk of a 'planned social order' aroused strong feelings, akin to terror, amongst academics, especially those who feared the introduction of Communism, and who were guided by the star of 'science for science's sake'. Thirty years later Neal Wood re-stated their fears with a piety that made it clear that the desire to efface Bernal's views was as vigorous as ever.[36] These were charges that Bernal was to hear time and again.

Wood accused Marxism and Communism of being the means best available of achieving the transfer of power to the scientist. 'Dictatorship by the scientist is the apotheosis of control, complete and totalitarian.' Bernal's vision was 'dreadful'. 'As a scientist he cannot agree to any limitation upon the scientific dynamic, even for the sake of saving science. His tyranny of mind over man is only for the purpose of a greater tyranny, until eventually both mind and man disappear into the void, a refinement to nothingness. Is this not the ultimate in nihilism?'

Wood was right to recognize Bernal as a leading protagonist in expressing something new – increasing political awareness in scientists in the thirties. There were others, such as Patrick Blackett, J. B. S. Haldane, Lancelot Hogben, and Hyman Levy: despite their brilliance, they were only a handful, but they were the ferment in the bread. They were asking questions, openly and deliberately, which challenged the traditions in which they had been raised, and doing so in an environment disturbed mightily by the gusts of the winds of change: questions such as, What is my science for? What is my responsibility as a scientist not only to society, but also to science itself?

Bernal's search for answers to those questions was to be a taproot of activities for the rest of his days, a search as unquenchable, and compulsive, as the enduring passion of his loves.

4

Soviet Challenge

Communism offers no one of this generation a
ticket to Utopia. But it does offer to intellectual
workers of every kind the one road of escape out
of a paralysing atmosphere of capitalist decay,
into a social environment which will give a limit-
less stimulus to the achievements of the mind of
man.

JOHN STRACHEY[37]

In the days when Bernal began to define his responsibilities as a scientist to society and to science itself, the history
of science as an academic study was primarily an amiable
diversion for retired scientists, or those about to retire. Only
a handful throughout the world were engaged full-time in the
subject. Thus, when announced, the Second International
Congress of the History of Science and Technology, to be held
in London from 29 June to 3 July 1931 in a lecture room of
the Science Museum at South Kensington, was only of routine
scholarly interest: a gathering of historians and scientists, each
pursuing his own branch with occasional attempts at correlat-
ing them.[38]

The congress was transformed, however, by the appearance
of a Soviet delegation, who arrived – in typically Russian
manner – at the very last moment, entwining their presence
in administrative problems for the congress organizers. It was
an important group of eight men, certainly the most know-
ledgeable, and responsible, about the role of science in a
socialist society. The leader was Nikolai Ivanovich Bukharin,

a classical Marxist thinker, the leading theoretician of the revolution after Lenin, co-leader with Stalin of the Party from 1925 to 1928, and head of the Communist International from 1926 to 1929. When he arrived in England he was an accepted decision maker and spokesman for the scientific community as director of research under the Supreme Economic Council, and a member of the Academy of Sciences, head of its Commission for the History of Knowledge.* But he had been expelled from the Politburo in 1929, and his political fate as the symbol of the anti-Stalinist opposition was already decided: he was to be executed in 1938 following a show trial.

The other members of the Soviet delegation were the physicist A. F. Ioffe, the economist M. I. Rubinstein, the physiologist B. M. Zadovsky, the mathematician A. I. Kol'man, the plant geneticist N. I. Vavilov, the electrical engineer V. F. Mitkcvich, and the theoretical physicist B. M. Hessen.** They had not been allotted any official time in the programme, but to meet their needs the congress was extended by a full half-day to hear their papers. Obviously that would not be sufficient to allow of a full presentation. Line by line, like fingers pointing a way in the darkness, translation of each paper into English was organized with back-breaking urgency, and within five days the necessary texts were available. These were assembled in the book *Science at the Cross Roads*, and published, replete with grammatical and typographical errors, ten days later.

Bukharin had positive views on the importance of science in a planned state. 'We must do our utmost,' he had written, 'to promote the union of science with technology and with the organization of production. Communism signifies intelligent,

---

* Bukharin had been named in Lenin's 'testament' as one of the collective of five to succeed him. The others were Stalin, Trotsky (exiled in 1927 and murdered in Mexico in 1940), Zinoviev and Kamenev (both executed in 1936.)

** Academician Vavilov was arrested on 6 August 1940 and died in prison on 23 January 1943. He was elected a Foreign Member of the Royal Society in London in 1942. Professor Boris Hessen vanished in the mid-30s. Academician Arnosht Kol'man (also spelled Colman), a colleague of Lenin, and a party member from 1919, in a letter to Brezhnev in 1977 returned his Party card and obtained political asylum in Sweden.

purposive, and, consequently, scientific production. We shall, therefore, do everything in our power to solve the problem of the scientific organization of production.'[39]

This approach, unburdened by any anchor of tradition, was stated vigorously, challengingly, by the Russians. They declare, 'In Soviet Russia absolutely new prospects are opening before science. The planned economy of socialism, the enormous extent of the constructive activity . . . demand that science should advance at an exceptional pace. The whole world is divided into two economic systems, two systems of social relationships, two types of culture. In the capitalist world the profound economic decline is reflected in the paralysing crises of scientific thought and philosophy generally.

'In the socialist section of the world we observe an entirely new phenomenon: a new conjunction of theory and practice, the collective organization of scientific research planned on the scale of an enormous country, the ever-increasing penetration of a single method – the method of dialectical materialism – into all scientific disciplines.

'Thus the new type of intellectual culture, which dominates the mental activity of millions of workers, is becoming the greatest force of the present day.'[40]

Although most of the participants at the congress rejected the radical approach, there were many who responded with great sympathy, particularly the group of young radicals present who included Bernal, Levy, Hogben, and Needham. It was the paper by Hessen entitled 'The social and economic roots of Newton's *Principia*' which startled them. Needham recalled it as 'perhaps the outstanding Russian contribution'.[41]

Bernal discerned two lines of argument from the contributions by the Russians. 'The first demonstration was a historical analysis of actual discovery, particularly detailed in the case of Newton, showing the dependence of his thought firstly on the dominant technical problems of the day in navigation, ballistics, and metallurgy, and secondly on the current political and religious controversy. Newton's work represents the scientific analogue of the Anglican compromise standing between the Aristotelianism of Rome and the rank materialism of

Overton and his Levellers. Thus, even mathematics becomes in a sense permeated with political and economic influences. This attack on the last sanctuary of pure science called forth a solitary protest from Professor Wolf, whose voice, with that of Sir William Whetham in the first session, were the only ones raised in defence of the academic ideal.'[42]

The only demonstration was of the close relation between science and technology in the Soviet Union's planned industry. 'In this relation both gain – not only industry from science through the rapid solutions of problems and the suggestions of new processes, but science gains from industry by the vastly greater funds at its disposal, by its more coherent organization, by the possibility of experiments on large-scale factory lines, but most of all by the inspiration from the problems of actual practice and by the intellectual cooperation of the workers.' He found the most convincing example was given by Vavilov, who with 2000 co-workers had established the seven chief centres of distribution of cultivated plants in the world. 'This work will not only be of great assistance to a rational agriculture, but at the same time throws light on purely botanical problems, and on the fascinating quest of the origin of civilization.'[43]

What was the effect of the Russians? 'In an immediate sense it was a failure,' wrote Bernal. 'The time was too short, the gulf between the points of view too great, for there to be any real understanding.' He was critical of the representatives of the Western world, who were 'an undisciplined host, unprepared and armed with ill-assorted individual philosophies. . . . The strength of the spirit of bourgeois science, particularly in England, lies in its avoidance of explicit statement.' The Russian appeal to the dialectic, to the writings of Marx and Engels, 'instead of impressing their audience, disposed them not to listen to the arguments which followed with the feeling that anything so ungentlemanly and doctrinaire had best be politely ignored.'[44]

But the congress did provide a seminal experience, from which was born a new morning in the historiography of science: and the twilight of that day is yet to come. It revealed for some a road out from the sterile labyrinth that was then the history of science, and one that was taken by J. G. Crowther,* by Needham,** and by Bernal, who contrasted the 'appalling inefficiency of bourgeois science' with a 'rapidly growing relatively efficient mechanized science' in the USSR. There were two questions that had to be faced: 'as to whether our individualist methods in science are not as obsolete and as effectively doomed as was the craftmanship of the Middle Ages, and whether after all they are worth saving.' He ended his review of the congress in his *Spectator* article with a key question: 'Is it better to be intellectually free but socially totally ineffective, or to become a component part of a system where knowledge and action are joined for our common purpose?' He had no doubts about the answer, and he was to devote all his energies, physical and intellectual, for the next three decades to making that clear.

During the congress, J. G. Crowther was occupied with Bukharin and Hessen, arranging visits to such places as the National Physical Laboratory. Ioffe took little part, but went off to visit Metro Vick who were engaged in the electrification of Russia. Bernal was provided with opportunities to meet Bukharin, and was much impressed with his intellectual worth and wit. Probably he heard from him about the first All-Union Conference on the Planning of Scientific Research Work in Moscow which Bukharin had taken part in three months before, in April. Bukharin insisted that 'the scientific research network must grow faster than even the leading branches of socialist heavy industry'. This was a view close to Bernal's

---

* 'Hessen's paper revealed to me a method of prosecuting the history of science which was more profound than the conventional one. I thought at once of applying it to other periods in British science.' He started 'precipitately, for fear of being forestalled' on a work, *British Scientists of the Nineteenth Century*, which took four years, however, to be written and published.[45]

** Joseph Needham was involved in the congress for personal, academic, and political reasons. His three-volume work, *Chemical Embryology*, was published that same year. The first volume carried a substantial 200-page survey of the history of embryology, based on lectures he had given in the previous year at University College, London. They had been entitled *Speculation, Observation and Experiment as Illustrated in the History of Embryology*. One of the points made in the lectures was the relation between biological research and embryological research in connection with society. Thus he was conscious at that time of the necessity to combine the history of science with economic and social history.

thinking; yet despite his other meeting with Bukharin in the Soviet Union, there is no reference to him in any of Bernal's writings on the organization of science because Bukharin had become a non-person in the USSR.

In retrospect, Hessen's paper is commonplace. It was over simple, and it was clear that Hessen was not up to date with much new research. 'But the limitation of the scope of Hessen's knowledge was irrelevant; he was a professor of physics at Moscow University, not a British historian', commented Crowther.[46] Intellectually he did something that no one had done before: he provided a new way of looking at the great Newton. It inspired the twenty-year-old undergraduate David Guest to break the submerging silence that followed the Russian statements.

Hyman Levy stated the situation as follows: after Hessen had read his paper, 'the audience was a little uncomfortable; it wished to give gentlemanly attention to what these foreigners had to say; it could not believe that anything they had to say would be at all significant; but at the same time it found the ideas presented to them so new and, from its point of view, so revolutionary as to make it impossible to form a judgment or to direct an intelligent attack. In short, at that particular moment, except to those of us who had already begun to think along these lines, the ideas were too novel to be absorbed, apparently too outrageous to be seriously considered or discussed. When the last speaker had finished and the time for discussion had arrived, those of us who might have spoken were temporarily tongue-tied by the difficulty of bridging the wide gap that had been disclosed between the speakers and the great majority of the audience, who so far as it was prepared to be tolerant, was silent because the ideas were too strange.

'At this awkward moment a pale-faced young boy, sitting behind me, bent over and whispered in my ear: "Do you think I ought to speak?"

' "Yes," I answered immediately, "if you have something to say," secretly delighted that someone from the English side should have the courage to make a contribution. . . . It is not easy for those who do not move in academic circles to visualize the forces at play in this and other situations connected with

university life. The vilification of Russia that had so persistent-
ly been pursued in the national press and that was being
focused on the delegates during the congress, implied an
atmosphere in which only a person who was prepared to
espouse an unpopular cause and to throw his academic future
to the winds would do battle.'[47]

'Guest suggested that, in keeping with the Soviet view of the
relation between science and society, it was possible that the
source of some of the profound contradictions in the logical
basis of mathematics was not to be found in mathematics
alone, abstracted from society, but was to be sought in prior
contradictions in the society from which mathematics had
arisen. Thus, argued Guest, the separation of the history of
mathematics from the history of society and politics might be
the reason why the fundamental contradictions in the logical
basis of mathematics appeared to be insoluble.'*

The Home Office in Britain kept a close eye on the Soviet
delegation. Telegrams sent by the London correspondent of
Isvestia were always intercepted. One that he sent on the
occasion of the congress showed good insight. It read, 'possibly
scientific congress become historic in sense that it involuntarily
provided tremendous impetus study dialectical materialism
especially England among growing generation scientific
workers.'[49]

A few weeks later, Bernal paid his first visit to the Soviet
Union. He was one of the twenty scientists in a group organized by J. G. Crowther for the scientific panel of the Society
for Cultural Relations with the USSR. Among the others
were W. Le Gros Clark, H. D. Dickinson, John Cockcroft,
J. B. S. Haldane, Julian Huxley, P. G. 'Espinasse, Glen A.
Millikan, and N. W. Pirie. For the medical panel of the SCR,
Crowther organized, also, a simultaneous visit for a group of
forty doctors. Bukharin acted as host for the government and
provided a lavish banquet and a large reception.[50] N. I.
Vavilov and Hessen were involved also, in discussions.

For Bernal, the visit – the first of many – confirmed his

* Guest died in 1938, fighting on the Republican side in the Spanish Civil War,
a tremendous loss to the intellectual world.[48] Bernal considered his book on
Dialectical Materialism to be 'the best short study in English'.

belief in the superiority of the planned society of socialism as against the opportunism of capitalism; he recognized the affinities that linked him with the dynamic changing new social and industrial forms. His attitude was reinforced by the view widely held in the early 1930s that liberal capitalist democracy appeared doomed. Two systems of government were presented as alternatives: either fascism, especially in the anti-humanist Nazi model created in Germany (essentially, capitalism reshaped in the most brutal, authoritarian form, as compared with the foretaste of Mussolini's regime), or the planned Soviet state. The former was favoured by key elements within the British establishment who stood for authority in politics to impose order and discipline, and who rejected the democratic belief in the equality, and brotherhood, of men. They sought an accommodation with Hitler. A number of dominant intellectual literary figures, such as Wyndham Lewis and Ezra Pound, supported the fascist cause openly, and others – W. B. Yeats, T. S. Eliot, and D. H. Lawrence – did so indirectly. A minor but popular novelist, John Buchan, whose works excited much feeling about the dangers of Bolshevism, expressed their view when he wrote in the *Morning Post* on 31 December 1929, 'But for the bold experiment of fascism the decade has not been fruitful in conservative statesmanship.'[51]

Scientists, by and large, rejected this view. It was not that they were left-wing. They were anti-Nazi. Dominating personalities, such as Rutherford, politically Tory in their outlook, were basically late nineteenth-century romantics expressing humanist values. Rutherford's colleagues in the Royal Society, for example, were active in aiding the German-Jewish refugees. The process of political radicalization was due very much to a few brilliant young scientists, consisting of Bernal, Blackett, Haldane, Hogben, and Levy. Three of them were Communists – Bernal, Haldane, and Levy: they made Communism, and Marxism, respectable in that atmosphere of crisis. 'There is no-one in politics today', Keynes said in 1939 to Kingsley Martin, 'worth sixpence outside the ranks of liberals except the post-war generation of intellectual Communists under thirty-five. Them, too, I like and respect.

Perhaps in their feelings and instincts they are the nearest thing we now have to the typical nervous nonconformist English gentleman who went on the crusades, made the Reformation, fought the Great Rebellion, won us our civil and religious liberties and humanized the working classes last century.'[52]

Bernal was one of the few under-thirty-fives whose culture was general, was informed by the new and the developing, and was enriched by the old, which he could not evade because it was always audible to him. He was, as Hyman Levy once put it, 'a sink of ubiquity'. In addition, he was politically aware: again in a minority, because most scientists were not. 'Scientists are queer fish,' he commented, 'but they are not all Reds!' That was true.* But they had begun to listen to those who provided an explanation of the way in which 'capitalism in crisis' was threatening them personally, and threatening their world of science.

Many of Bernal's scientific colleagues, he wrote, preferred not to think about such disturbing matters, but shut themselves away from the world of politics. 'Science was to them, if they were of the sober and serious kind, a form of religious personal duty, or, if they shared the cynicism of the age, a very amusing pastime. I saw in these attitudes something of the reflection, even among the scientists, of the struggle which I had witnessed at home and at school between reaction and liberation. To isolate science, or to treat it lightly, were both ways of diminishing its real impact, and particularly of diminishing the range of its applications, and the responsibility of the scientist for them.'[54]

The essence of the ideology of natural scientists in capitalist countries, he wrote in 1932,** was expressed in such common phrases as 'seclusion of the laboratory', 'pursuit of knowledge and truth for their own sakes': 'science' was divorced from

---

* C. P. Snow guessed that a poll of the 200 brightest physicists under the age of forty, if taken in 1936, would have revealed about five as Communists, ten fellow-travellers, fifty left of centre, 100 passively sympathetic to the left, the rest neutral, apart from five or six on the eccentric wings of the right.[53]

** In the Communist *Labour Monthly* under the pen-name of 'B.Sc.' in an article 'British scientists and the world crisis'.

life in general, as if it existed in a watertight compartment and doses of it could be 'used' and 'applied' in other fields. He saw that outside the laboratory the careful and accurate observation of facts disappeared, to be replaced by traditional beliefs and attitudes. The scientist in capitalist countries was saddled with an ideology that separated 'science' from life in general. He concluded, 'Science can only become free by breaking the limitations that capitalism imposes on it; scientists must realize that a path free from these limitations can only be achieved by adopting a scientific outlook towards all aspects of life and by realizing that none of them can be separated off as natural science is by capitalism from the others. How in fact can science become freed from the fetters that now bind it, *how* is the *cause* of the crisis to be removed? There is only one way – by the complete overthrow of capitalism and the building of socialism. History has given this task to the vast mass of the exploited – the workers of the world. The individual scientist must learn that the limitation of science is inherent in capitalism, and that the further evolution of science demands social revolution. Only by working on the side of the revolutionary proletariat can the individual scientist give expression to the revolutionary nature of science.'

This was rather immature Marxism, but it reflected the monochromatic vision with which the left-wing radicals looked at the Soviet Union, 'the fatherland of socialism'.

In 1932 Bernal made his second visit. 'I went around the Soviet Union in those rather rough primitive and casual days when one saw very much of the difficulties as well as of achievements. I saw the construction camps for the Dnieper Dam, and at the same time saw something of the hard times that were produced in the period of early collectivization – a consequence of the concentration of all efforts for the building of heavy industry, very remote from immediate enjoyments.' He recalled the 'conditions of incredible difficulty' that the capitalist slump imposed: 'mechanical equipment had to be purchased abroad at high prices, and the necessary money obtained by selling at very low prices the food which was badly needed at home'.

But he did not mistake 'the sense of purpose and achievement in the Soviet Union in those days of trial. It was grim but it was great. Our hardships in England were a hopeless misery; theirs were deliberate and undergone in an assurance of building a better future.'[54] For him the Soviet people offered a lesson without parallel in the story of the liberation of mankind; they were pursuing, also, the expression of a morality which, he believed, was destined to transform human behaviour.

In the winter of 1934 he made his third visit, this time in the company of a young woman, Margaret Gardiner, with whom he had lived for many years, but never married, and who bore his son, Martin. He was introduced to her by Solly Zuckerman. She was attractive, had some private money, and was active in progressive causes, such as the anti-fascist body, For Intellectual Liberty, of which she was honorary secretary,* and in which Bernal played an important part. They had arranged to travel together on an Intourist package to see the November celebrations in Red Square. Bernal was to give some lectures at the University of Moscow. She travelled down by train on her own to the ship at Tilbury where he was to meet her. 'I looked around for Desmond but there was no sign of him. I got my luggage stowed in my cabin but still no sign. In consternation I saw that they were pulling up the gangway and then there he was below, wild-haired and shouting to me against the wind. "I haven't got my visa," he yelled. "They haven't given me my visa. I'll have to wait. I'll fly out as soon as I can." As the ship left, he stood there, waving apologetically, as though it were somehow his fault. It was a first taste of muddled, incompetent bureaucracy, for after all he was the honoured, invited guest, whereas I was merely a tolerated tourist.'[55]

For Margaret Gardiner it was an exciting, and sobering, experience. She disliked 'the heroic "socialist" statues and

---

* The President was Aldous Huxley, and members included E. M. Forster, G. H. Hardie, F. Gowland Hopkins, William A. Jowitt, and Henry W. Nevinson. It was linked with the Comité de Vigilance des Intellectuels anti-Fascistes in France. In 1978, Margaret Gardiner gave her private collection of paintings and sculpture, valued at £365,000, to create the Pier Gallery Collection in the Orkney Islands. Many of the works were by such friends as Barbara Hepworth and Ben Nicholson.

friezes. But most of all I disliked the ubiquitous, inescapable, huge portraits of Stalin. "I hate that man," I said to Desmond. "But why?" he asked mildly. "I don't quite know. I hate his face, it's a horrible face." "It's just a nice, simple Georgian peasant face," he said. And I felt slightly ashamed of my intolerance, which was not, after all, based on knowledge.'

They were still in Moscow when Kirov was assassinated. Margaret heard that apparently Stalin had been involved in the murder. 'When I told Desmond about this conversation, he shrugged it off as malicious gossip.' But the general atmosphere had changed, so that there was 'a heavy pall of suspicion and fear. . . . "Don't you feel it?", I asked Desmond. "No, I don't," he answered. But many years later, when deeply disturbed by the happenings in Hungary, he said to me, "You know, you were right that time in Moscow, only I didn't want to admit it. I wanted to give them the benefit of the doubt." ' That was his constant attitude. If he had doubts, these were known only to those most intimate with him; public objection was impossible for him.

This was made clear in his attitude to Tito's Yugoslavia. After the Second World War, there was in that country a period of reconstruction similar to that which occurred in Russia after the First World War. It was built around the work of the Youth Brigades. Many Britons, including at least two members of Bernal's laboratory, were involved, and their experience had a great effect on the course of socialism in Britain. The seeds of the whole new left movement appeared in 1947 on the youth railway in Bosnia, and began to grow when, in 1948, Yugoslavia was expelled from the Cominform. There was much discussion in his laboratory, in which Bernal took little part. Eventually, he visited Yugoslavia, but expressed no enthusiasm and showed little curiosity.

C

5
Commitment Decade

Young men late in the night,
Toss on their beds,
Their pillows do not comfort
Their uneasy heads,
The lot that decides their fate
Is cast tomorrow,
One must depart and face
Danger and sorrow.

W. H. AUDEN[56]

In the 1930s Bernal was the acknowledged guerrilla *guru* of science. But he did not provide leadership: that was not his style. He provided the charisma (and machismo), and the intellectual strength; he was the unreasonable evangelist of reason, proclaiming the unlikely vision of a future based on science and technology in opposition to the apostles of destruction, who were for him the defenders of an unjust, dying economic system. 'During the years of the great Depression and after I began to study in a more serious way the works of the founders of Marxism, and there I found a philosophy that was not merely descriptive, but also purposeful – one that could be lived and could be a guide to action.' ‡

The richness of conflict in the 30s filled him with a passionate activity which consumed his energies to the full: his territory between departure and bed-fall ranged from the sombre excitements of the laboratory through the groping application of Marxist ideology to political/economic problems to the daunting explosiveness of the social responsibility of scientists.

By the end of that decade he was a member of over 120 committees, establishment-based and revolutionary.[57]

Late in 1931 the Japanese invaded Manchuria, and the League of Nations demonstrated its impotence; at Invergordon in Scotland in September of that year there was a strike of sailors; and there was unemployment. The unemployed were organized against the destructive means test through the National Unemployed Workers' Movement, a strongly left-wing lobby, whose activities resulted in a memorable hunger march in 1932. Between 1921 and 1939 there were never less than a million – one-tenth of the insured population – out of work; in the winter months of 1932–33 there were some three million unemployed, and these official figures did not include agricultural workers, the self-employed, and many women.[58]

And there was the appeasement of the fascist dictators. In his travels in Europe, Bernal had seen something of what was going on in Germany. 'From the middle of the 1930s to the end of the war [in 1945] that new appearance of reaction in its most brutal and intolerable form is the dominating experience of my life.' With that was linked the inevitability of another war, for he had no doubts that the capitalist powers would join together to seek to put an end to Soviet socialism. Basic to his behaviour was his belief in the superiority of the Soviet system. He accepted fully the view that 'under capitalism, cultural decay everywhere; in the Soviet Union mighty cultural progress. Under capitalism, the inescapable impoverishment of the masses; in the Soviet Union, joyous work in the clearly outlined road towards a classless society.'[59] 'In science, in education, in religion, in the family, in the prisons, the USSR gives practical embodiment to the progressive ideas of the nineteenth and twentieth centuries. The Communists are the heirs and the only defenders of the liberal tradition', he wrote in 1933.[60]

He had no doubts that the Soviet achievement was the nearest practical embodiment of the ideals for which scientists worked. But to break the power of capitalism, the workers had to seize power, to expropriate capital, and do away with production for profit. How could scientists be involved in this? He thought them so rooted in their class that 'in the main, rather than face this, they will give up their liberal traditions and wait resignedly for the reaction of fascism'.[61] However, events had brought more scientists to recognize that necessary action was required, and the first step was to acquire effective knowledge, which could be obtained only through taking an active part in ongoing activities.

It was in 1931 that the first Communist student groups appeared: in Cambridge (as a breakaway from the Cambridge Labour Club), in London at the LSE and at University College. In 1932, the October Club was formed in Oxford, as were other Communist groups in Bristol, Liverpool, Manchester, and Newcastle; a national co-ordinating committee for student activity was set up, and in November the first number of the *Student Vanguard* appeared. Bernal was much involved. Some time in 1932 he and Maurice Dobb were summoned from Cambridge to party headquarters in London for a discussion on how to stop what was described as 'an inefficient and inept attempt' to organize a student Communist movement. Emile Burns, the CP official responsible, was insistent that the students should be organized centrally through London, and he named two trusted party members to take charge. But despite misunderstandings and mistakes, 'we were forging the elements of that approach which in the period from 1933 onwards was to build up a powerful democratic movement, not only among the students, but also among the intellectuals at large, among architects, artists, writers, actors, musicians, doctors, scientists, and technicians'. The issues basic to the approach were insistence on science for the furtherance of welfare, and the preservation of culture and human dignity from fascist barbarism and war.

The 1930s have been called, also, 'the Auden years', for under his influence, as a Communist at Oxford, discussion of revolution on the Russian model began to occupy the younger writers, especially the poets. In December 1933, Julian Bell wrote that 'it might with some plausibility be argued that Communism in England is at present very largely a literary phenomenon – an attempt of a second "post-war generation" to escape from the Waste Land'. In February 1934 a British section of the radical Writers' International was formed, and in October the first issue of *Left Review*, its official journal, appeared. Also, in October the British section of the Artists' International held its first exhibition.

Students were living as in a world besieged, resentful rebels against their elders. J. M. Keynes 'could not but observe the tendency towards communism amongst the young at Cambridge, and most markedly amongst the choice spirits. . . .'[62] The Cambridge Socialist Club had 200 members in 1933, over 600 in 1936, and almost 1000 in 1938 (in a university with less than 5000 undergraduates). The October Club had 200 members in its first year.[63] This growth of radicalization was reflected in CP membership: in 1935 nearly 8000 members; in 1939, nearly 20,000.[64]

Bernal was concerned with the lack of an effective organization of scientists. The Association of Scientific Workers (AScW) was the obvious body which he could help to develop. Indeed, between 1931 and 1933 it lay waste, the ground prepared but not cultivated. It had been formed in 1918 as the National Union of Scientific Workers (NUSW). It differed from other organizations of scientists in that it was not based on one profession, as was, for example, the newly formed British Association of Chemists. It was expressly a trade union ready to act on behalf of all scientists.

The NUSW was conceived in Cambridge,* following the publication of *Science and the Nation*, a collection of essays, edited by Albert Seward, FRS, urging adequate support of pure science as a basis for post-war recovery. The essayists included such distinguished individuals as W. H. Bragg and F. Gowland Hopkins. In the *Cambridge Magazine* in May 1917, E. E. Turner, reviewing the book, had drawn a depressing picture of the bleak future for the young researcher. It led Harold Jeffreys to call together a number of young Cambridge and London scientists, who then wrote to colleagues in univer-

---

* I am indebted to Dr Elizabeth Kay McLeod, for the information on which this section is based. She kindly allowed me to read her MS 'Politics, professionalization, and the organization of scientists: the Association of Scientific Workers 1917–1942', presented in partial fulfilment of requirements for the degree of Doctor of Philosophy in History of Social Studies of Science, University of Sussex, 1975.

sity and government laboratories. Their argument was 'that the position of those who wish to devote themselves to scientific research is unsatisfactory. The research worker does not enjoy, as he is entitled to do, a standing equal to that of the other learned professions, and in many cases he has to engage in additional work in order to supplement his income.' At the end of 1917 a new organization was formed, to be called the NUSW. A provisional executive included four of the original Cambridge group. The aim of the association was 'the promotion by corporate action of the economic interests of its members', and 'the first step in obtaining a proper recognition of the vital importance of science in all departments of national life must consist in securing conditions for scientific work which will attract the best brains in the country, and command respect in a community which tends to regard wealth as a measure of worth'.

By the time Bernal began to be active in the Cambridge Branch in the early 1930s, the NUSW no longer existed in that name. It had become the Association of Scientific Workers (AScW),* a name adopted in 1927 to seek to resolve the basic conflict of interests between 'the right' and 'the left' within its ranks. By that time it was clear that the NUSW could no longer function effectively as a trade union: between 1927 and 1929 the AScW finally lost its remaining industrial members, and government scientists were taken over by the Institution of Professional Civil Servants (IPCS). The group within the AScW who were determined to remove its reputation for sympathy with the Labour movement, to make the association 'politically respectable', succeeded in ensuring that it was no longer affiliated to the Labour Party, or legally a trade union.

Those who were concerned about the association had to deal with the question: What function could the AScW perform in the interests of science and scientists? An answer became clear, especially after 1933. Conditions were ripe to develop politically conscious scientists, especially the young who argued that not only were they and science being frus-

---

* The c was added to distinguish it from the ASW (Amalgamated Society of Woodworkers).

trated, but also their potential was being denied. Bernal had begun to investigate 'the way in which science was organized, the way it worked. I studied the way in which throughout its history it had developed from the phase of primitive magic up to the control of the natural forces in modern times. And I saw that science, which started in some refined and unimportant part of the pattern of life – in astronomy, in the study of precious metals – had become something on which the whole of modern civilization depended. In doing so, it had lost its old abstraction. Abstract science had been a support for the established order in a hierarchical society: the early scientists were the privileged protégés of Kings and Churchmen. But now, since the Industrial Revolution, it had been turned into a servant of industrialists. It had become in our own century an essential support in peace and war of the great monopoly industrial states that had succeeded the free competition of capitalism of the nineteenth century. I saw something of what this meant towards the development of science itself, and I put this into my first big book, *The Social Function of Science*.' ‡ But that was not to appear until the eve of war: it was to be his key to open the door leading from the labyrinth of confusion that was then the accepted understanding of what science was.

An approach to this was made clear in his survey – written anonymously in the early 1930s – of science and education in Britain in the collection, *Britain Without Capitalists*.[65] The book was an important statement, the first of its kind, as an attempt by a group of (about twelve) economists,* scientists, and technicians – all anonymous – to apply Marxist principles to 'a critical analysis of the condition of British industries today, and the possibilities of achievement open to the working people of this country once the capitalist class was removed'. It was basically a study of Britain's productive system, and it stated boldly that science must be thought of as an industry, as the chief transforming agent of production, which had arisen because of the importance of its contribution to industrial profits and the necessity of maintaining imperialist military

---

* H. D. Dickinson was the economist.

strength. It concluded that in a Soviet state science would be 'an unmixed blessing, for it can no longer be made use of to increase exploitation or to intensify the horrors of war. This is the use which all the great scientists of the past have thought of as an ideal, but they have had either to blind themselves to the social realities, or to accept the fact that up till now the ideal has had to be sacrificed to practical necessities. The socialist State will be the first to give the scientist the full material and organizational possibilities for his work. It must also be the first to allow him to turn his work to its true end.'

For the younger generation of scientists, those in their early twenties, Bernal was already a legendary figure. His appearances at AScW branch meetings were rare, but when he took part he did inspire activity. John Fremlin recalled that in the mid-1930s Bernal was 'the general stimulator' in a vigorous AScW recruitment drive. Nationally, he was one of the guarantors of the AScW, 'for a sum of about £200', according to Reinet Fremlin, who was national secretary of the association from 1937 to 1945. As a speaker, frequently she found him in his opening statements 'a bit woolly, as if *en route* he had had some new thoughts and had not quite worked them out: often, his talk was somewhat above the level of his audience. But he was very good at answering questions. Then he was discerning and clear, establishing a good personal relationship.'[66]

He was then a member of the AScW National Executive Committee, and when he did attend he would concern himself with, say, two or three items on the agenda, which were his reasons for being present. His activities in the association were his attempt to shape an instrument by which to translate the actual world into the world he wished to see around him. He was so confident, so filled with knowledge: he promoted confidence because he had a philosophy of life, a determined viewpoint. He was a rebel who made demands on those who wished to be involved in his causes. Thus, John Fremlin, self-confessedly shy, uncertain, and politically ignorant, was asked to go out and give talks, anywhere and everywhere, on the anti-war campaign. 'I did, although I was scared. Yet I developed the necessary courage, and this aided my own independent development,' he remembered.

It was during the 30s that Bernal was engaged, also, in polemics with such shapers of opinion as Lancelot Hogben, Gerald Heard, and Julian Huxley. They argued vigorously, mainly in a series of letters, about 'means and ends', 'opportunism and Communism', 'Marxism as a philosophy for a non-acquisitive society', 'just wars, morality, and the struggle for peace'. Hogben always approached Bernal cautiously, seemingly a little intimidated by what he referred to as 'the recesses of your erudition'. He divided Marxists in Britain into two sharply contrasting groups: the one made up of men such as Bernal, 'who are sincerely examining the impact of technical innovation on the society in which they live, as Marx examined the impact of technical innovations in the society in which he lived'; the other consisting of individuals 'who regulate their conduct in the light of conclusions which Marx drew from his own studies without regard to facts which he could not possibly have known in his time'.[67] Of course, Bernal did not agree with his view that 'at the present Marxist phraseology is a powerful incubus, destroying lucid discourse devoted to the advancement of human wellbeing, and it is not less so than Fascist ideology which employs emotive language to mobilize the retreat into barbarism'.*

Hogben argued, also, that the Labour Party, whose policy was based on the block vote of the trade unions, could not become an instrument for promoting a planned economy of abundance. Industry, from the trade union viewpoint, existed to pay wages. And, from the viewpoint of the stockbroker,

---

* Hogben letter to Joseph Needham dated February 1st (year not given, but about 1934). This letter contains the following puzzling comments: 'And though I hate war above everything else, and next to war Jew-baiting, I will not have immigrant Yids dictating to me what language I shall use, unless the discussion is on the level at which language is of a purely informative character. The Russians have had the sense to realize this profound psychological repugnance to foreign forms in handling their cultural minorities . . . I think this difference is a very fundamental one . . . I read your essay on Harvey and feel this is in the English tradition. I read Bernal in the Labour Monthly and get as near to feeling anti-semitic as I ever could get. The fact that Woolf does not wash does not worry me; when he wants to rob me of my linguistic birthright he evokes sentiments bordering on sheer hatred. I think, by the way, that this is a main factor in the social disease of Jew hysteria . . .' When, in January 1978, I discussed this with Needham, he could not provide any enlightenment, but stressed that it was easy to upset Hogben.

industry existed to pay dividends. Neither saw industry as a means of making natural wealth available for human uses. When Bernal insisted that the only choice before them lay between fascism and Marxism, Hogben countered that the attempt to establish a planned economy of human welfare by reasonable persuasion had not failed, because it had not yet been tried. Bernal could not accept that before 1939, despite his support for a popular front. After 1945, although still critical of social democratic parties, he gave measured support to Hogben's insistence that the policy of peaceful progress might prosper if redistribution of wealth kept pace with public acquisition of resources for creating new wealth.

The country was living through a slump which did not fit into a Communist analysis of the crisis of capitalism. Income per head rose from 107·5 in 1925–26 to 134·9 in 1936–38; in 1920, only one house in seventeen had electricity: by 1939, two homes out of three were supplied; Marks and Spencer opened 129 stores between 1931 and 1935, their turnover rising tenfold between 1929 and 1939; in 1920, there had been about half a million motor vehicles of all sorts: in 1930, there were three times as many, and by 1939 that figure had doubled: of those three million vehicles, two million were private cars; in 1931, one and a half million were entitled to paid holidays: by 1939, the figure was 11 million.

But the forces of reaction were scared. They saw in the demands for a Popular Front a threat which could be met only by strengthening Hitler and Mussolini. The Spanish Civil War provided the decisive traumatic experience, which revealed openly the true savagery of fascism. Bernal was active in support for the Spanish people, in programmes for medical aid, in political activity for a people's front. And, in particular, preaching to fellow scientists that science could not develop or function without liberty; that, for the first time in history, science could be directed consciously for human welfare, but the scientist had to recognize this could be secured only by linking with the progressive forces, who in their turn had to learn to use science in their struggle for liberty and democracy.

This was the dominant theme to which Bernal addressed himself throughout the 1930s: the relationship between the laboratory behaviour of the scientist and the public experience of science. In so doing, he was to help a generation of scientists to discover themselves – not only in Britain, but also throughout the world.

6

Blast and Counterblast

To break out of the chaos of my darkness
Into a lucid day, is all my will.
STEPHEN SPENDER[68]

In January 1939, Bernal opened his Friday evening discourse at the Royal Institution by describing the structure of proteins as the major unsolved problem on the boundary of chemistry and physics. 'We have not yet found the key to the problem,' he said, 'but in recent years a mass of new evidence and new lines of attack have enabled us to see it in a far more concrete and precise form and to have some hope that we are near to solving it.'

In that same month there appeared his first major work, *The Social Function of Science*, which he might have described, also, as a major unsolved problem, but on the boundary of science and society. It took the war – its beginning only a few months away, September 1939 – to present solutions which, years later, caused him to comment, 'A prophet can so easily be deflated by the fulfilment of his prophecies. I feel very much the same in relation to myself.'[69]

The Social Function, an optimistic book, consists of two parts, headed: what science does; what science could do. Its concern was with the potential of science to satisfy material needs, and the changes necessary in society and in the organization of science to realize this potential. In retrospect, its publication is assumed to have caused more of a stir than it did at the time, although it was widely reviewed. Lord Ashby revealed that 'in common with thousands of my generation I was driven to think about these matters' by the book.[70] And Lord Zuckerman stated, 'More than anything else it made him known to a wider world.'[71]

Despite the difficulties of the war years, it was reprinted in each year from 1940 to 1946 (except for 1945), and its 500 pages were translated into the major languages. It arrived just in time for it to be the textbook of French and Dutch scientists, many of whom read it in internment. After liberation, they put it into practice. The book has never been published in the USSR, maybe because it is regarded as somewhat subversive with its clear 'Bukharinist approach'. Besides, the Russians had Bernal himself as a frequent visitor.

Bernal inscribed Zuckerman's copy of the book, 'To Solly, Quot Homines, Tot Sententiae, D'. Of course, Bernal had benefited greatly from many discussions with Zuckerman, who is one of those acknowledged in the preface, and as a member of that remarkable and exclusive dining club, the Tots and Quots, founded and inspired by Zuckerman.*

The Social Function is the quintessence of Bernal as 'a subversive', expressing the originality of one who is 'chosen' to perform an historic role. Hogben, a critic of Communist performance, was delighted by the book. In a review in February 1939 in *Controversy*, a socialist monthly, he stated, 'The concluding paragraph of a book packed with statistics reaches a moving eloquence which revealed his personality to me in a new and vastly attractive light.' It was – and still is – a remarkable work. The footnotes contain a wealth of ideas and facts on a multitude of topics on which Bernal might depart from the main argument. Many minor sections contain major proposals and analyses. For example, the section on science information is the key document for modern information science. It might be regarded as the parallel of Einstein's relativity theory, the expression of an advance into a new understanding based upon a reshuffling of the existing patterns of behaviour. Certainly, it represents the essence of progressive thinking of

---

* See *From Apes to Warlords*, Appendix 1, for Zuckerman's description. The club name arose from a quotation used by J. B. S. Haldane, *Quot homines, tot sententiae*, which Lancelot Hogben, recently returned from South Africa, corrupted into the quottentots, and this became the Tots and Quots.

the 1930s about the function of science in society. It was a first bold attempt at a Marxist analysis to consider 'how the work they [the scientists] are doing is connected with the social and economic developments which are occurring around them'.

Bernal saw how science had changed from being the domain of gifted amateurs into an industry with its own scientific workers. But because of the haphazard and uncontrolled way in which science had grown it had become 'a structure of appalling inefficiency' in terms of its internal organization and the means of applying it to production or welfare problems. His cry was, 'If science is to be of full use to society it must first put its own house in order'.

Bernal throughout the 30s saw the threat of Nazism also as the threat of war: for him, this reinforced the particular responsibility of the scientist 'because another war would be predominantly a scientific war. . . . And there the questions of the union of scientists, the question of the need to stir the social conscience of all scientists became a most urgent one'. His activity in the AScW was concerned first with reviving the Cambridge branch, basing the new membership on the Cambridge Scientists' Anti-War Group (CSAWG), of which he came to be president in 1937.* He was nominated for the executive of the AScW in February 1934, and at the same council meeting the Cambridge branch put forward a resolution urging members 'to find a means which may assist towards a better adjustment between scientific advance and social progress'. Under the stimulus of Bernal, the branch formulated a new policy statement, accepted by the executive, to appeal to 'new circles of scientific workers', and to make clear what the AScW stood for.

The new policy was in two sections: the professional sphere, and the social sphere. The aims for the professional were 'to promote a spirit of unity among scientific workers and to do what the BMA and the Law Society have . . . done for members of the medical and legal professions . . .' and 'to collabor-

---

* This included E. H. B. S. Burhop, R. C. Evans, J. Fremlin, F. W. Hughes, A. E. Kempton, R. Maasdorp, C. B. Mohr, J. and D. Needham, N. and A. Pirie, R. L. M. Synge, C. H. Waddington, A. Walton, M. Wilkins, and W. A. and N. Wooster.

ate with other professional and qualifying groups and to act on behalf of the interests of any class of scientific workers . . . not yet provided for by special organizations. . . .'

In the social sphere the association sought to ensure: '(a) that scientific research is adequately financed; (b) that scientific education is improved and its advantages made more widely accessible; (c) that science should be intelligently organized, both internally and in its applications, to ensure the maximum of initiative and the minimum of waste and confusion; (d) that scientific research should be directed primarily to the improvement of the conditions of life.'

To attain those ends, thirty-two detailed actions were proposed, ranging from '(1) to secure that the practice of science for remuneration shall be restricted to persons possessing adequate qualifications', to '(31) to endeavour to secure that the results of scientific research are not applied for purely destructive purposes', and '(32) to study the protection of inventors by patent law'.

This A Sc W attitude, formulated largely by Bernal, presented a direct challenge to the traditional attitude fostered by the elders of science, who based themselves on Robert Hooke's draft preamble to the Statutes of the Royal Society: 'The business of the Royal Society is: To improve the knowledge of natural things . . . (not meddling with Divinity, Metaphysics, Morals, Politics, Grammer, Rhetorick, or Logicks).' Allies were found within the Royal Society: in 1935 there appeared a collection of essays, *The Frustration of Science*, 'indicative', wrote Frederick Soddy in a foreword, 'of the growing sense of social responsibility, among some individual scientific men at least, for the world the labours of their order have so largely created'. His words merit further consideration for they make clear the serious concern that was emerging. 'The public expect far more from scientific men in this respect than they have as yet contributed. Individually most of them in this field are still utterly unscientific, and quite as apt as the public themselves to regard original thought on these subjects as socially dangerous and to be suppressed and those who have strayed from the path of "pure" science in these directions as cranks or impostors. As for the official and professional bodies representing science and medicine, as yet they have hardly emerged from the easy but very questionable attitude that it is no concern of theirs what they are hired out for.' The book, six of whose seven contributors were associated in some way with the AScW,* showed how science was frustrated through lack of funds and neglect, and how it was abused in use for war.

Bernal was much in demand as a public speaker, and he appeared at many meetings on the relationship between scientific research and war. He shared a platform with Needham in May 1936, when the AScW University College branch in London organized a meeting, attended by 250, on the utilization of science. Needham stated that the budget of £150,000 per year for poison gas research was larger than the total sum devoted to medical research. Bernal showed that the total expenditure on research in industry of only £440,000 annually produced an estimated saving of £3,500,000. How much more, he asked, might be achieved by careful investment in scientific research?

The main features in *The Social Function* were worked through in the preceding years. Activity in the AScW provided the keys. In October 1936, an editorial in the *Scientific Worker* called for 'the wider application of science and scientific method to the welfare society', and 'to secure the direction of scientific research and scientific work primarily to the improvement of conditions of life'.[72] These were aims which in the immediate pre-war years excited not only scientists, but also other sections of the community, puzzled and perplexed, and above all, afeard of the growth of fascism.

The British Association for the Advancement of Science (BA), through the vigorous leadership offered by Sir Richard Gregory, editor of *Nature*, and through the columns of that prestigious weekly, was seized of the concept of 'the planning of science and its social relations'. At the 1936 meeting, the president, Josiah Stamp, dealt with the impact of science on society. Also at that meeting, Sir Daniel Hall suggested that an institute for the investigation of the influence of science on

---

* Sir Daniel Hall, J. G. Crowther, J. D. Bernal, V. H. Mottram, P. M. S. Blackett, and Enid Charles (Mrs Lancelot Hogben).

society should be formed. His proposal was heard with interest by a delegation of American scientists, who included E. G. Conklin, the president of the American Association for the Advancement of Science (AAAS). It was agreed that the collaboration between the two associations should be encouraged. And in that encouraging atmosphere, Ritchie Calder proposed the formation of a World Association for the Advancement of Science. By 1938, the key BA officers, recognizing that, if they did not act, an independent body for the study of the social relations of science would be set up, decided to form a division for the Social and International Relations of Science. This was done at the Cambridge meeting in that year. Gregory was appointed chairman of the committee of the division, and Bernal was amongst the thirty or more members.

The high hopes held by Bernal for the success of the new division – success to be measured in terms of an extension of an understanding of social responsibility by scientists – were not met. Gregory was a traditional Low Church supporter of the Labour movement, and consistently anti-Marxist. This was reflected in the writers he invited to write for *Nature*. The well known left-wing radicals, including Bernal, contributed less than one per cent of leading articles in the 1930s. (Hogben wrote three; Bernal and Levy one each.)[73]

There was a central debate about the social relations of science within an overall debate about the nature of the social order to which such protagonists as Gregory and Bernal, seemingly in accord, presented different solutions: their roads coincided only under the pressure of national needs: basically, they were on opposite sides.* Bernal argued that science had advanced from 'the large and simple to the small and complex'. The first stage – 'the description and ordering of the available universe' – was completed, by and large. On the way to completion was the next stage – 'understanding the mechanics of the universe'. There remained 'unknown, and indeed in part necessarily unknowable, possibilities beyond this . . .'. He saw

* On student days in Cambridge, Barbara Wootton wrote, 'J. D. Bernal whose intellectual stature is such that not even a reputation for Communist sympathies can diminish it.'[74]

that humanity would 'have to tackle a universe which will itself become more and more a human creation', and that 'the chief difficulties both in the theory and practice of science lie in the problems that human society has created for itself in economics, sociology, and psychology. In the future, as the simpler conquest of non-human forces is brought to its conclusion, these problems will become increasingly important'.[75]

To master and direct the world, humanity had to learn how to cope both with the orderly and with the novel aspects of the universe. Here, Marxism 'as a method and a guide to action, not as a creed and a cosmogony' was the key. Its relevance to science was to remove it 'from its imagined position of complete detachment', and to show it 'as a part, but a critically important part, of economic and social development'. Bernal then stated directly, 'It is to Marxism that we owe the consciousness of the hitherto unanalysed driving force of scientific advance, and it will be through the practical achievements of Marxism that this consciousness can become embodied in the organization of science for the benefit of humanity'. Given that, science will come to be recognized as the chief factor in fundamental social change. The social function of science should be to 'provide a continuous series of unpredictable radical changes in the techniques concerned with the economic and industrial system'. He foresaw that 'science itself will change and develop, and in doing so will cease to be a special discipline of a selected few and become the common heritage of mankind'.

His final paragraphs in *The Social Function* merit full quotation. Hogben was impressed greatly with them. He wrote, 'Of the new social order which may emerge if truth prevails no one has written with more eloquent lucidity than my friend J. D. Bernal, himself a Marxist.'[76] Bernal stated, '*Science as Communism.* Already we have in the practice of science the prototype for all human common action. The task which the scientists have undertaken – the understanding and control of nature and of man himself – is merely the conscious expression of the task of human society. The methods by which this task is attempted, however imperfectly they are realized, are the methods by which humanity is most likely to secure its own future. In its endeavour, science is communism. In science men have learned consciously to subordinate themselves to a common purpose without losing the individuality of their achievements. Each one knows that his work depends on that of his predecessors and colleagues, and that it can only reach its fruition through the work of his successors. In science men collaborate not because they are forced to by superior authority or because they blindly follow some chosen leader, but because they realize that only in this willing collaboration can each man find his goal. Not orders, but advice, determines action. Each man knows that only by advice, honestly and disinterestedly given, can his work succeed, because such advice expresses as near as may be the inexorable logic of the material world, stubborn fact. Facts cannot be forced to our desires, and freedom comes by admitting this necessity and not by pretending to ignore it.

'These are things that have been learned painfully and incompletely in the pursuit of science. Only in the wider tasks of humanity will their use be found.'

In a review entitled 'Counterblast to Bernalism'[77] in the *New Statesman & Nation*, John R. Baker, described as an 'eminent Oxford biologist', expressed the viewpoint of many who regarded Bernal and his views as leading to an authoritarian society. He coined the term 'Bernalism', which never caught on, and which he defined as 'the doctrine of those who profess that the only objects of scientific research are to feed people and protect them from the elements, that research should be organized in gangs and told what to discover, and that the pursuit of knowledge for its own sake has the same value as the solution of crossword puzzles'. He asked the reader to 'try to imagine Charles Darwin told off by the Bernalist-in-charge to organize a gang of PhD students. The mind reels before the thought.' For Baker, a scientist should have 'an ethical concern for the judgment of his own conscience. Those to whom one listens with respect when they speak of verifiable matters (e.g. in crystallography) compel attention much less inevitably when they try to lay down the law on moral issues.'

Bernal replied in the *New Statesman* a week later.[78] He found Baker easy to deal with. 'I do not know where Dr Baker has

met the Bernalists; I have never been one myself, and I don't
believe they exist,' he began. But he had already replied to
such criticisms in 1938 in an article in the American Marxist
quarterly *Science and Society*, for which he was a contributing
editor (responsible for the English contacts) with Hyman
Levy. His article entitled 'Science and liberty' began, 'There
is no branch of human activity more dependent than science
on the maintenance of liberty'. His reasoning, however, was
simplistic: for example, 'the decay into which science fell in
the twenties and thirties of the nineteenth century was largely
a result of the reaction of the wealthy and powerful against its
atheistical and Jacobin association'. The 'solution' lay in a
separation of science from the liberal movement; the development of the nineteenth-century fiction of pure science, which
'enabled the wealthy to subsidize science without fearing to
endanger their interests, and scientists to avoid having to ask
awkward questions as to the effects of their work in building
up the black hell of industrial Britain'.[79]

He ended, as he began, 'The fate of science depends upon
the preservation of liberty.' Science 'consciously directed and
planned for human welfare could transform the world in half
a generation'. But the scientist and the forces of liberty and
democracy must work together.

Bernal developed this approach in a more sophisticated form
in the *New Statesman* article. He argued there was no contradiction between science in practical use in a community and the
scientist working 'for what he thinks is a sheer love of truth and
beauty'. The former was a question of social economics, the
latter of psychology. The problem was not to decide whether
science was to be a directed activity, but what its direction
should be; not to decide whether it should be organized, but
how to organize it so as 'to avoid confusion and obscurity
without damaging the freedom of thought and activity of the
individual worker, on which ultimately everything depends'.

Baker was far from satisfied. On 2 March 1940, he attacked
again in the *New Statesman*. He declared, 'Let those whose real
interest is politics be politicians and not masquerade under
another name'.[80] He never really understood Bernal. He saw
him only as an enemy, as a threat, as did the Society for

Freedom in Science, of which Baker was secretary. In his book *The Scientific Life*, published in 1942, Baker declared that science was under attack, and the attack came 'subtle and indirect from within'. He saw 'the spirit of free enquiry' as under threat 'by those who would plan other people's researches and confine investigation to crudely practical ends'.[81] The message of Bernal's *Social Function* was to have scientific research workers treated as sheep. 'Anyone who reads this book must become aware that it preaches a doctrine of the reduction of freedom for research workers. It is true that here and there the book contains passages which pay lip service to the ideal of freedom; but these passages are contradictory to the whole tenor of that book.'

Michael Polanyi, a most capable intellectual figure in the society, and himself a crystallographer, challenged 'the new radically utilitarian valuation of science', which rested on 'a consistent philosophical background, borrowed mainly from Marxism'. This could lead only to scientists being placed 'under the guidance of authorities who know the needs of society and are generally responsible for safeguarding the public interest'. A materialist interpretation of history reinforced the plea for the planning of science, as science has always advanced only in response to social needs. 'The protest of those who would defend the freedom of science against planning is rejected and branded as an expression of an obsolete and socially irresponsible attitude.'[82]

That was first written in 1945. Three years later, Polanyi declared that although the books which started the movement for planning were still read, their message was no longer taken seriously, for 'the movement had petered out'. Of course, it had not: it had changed its form, and the devotees in the Society for Freedom in Science could no longer recognize it.

The Social Function appeared at the conclusion of a decade of tremendous activity by Bernal, and on the eve of a six-year period during which he was to fulfil himself as never before or since. He took a full part in the Bohemian life of the 1930s, especially in London, at, for instance, the many bottle parties. He would either appear with a woman, or leave with one. Many who saw him regularly were unaware that he was married. On the occasion of a Royal Society *conversazione* at Burlington House, the noisy chatter suddenly and strikingly ceased – 'a pin dropped would have been heard', according to Charles Goodeve – as 'Professor and Mrs Bernal' were announced: all eyes were turned for very few had ever seen a Mrs Bernal, or knew that one existed.

His acquaintances were as numerous as his interests. In the summer of 1927, Francis Meynell made 'anxious inquiry' of Bernal on a matter concerning flying and cricket. At Great Yeldham, a few miles from Cambridge, a new cricket pavilion had been finished. Meynell wanted to make a grand occasion of its opening. His friend, David (Bunny) Garnett had just learned to pilot his own plane. 'I thought it would be gay and exciting to have him fly over and drop a cricket ball from the air for our opening match', Meynell recalled. 'Then, knowing nothing of ballistics, I had a sudden fear that the ball would gather such speed in falling that it would have a cannonball effect and might go through the roof of the new pavilion.' Bernal reassured him there was no likelihood of that: 'but I had not realized how difficult it would be to aim from an aeroplane, even at so large a target as a cricket field. We saw Bunny fly over, but we never found the ball', wrote Meynell.[83]

In the summer of 1932, he was staying with John Strachey and Celia (the second Mrs Strachey) at their country home.[84] Strachey had broken with his old friend, Sir Oswald Mosley, and he, imagining that 'Mosley might have his own back on him', discussed with Bernal, the physicist John Pilley, and the solicitor to the *Daily Worker*, Harry Thomson, as they sat under an apple tree, 'the best way to get rid of Mosley'.

There were also the artists – particularly Barbara Hepworth, Ben Nicholson, and Henry Moore – with whom Bernal spent many hours. At that time they formed the Belsize Park Group, and were concerned primarily with geometrical constructivism as part of their desire to express in visual terms 'a comprehensive nature-and-social philosophical synthesis'.[85] Waddington pointed out that they expressed an aspect of the real world which had not been made clear previously. 'The sense of the real world as an area of interlocking energies, of a line as a path of minimum energy through orderly fields of force, is, of course, an expression of some of the basic notions of modern science; notions, moreover, that were not at all fully expressed in the earlier geometricizing developments, which were either predominantly static, or, as with the futurists, kinetic, with an emphasis on movement, but hardly at all dynamic, with an emphasis on force.'[86]

Barbara Hepworth often told me, at her studio in St Ives, of how she loved the visits of Bernal, who would examine her works and explain their mathematical and geometrical forms. For many years, Bernal had in his flat a rather bad drawing of a crystal by Barbara Hepworth.

In 1937, there appeared a major international survey of constructive art called *Circle*. The editors were J. L. Martin, Ben Nicholson, and Naum Gabo. Their aim was to allow painters, sculptors, architects, and writers to express their views, and to maintain contact with each other. Contributors included Piet Mondrian, Herbert Read, Le Corbusier, Barbara Hepworth, Henry Moore, J. M. Richards, Maxwell Fry, Marcel Breuer, S. Giedion, Walter Gropius, Leonide Massine, L. Moholy-Nagy, Lewis Mumford and Bernal on 'Art and the Scientist'. He pointed out how one of the features of present-day civilization ('out of which we are now passing') was the separation of art and science, so that 'for the official scientist a picture or statue might just as well not exist'. That had always been so. Interest in the visual arts led to the birth of accurate observation of nature; the problems of architecture gave rise to the science of mechanics. But bourgeois culture separated the useful and the ornamental.

The full implications of modern science for art, he went on, had not been thought out. He put forward some 'notes and suggestions of the lines along which such an analysis might be made'. In surrealism, the rules of composition were no longer mathematical, but psychologically guided: it drew also on biological structure, a new field of content for art. Artists were becoming discontented with solving only problems of presentation. 'Socially, art is not complete unless it passes from the solution of problems to something of more immediate social utility.' He went on to develop the theme of the social responsibility of the artist, which was akin to that of the scientist. 'Even a civilization in a state of transition must be able to find expression through its arts for the struggles that are going on. The expression need not, in fact should not, take the obvious and hackneyed forms of revolutionary art. Nor, on the other hand, can it be left to the artists in isolation to discover what form it should take. Scientists and artists suffer not only from being cut off from one another but being cut off from the most vital part of the life of their times. How to end this isolation and at the same time to preserve the integrity of their own work is the main problem of the artist today. There are no ready-made solutions, but if the goal can be seen the way to it will be found.'

The main goal he had in mind at that time was the struggle against fascism and the fight for peace. He was already heavily involved, and soon he was to be given the opportunity to move into action.

7
Days of Fulfilment

Your science will be valueless, you'll find,
And learning will be sterile, if inviting,
Unless you pledge your intellect to fighting
Against all enemies of mankind.

BRECHT[87]

Science and war was a theme which occupied Bernal strenuously until death; and he was to live on, memorialized institutionally, in the struggle to establish and maintain the conditions for peace. He showed, in *The Social Function*, that the connection of science and war was not a new phenomenon, they had always been linked most closely; 'the novelty is in the general recognition that it is not the proper function of science'.[88] The chapter on 'Science and War' (Chapter VII) was a most remarkable statement, the first of its kind to examine quantitatively the expenditures on scientific research for military purposes, and to relate these to the nation's civilian expenditures and needs. He made clear how during the First World War, 'scientists found themselves for the first time not a luxury but a necessity to their respective governments'. He deplored the wastefulness, for example, the death at Gallipoli of H. J. G. Moseley ('who might have become the greatest experimental physicist in England'); he spoke of how a leading physicist, who offered to organize a meteorological service for the army, was told that the British soldier fought in all weathers. Despite the wastefulness, 'under the stimulus of war it was possible to increase the rate of application of science by many times what had appeared to be the limit of peacetime activity. This showed that the progress of science had been limited in peace not by any intrinsic factors but rather by the external economic and political factors.'

Under the pseudonym 'X-ray' in 1927, Bernal had contributed to *The Communist*[89] an analysis of 'The Great Poison-Gas Plot'. His thesis was that the new weapon of poison gas was a military success, that the science and art of poisoning people had made very rapid progress, and that a new type of chemist – the professional poisoner – had appeared. The British government, whether Conservative or Labour, was developing a powerful chemical warfare machine, involving civil institutions such as the universities and the Department of Scientific and Industrial Research. He concluded the lengthy article, which contained much statistical and financial data, by forecasting that there would be no front in the next war as there had been in the last: the front would be limited only by the distances to which aeroplanes could fly. He insisted that protection against gas would be very difficult: and asked, 'why should the workers of the world who have no quarrel be poisoned by the million?' The only way to prevent the holocaust was 'to smash capitalism. . . . The task is difficult and urgent, but Lenin's Communist International can do it, if we build up strong Communist parties and give it enough power.'

The Cambridge Scientists Anti-War Group (CSAWG) was formed by some eighty scientists, mainly from the Cavendish Laboratory and the Biochemical Laboratory, and from 1934 they were active in study groups, organizing public meetings, and various research activities concerned with air raid precautions and the dangers of gas warfare. They took space on hoardings to proclaim the danger of war. One poster that was prepared read, 'Fascism means mass murder and war', but it was never displayed, because those who rented the CSAWG the advertising space feared it might be held to be libellous to fascists.[90]

There is little doubt that although Bernal was one of the first names that came to mind when mentioning the group, his practical contribution was limited. 'I do not remember that Bernal took part in any of the experimental work, supervisorly or otherwise, although it may well be that he suggested it, and certainly he was instrumental in getting hold of some of the gas masks which we tested, and I suspect through some unofficial channels.'[91]

The Woosters were the activists, and many experiments were done in their house. Almost all of the incendiary bomb tests, and much of the gas mask research, were directed and carried out by John Fremlin and one or two colleagues. 'The gas-proof room experiments hung heavily on Reinet (Mrs Fremlin) who, as a graduate at Newnham, was not at that time a member of the university, and (being in lodgings) could therefore take readings between midnight and 6 a.m., which was not permitted to junior male members of the university', recalled John Fremlin.

In 1937, the CSAWG published their book, *The Protection of the Public from Aerial Attack*, giving details of the various experiments they had carried out. It is interesting to note that Bernal is described in it as one who had 'personally carried out and supervised the experiments recorded'. The conclusions in the book were challenged in a lengthy review by C. H. Foulkes* in *Nature* of 10 April. General Foulkes declared the book could do nothing but harm, because it was calculated to destroy confidence in the Home Office defensive measures, and to create panic. Bernal and his colleagues** replied in a letter published in *Nature* on 1 May. They declared that they 'had no desire to create panic, but those who persuade the people of Great Britain to believe that they are safe when they are not are inviting panic and worse than panic in the case of war'. As scientists and citizens, they would be lacking in their duty if they accepted assurances whose validity they had not been convinced of. Finally, they urged that the protection of the population from aerial attack should be studied openly by representative scientists, so that a rational estimate could be

* Maj. Gen. Charles Howard Foulkes, Col. Comdt. RE since 1937, a distinguished, much decorated soldier, b. 1875. Author of *Gas! The Story of the Special Brigade*, 1934.
** J. H. Fremlin, Shirley Glasstone, A. F. W. Hughes, A. J. P. Martin, Joseph Needham, N. W. Pirie, R. N. Roberston, R. L. M. Synge, J. S. Turner, D. H. Valentine, C. H. Waddington, Arthur Walton, Nora and W. A. Wooster.

made of the probable efficiency of measures finally adopted.

Two years later, on the eve of war, Bernal was still accusing the government of a lack of realistic discussion of the problem of air-raid precautions (ARP). A memorandum on air-raid precautions in St Pancras, London, dated 20 May 1938, made clear how effectively Bernal was involved in such activity. The objects of the precautions were the protection of lives and of property, and the maintenance of essential services. Government proposals were stated, and followed by '*Our proposals: Gas*. This is a secondary danger, but becomes a primary one if there is no adequate protection.

Dispersal. We propose full public shelters giving really adequate protection.

Wardens. We insist on democratic control and of all ARP schemes, and recommend that the trades unions, etc., ask their members to volunteer.

Evacuation. We insist that this be a government responsibility.

Finance. We insist that the government shall accept and pay for adequate shelter and precautions in the boroughs.

Policy. Peace and protection.'

Although described everywhere as one of the Cambridge 'reds', Bernal had come to be regarded as an authority on the effects of bombing. Thus, he was taken by Zuckerman in the early summer of 1939 to a luncheon at All Souls given by Sir Arthur Salter, then M P for Oxford University, to discuss this difficult problem. At the lunch was Sir John Anderson, the Lord Privy Seal, with responsibility for civil defence, who was to become the Minister for Home Security when war was declared. Bernal was eloquent and persuasive when demolishing the measures proposed by the government. He impressed Sir John, who, later, described the discussion to his newly appointed Chief Scientific Adviser, Dr Reginald Stradling, the director of the Building Research Station. Stradling warned that Bernal was a security risk, and Sir John commented, 'even if he is as red as the flames of hell', he wanted him as an additional adviser on civil defence.[92]

When war began, Bernal was attached to a new department (Research and Experiments) at the Ministry of Home Security, then housed at the Forest Products Research Laboratory at Princes Risborough. This was only twenty miles from Oxford, and in those early days of the phoney war he went frequently there to tell Zuckerman about his work on the physics of explosions and the resistance of structures to various types of shock. Zuckerman listened, without finding it easy to understand, until he himself came to be involved actively in war work as a result of an introduction by Bernal to Dr Stradling. He came to be concerned with research on the risk of concussion to people in underground shelters from bomb-explosion shock-waves passing through the earth.[93]

As a team, Bernal and Zuckerman transformed the study of bombing and its effects from rumour and guesswork to a policy based on thoroughly scientific and practical principles. Bernal was regarded as an imaginative, yet thoroughly practical, person. For instance, early in the war he was involved in a discussion on how to deal with the fuse of an unexploded bomb. Speedily, he hit on a solution, based on the schoolboy practice of egg-blowing. This gave him the idea of making the bomb harmless by emptying the explosive with steam from a safe distance, thus ignoring the fuse completely. By the end of 1940, he and Zuckerman were both members of various committees: for example, on body armour and steel helmets, and on air-raid casualties, both committees linked with the Medical Research Council.

Bernal was a brave man: he seemed to have conquered the angel of fear in his effort to understand and gain knowledge from everyday experience. In 1940, when it was agreed officially to start a bomb census, that is to keep a record of every bomb dropped on Britain, he was with Stradling and Zuckerman in a civil defence war room in London when news came that following a daytime raid St Pancras station had had to be closed. 'That's for us,' said Bernal, and they dashed off. The reported unexploded bomb which had caused some damage turned out to be one of the army's anti-aircraft shells. Bernal, who had gone out to inspect the bomb, disappointed, strolled back to the station master's office, and said, 'Mr Station Master, you may now open your station'.[94]

On another occasion, in the Luton area, Zuckerman, who

was seeing his first human casualties, was impressed deeply by Bernal's objectivity as he tried to reconstruct exactly what had happened when the bomb burst. To Zuckerman 'destruction was still destruction, and so far as I was concerned, it lent itself to no possible order'.[95] During 1940 and 1941, Zuckerman began to develop the concept of 'vulnerable area', or 'standardized casualty rate'. In this he was aided by the statistician Frank Yates, who had been introduced by Bernal.* Another nominee of Bernal's was Jacob Bronowski, who was not highly regarded for his scientific quality by Zuckerman.

By mid-1941, Bernal and Zuckerman were accepted as the country's experts on the effects of bombs. Then, one Saturday night late in August 1941, Zuckerman, who was dining with Cherwell in Christ Church, as he did usually when they ran into each other there, suggested a survey of the overall effects of bombing on Hull and Birmingham, because the bomb census was almost complete for those cities, and because one was a manufacturing, and the other a port, centre. An official request went to Stradling, and Bernal and Zuckerman were asked to undertake this: the latter to deal with the casualty and social aspects, the former with the rest. The inquiry was generally to cover physical damage, casualties, effects on production, absenteeism, evacuation, and morale. It turned out to be an historic report,[97] whose final preparation was hectic for the two chief investigators.[98] Its conclusions denied a breakdown of morale due to the intensities of the raids: further, that loss of industrial production was caused almost entirely by direct damage to factories, and these were more seriously damaged by fire than by high explosive.** This report was regarded by Cherwell as a challenge to his view that massive bombing of German cities would destroy morale and cripple production. The dispute about area-bombing still goes on. Neither Bernal nor Zuckerman changed their minds re-

* 'Standardizing destructive power seems very simple now, but before Yates showed how it could be done, broken buildings and shattered bodies were only broken buildings and shattered bodies.'[96]
** The diary entry of Sir Henry Tizard for 17 February 1942 reads, '. . . Bernal left his summary of the results of German bombing of England. Taken as a whole the effect on production and morale has been surprisingly small.'[99]

garding its limited usefulness and extravagant wastefulness. But Bernal was not as deeply involved as Zuckerman in this particular controversy. In fact, his years of apprenticeship were ending. He was moving on to other – seemingly more glorious – fields of wartime activity.

Even in those years, when the day's rumours were of sacrifice and death, he still maintained his activities in the promotion of science in the service of a new world. In September 1941 he was involved in a conference on 'Science and World Order', arranged by the Division for the Social and International Relations of Science of the British Association at the Royal Institution in London. It was an important meeting in which scientists from twenty-two nations, including the USA, the USSR, and China, 'met to discuss the kind of world that must come out of war, a world in which the plenitude of science would be used not for destruction, but for the emancipation of mankind from want and fear'.[100] The conference might be regarded as a triumph for Bernal's views. Even right-wing scientists, such as A. V. Hill, subscribed openly to the need for 'scientific planning and the planning of our national resources . . . planning, however, in which any new order we arrive at is fitted to our traditional freedom'.[101]

Bernal, as always the visionary, pointed out that they were in the middle of a complete transformation of the position of science in social affairs, that war conditions had speeded up that transformation, and that it had become clear that science had a wider and more thoroughgoing application to governmental affairs. Science was helping to decide the direction in which policy should go, and also in carrying out the policy itself. He warned that 'in conditions of war we have not the leisure to discover what our problems are. Disaster comes too rapidly in wartime, and the job is to anticipate disaster rather than to react after it.' He urged the necessity for speedy availability of information, using the latest techniques for decision makers, and giving people the information they ought to have even before they knew it existed, or that they wanted it. He advocated the extension of operational research, a wartime discovery, to peacetime problems. What was needed, he insisted, was 'not a government of scientists, but a scientific government, alive to the possibilities of science . . . the most urgent requirement is not that our scientists should become administrators, but that our administrators should become scientific'. He went on to develop his strongly held belief hat a modern industrial state could develop only if its activities were co-ordinated in a common direction.

Those present at the conference, listening keenly to him, were aware that the Luftwaffe bombers were only half an hour's flying distance away. They responded to his words of defiant hope, calling after the war, as during it, for 'a common purpose and a new motive which will transcend all the limited motives of private profit or individual security that have dominated men in the past. But science and human goodwill cannot march separately; they must go on together if they are to escape the futility and destruction of the present day. For this, science must cease to be the preserve of a few people. As the scientist comes more and more to interest himself in all human problems, so must the citizen learn a wider and deeper application of science.' An interesting example of the kind of exciting vision he was so able to generate was his proposal for an International Resources Office to conserve material resources through their full and co-ordinated, but not wasteful, use.[102]

Bernal continued to be active in the Association of Scientific Workers, which during the war years came to have a key influence in the organization and deployment of scientific manpower. By 1940, the AScW had agreed to allow laboratory technicians into membership, and to register as a trade union. The drive to develop as an industrial union was successful: membership rose from 2000 in April 1941 to 10,536 by March 1943.

In January 1942, in the middle of the war, the AScW organized in London a conference on the utilization of scientific manpower and the application of scientific knowledge to problems of industrial production and of the armed forces. In a summing up, Bernal said that although the scientific way of doing things was forcing its way against opposition, 'the attitude in many of the departments was equivalent to sabotage'.

He was convinced that scientific workers were 'at least co-operatively conscious of the job they have to do in society, and they will do it, and not stop doing it, when the war is won'.

His links with the AScW provided him with a good mechanism for keeping in touch with the grass-roots scientific worker. Thus, he was interested in the critical review of the actual and potential war function of university research laboratories which was provided by the Cambridge University branch. On 28 July 1942 he spoke on 'Science and the war effort' to the staff associations of the National Physical Laboratory and associated laboratories. He pointed out that all available forces had to be applied to definite ends. In military affairs, 'owing to the difficulty of changing over, unless, say, a 100 per cent yield is to be expected in a year, the work is not worth doing'. He commented, also, on 'perhaps the greatest handicap', the lack of direct contact between scientific workers and their opposite numbers in the services.[103]

Some time in 1942, Zuckerman ceased to organize the dinners of that remarkable institution, the Tots and Quots, because of pressure of war work. About mid-April of that year, Zuckerman heard from Bernal, who had received a letter from Lord Louis Mountbatten, the Chief of Combined Operations (CCO), inviting him to serve as scientific adviser to 'Combined Ops'.* Bernal said he would agree only if Zuckerman was invited. The invitation went out almost immediately, and within two weeks they were installed in Richmond Terrace, off Whitehall. The suggestion to employ them was based on the advice of Sir Henry Tizard. Mountbatten had said he wanted two first-rate scientists who would be put on the operational analysis of devices, equipment, and techniques for the landing in Europe to come. They were preceded by Geoffrey Pyke, another civilian, recommended by Leo Amery, Secretary of State for India. 'He was a chap with no scientific qualifications, but a crazy, independent

---

* On 18 March 1942, the Chiefs of Staff had approved the appointment of Commodore Lord Louis Mountbatten as CCO with the acting rank of Vice-Admiral, Lieut-General, Air Marshal. COHQ was given new and wide-ranging terms of reference.

D

thinker, and something of a genius.' § He was filled with the most original ideas, which, he insisted, required to be promoted with 'ferocity of purpose'. He was, to put it modestly, a most controversial person. He and Bernal, already known to each other, were to work most intimately together during the next two years.

Bernal, Zuckerman, and Pyke were Mountbatten's 'Department of Wild Talents'. Zuckerman, known for his studies of baboons, was 'the Monkey Man'. More seriously, Bernal and Pyke were regarded as bad security risks by the Americans. This meant that their proposals were regarded with great suspicion, and made for serious working difficulties. Vannevar Bush, Roosevelt's scientific adviser, loathed Pyke, and his name was not mentioned in Bush's presence.

Mountbatten himself was an original. He made possible for Bernal the finest hours of his life, a period during which he was enabled to work out in practice what he had up to then considered only in theory. During his period of work for the Ministry of Home Security, he had observed the effects of bombing on great cities. 'I lived among ruins. I counted and analysed casualty figures. I saw something of the senseless misery of war at first hand.'[103] But now he had become involved in one of the most technologically complex and difficult of military operations: the Allied cross-Channel invasion of France in June 1944 (code-name, 'Overlord').* Mountbatten was called in to take on the job of CCO against his will. 'After having had an exciting first two years of the war in command of a destroyer flotilla, most of which had been sunk, I was delighted to be given command of an armoured aircraft carrier and get back to sea at once. Suddenly, I was pulled out of this on the order of Winston Churchill. The other chiefs of staff were much older than me: the First Sea Lord was twenty-four years my senior, and Alan Brooke about

§ This reference mark indicates direct quotations from an interview afforded to me by Mountbatten on 17 November 1977, later corrected by him, and returned to me on 3 January 1978.
* '. . . it can be equated to moving two cities the size of Chicago, USA, and Birmingham, England, across the storm-swept English Channel to Normandy in the face of German naval, army, and air opposition.'[104]

twenty years older. I came in very reluctantly. However, without my organization, many people have told me, there would have been no invasion in 1944, and not even in 1945.' §

As CCO, he had 'the tremendous job of thinking out, and developing the special equipment and techniques for an opposed landing across the Channel on a scale unknown anywhere before. There had been no study of this kind since the Dardanelles, and that was on a far lesser scale. I began to put my staff together, and I soon came to the conclusion that I must have amongst them the best available non-service men, preferably scientists. These would not have been trained in conventional Service Staff Colleges, and they would have minds open to work on entirely new problems.' § Mountbatten had a difficult task in getting his civilians accepted. Zuckerman was always presentable, but Bernal was more of a problem, mainly because of his very long hair and his political views. On one occasion, the Combined Ops staff was to be reviewed by King George VI on the terrace of Montagu House, overlooking the Embankment and on the Thames.* Bernal and Zuckerman had been told to be on parade, but when Zuckerman arrived, after most of the staff had already formed up, 'Des was not there. Mountbatten greeted me by saying that he was worried lest Bernal, who usually wore his hair very long, might have gone to have it cut. Fortunately, Des turned up in time, with his hair in its pristine state, and the King, who had been told what to expect, was not disappointed.'[105]

R. V. Jones, professor of natural philosophy at Aberdeen University, recalled how although he, like Bernal, was involved intensely in war work, their paths hardly crossed. But in 1943 they visited the same RAF station at Medmenham, the HQ for examination of air reconnaissance photographs, within a week of one another. Jones knew the officers there very well. On that visit, some of them asked whether he knew a Professor Bernal. When he said he did, they asked what kind of chap he was. Rather guardedly, Jones replied that he was a very good physicist, but why did they want to know? It appeared that a week or so earlier he had visited them in connection with his

---

* Since demolished to make way for the Ministry of Defence.

work on the assessment of bomb damage. The officers had been a little put out because, as one of them, a reserve officer as they all were, said, 'We *are* a regular Air Force station, and we thought he might have put on his best suit to come and see us. However, when we got to know him he seemed quite a pleasant chap, and at the end of the day he invited us to pay a reciprocal visit to his own establishment. We went yesterday, and directly we saw him we realized we had misjudged him because from the clothes he was wearing there he *had* put on his best suit to come and see us.'[106]

As with Bernal, stories about Pyke are legion. During a stay in North America, Pyke, in the company of a group of high-ranking officers, walked about in the snow in a shabby suit and a thin overcoat – and sockless. Again, for a meeting with Mackenzie King, the Canadian Prime Minister, he had bought a suit, fitted with a zip, then a new device, instead of the usual fly-buttons. Before the meeting, he had gone to the lavatory, and the zip had stuck. Pyke walked into the PM's office, drawing attention to his open fly, saying, 'Prime Minister, I would not have to present myself to you in this state were it not for the fact that Canadian engineers are totally inefficient.'[107]

Pyke, of course, was not asked to be present at the Royal review. The first time he was shown into Mountbatten's office his beard needed trimming, his shirt collar was grubby, and it was clear he never wore a tie; his jacket was unpressed, as were his scruffy flannel trousers inches above his battered crepe-soled shoes.*

'You have no idea of the prejudices I was up against to get them accepted as members of my staff,' said Mountbatten. 'A key soldier, one of my directors of planning, at a meeting asked whether we had got to take "these civilians". I knew that he had been a territorial, therefore a civilian, not a regular. I reminded him pointedly of this. Another chap had been on a staff course, and felt superior because of this. I asked him whether I should give the civilians authority by giving

---

* When I met Pyke for the first time, on a winter's day after the war, in an ABC teashop (long gone) in Vigo Street off Regent Street, London, I was shattered by his appearance, just as described, but with open sandals. [MG]

them a rank, or continue to treat them as civilians. In the end, I said I had had enough of such nonsense.' § He was convinced that the scientists could help with their ideas, and he had to get them involved. Just over a month after they had moved in, Mountbatten circulated to his staff the following minute: '1. I have decided that the two Scientific Liaison Officers, Professor Bernal and Professor Zuckerman, should be allowed to act as scientific observers at the meetings of the planning syndicates, each taking a different operation in turn. 2. This is an experiment to which I attach great importance as I am anxious to link up the scientists from the very beginning of operational planning so that when their scientific knowledge is required, they may be completely in the picture. 3. For planning they work directly under CXD.'

Bernal did not work on the same projects as Zuckerman; half the time each did not know where the other was or what he was doing.[108] Bernal was concerned with a very large number of different problems, but all with the same general theme – how to facilitate landings in any part of the world. He found this most interesting – militarily, scientifically, and historically. The idea of a major landing on an open coast was novel. Past efforts were mostly attempts at landings at ports: the one great exception of the disastrous 1915 Dardanelles expedition had shown the extreme difficulty and danger of coastal landings. Bernal found that little could be learned from past experience. The principles of organized landings had to be worked out afresh.

Looking at the basic problem, Mountbatten used only commonsense. 'I did not need to ask any involved questions. There was the clear objective of making an amphibious landing. Obviously, first, we had to learn the technique of landing against opposition; second, the record of the English weather meant we could not have a reliable forecast for more than four days, and the invasion had to continue regardless of the weather. To try to take an enemy-held port was to start with a great difficulty. The others wanted to invade the Pas de Calais. I was against this. I did not believe we could hope to capture Calais or Boulogne. I was interested in the Baie de la Seine, and the nearest point at which I wanted to start an experiment was Dieppe. The RAF objected because they could not give fighter support at that range until drop fuel tanks could become available.

'I insisted we could secure a lodgement, but then we would have to ensure we could build up reinforcements more speedily than the enemy could reduce us and push us back. The deception plan I proposed was to give the impression we were after the "obvious" landing place at Calais, but to go for the Baie de la Seine. I was fought bitterly by opponents of this. At this stage I felt I needed some help from extraordinary brains.' §

Bernal did not take part in the abortive Dieppe raid in 1942, with its very heavy casualties, but, with Zuckerman, was present at a rehearsal in the form of a dawn landing at West Bay in Dorset. They had asked to be observers in a support ship in the Dieppe raid, but Mountbatten had refused this. Bernal commented, 'It is surprising that room can be found for war correspondents, but not for your two scientific advisers.' Mountbatten explained to Bernal that he did not want to risk losing him and Zuckerman on a raid. They were much too important in preparing for the main invasion, and there were several military members of his staff who would give them a first-hand answer to their questions. Both were involved in the post-raid enquiry; Bernal was concerned with the damage suffered by naval and assault craft.[109] The raid made it completely clear that a sufficiently heavy bombardment of a port would destroy its facilities, thus nullifying the success of its capture. Thus, bit by bit, the idea grew of developing an alternative in the form of a sheltered stretch of water with mobile port facilities. Bernal helped with the development of an artificial harbour. As early as the summer of 1943, he came to have some idea of the place and plan of landing. He looked into the question of the suppression of waves by introducing barriers. He examined a Russian scheme for putting along the sea-bed perforated pipes through which compressed air could be pumped. This caused an aerated barrier of water, which as it was compressible would not transmit wave motion. Mountbatten turned this down, because it required a great air compressor to be moored off an enemy beach: clearly, it could be knocked out easily by a single bomb. Bernal then examined *lilos,* which were inflated canvas bags, moored as a breakwater so that they would yield to the pressure of the waves and not transmit them. This scheme, too, was rejected. 'Finally, we turned to the simplest, but most expensive, project: to sink ships and concrete caissons. The more these were bombed, the more a breakwater would be formed.' §

In August 1943, Bernal was on board the *Queen Mary,* en route to Quebec for the top-level Quadrant conference. How this came about was one of Bernal's favourite stories. 'That chap, Mountbatten, sent for me. I said to him, "You know I want to go to Canada." He said, "Get your hair cut, and pack a suitcase for a fortnight." We got on a train from a siding near Olympia. On board the *Queen Mary,* he said to me, "You haven't had your hair cut." He put me under guard, and I was taken down to the official barber, who cut about one inch off. When Mountbatten saw me, he said, "You still look odd. Plaster your hair down. Try and look normal!" '*

For the first day, Bernal almost the only civilian aboard, apart from a Mr Wingate[111] – was on his own. Mountbatten then sent for him and met him outside a large stateroom where Churchill and the Chiefs of Staff, with some of their advisers, were waiting for a demonstration of the merits of an artificial harbour to provide enough shelter for effective disembarkation. Mountbatten said, 'I have just told them that by the most extraordinary coincidence the greatest expert in the world happens to be on board. It's you . . . Yes, I know you know nothing about it, but you are the world's greatest expert. That's an order.'[112]

They entered the stateroom, then – recalled Mountbatten – 'we went into one of the big bathrooms, where Des had made some paper ships. They were put at one end of the bath, and Pug Ismay made waves on one side. Then Desmond used an inflatable swimming collar, which he stretched across the bath to absorb the wave movements. And his very able exposi-

---

* Mountbatten, in telling me this, said it was exactly the way in which Bernal told the story many times afterwards. According to Bernard Fergusson, Mountbatten said one day that he had been thinking Bernal ought to go to Canada at some time. He called in Bernal, and said 'I think you ought to go fairly soon. In fact, I have arranged for you to go this afternoon.'[110]

tion helped to tip the scale with the Chiefs of Staff, and made Winston more enthusiastic than ever.'* Bernal gave the credit for the first idea to a marine officer, Major Salter. Its development was really a team effort at COHQ.

By 1942, Arromanches in Normandy had been selected as the place where the Allied forces were to make their landing in Europe. But this, of course, was very secret, known only to a select few, certainly not to Bernal. The artificial harbour, the *Mulberry*, was designed to enable the troops to be landed with their equipment and supplies, and to be kept ashore. The next task was to build up the force at a faster rate than the enemy could rush up troops to meet that attack. That could be secured by cutting his lines of communication.**

It was Bernal who began a long scientific investigation which led to a deeper understanding of the physics of beach formation. It led, also, to an appreciation of the importance of the records of social behaviour in helping to understand the present. His approach was impressive. Mountbatten took advantage of this to fight the great prejudices shown by members of his staff against the remarkable civilian brains he had introduced. To begin with the military were unwilling to inform the civilians. A young naval officer went to Bernal, and asked him what he thought of the possibility of making a very small, light, portable echo-sounder to measure very shallow

---

* Fergusson stated that there were twenty newspaper-made ships, that the First Sea Lord (Admiral Pound) stood on a lavatory seat to get a view, that Bernal said the shallow end of the bath represented the coast of Normandy, and that a junior officer made waves with a back-brush in the deep end, and 'the Fleet' sank. Bernal said, 'That, gentlemen, is what will happen without an artificial harbour.' He then borrowed a lifebelt, which he laid across the shallow end, to represent the *Mulberry*, set up another fleet of twenty paper ships, and called for more waves. Nothing sank. The Chiefs of Staff were impressed.[113]

** Zuckerman produced a plan called *Interdiction* for that purpose. Basically, his proposal was to bomb everything that could be of help to move Hitler's 25 divisions in the Calais area following invasion. This was not developed in COHQ. 'It was Solly's plan, but we had to fight the obstinacy of Harris,' Mountbatten told me. By that time, however, Mountbatten was well-established in SE Asia, having left Combined Ops. in 1943. I will not go into the bitter controversy at the highest military levels engendered by Interdiction. It is important as an aspect of the difficulty there was – and still is – in taking 'the gusts of emotion', to use Blackett's phrase, out of decision making. To the interested, I recommend Zuckerman's book, *From Apes to Warlords*.

depths. Bernal asked why. The officer replied that the matter was too secret to explain, and that it was up to him to answer the question. To this Bernal replied, 'No, that is the wrong way to use a scientist.' Besides, the CCO had given an instruction that the scientists were to participate in the formulation of the questions to be investigated. He wished to know more. Reluctantly, the officer told him that what was wanted was a way of finding out, without the Germans knowing what we were doing, how to measure beach gradients, the runnels, and the consistency of the kind of beaches we might assault. His own idea was to put a lightweight echo-sounder on a board, and at night to push it from a submarine with a swimmer who would try to obtain this information. Bernal said, 'You have asked the wrong question. You should have asked, How do we measure the beach gradients and runnels without the Germans knowing?' His answer was that photography should be used, taking vertical photographs of the desired beaches at various stages of the tide and wind directions, and that the coverage should extend beyond the desired beaches so as to disguise what they were up to from the Germans, that is to photograph between Le Havre and the eastern base of the peninsula.

'This incident has been quoted before,' said Mountbatten, 'but it shows the importance of the stand taken by Desmond in insisting on participating in the formulation of questions. This was a very great pioneer service he performed. The effect was very good, for it showed my staff how the unusual brain could be of real help to them. This helped to alter their whole outlook, and Combined Ops became the only HQ where staff thought critically in an unconventional way.' §

By chance, the beach at Arromanches was known to Bernal. He had been on holiday there some years before with one of his girlfriends. He was given the task of examining some of the physiographical information that might be useful for the landings. He had noticed that the beach was very flat and slightly muddy. His first impulse was to see what the guide-books said, and in them he found confirmation of what he had observed. His *Guide Bleu* informed him that, 'The beach at Arromanches is very sloping, indeed the sea goes out a long way, and at extreme low tides the peasants go down to the end of the beach and pick up a kind of material they call *gourban*, which they use as manure in their fields.'

It was apparent to him immediately that that kind of beach might be treacherous, and that it was laid down probably on an old forest of glacial times, that is on a base of clay and peat. (He learned later that that was characteristic of all the sloping beaches around the French and English coasts.) He asked, What was the character of the sand deposits on such beaches? How thick were they? And how safe to allow military vehicles to use them? The provision of answers gave much work for researchers in many laboratories. For example, experiments were carried out at Brancaster, Norfolk, which had an identical beach structure, to discover whether it could carry the biggest tanks.* Brigadier R. A. Bagnold, an expert on sand, was able to show that the waves themselves are responsible for moulding beaches: on a normal, gentle day the waves do not produce simply circular movements of the water, but have a residual, progressive movement: that is, both the water at the top and that at the bottom move in towards the beach. The excess water is carried away by the undertow, which is a current flowing between top and bottom. In gentle weather the water at the bottom carries up grains of sand to build up the beach, and so long as there is sand the beach will grow; or, it will add sand at the bottom which, when winds are strong, may be blown away at the top to form sand-dunes. In a storm, however, the opposite occurs. The waves stir up the sand, which is lifted into the returning stream and is carried out to sea to be deposited in deep water. A beach may build up three or four metres in a season, and then a single, stormy night in winter may sweep it clean.

Bernal realized that to understand the beach structure it was necessary to reconstruct its history: over time, considerable variations in the coastline occur when processes of beach building are combined with land movements and slight risings and sinkings. He gathered information on the local geology and history, seeking out the artery of change. He was fortunate

---

* After the war, Zuckerman was puzzled as to whether there might not be confusion about the beach. He had inspected craters after a special bombing test at Thornham, on the north coast of Norfolk.[114]

enough to have available every volume of the *Proceedings of the Linnaean Society of Caen*, published since about 1844. He paid particular attention to accounts of summer excursions, usually made to the seaside. He found entertaining details of the dinners eaten, and speeches made, on those occasions, but most precious was the information provided by geologists, botanists, or zoologists, as the character of a snail or of a plant would indicate the nature, marshy or otherwise, of the particular area. Thus, he thought it likely that the Bay of Calvados had been farmland not later than 230 AD. And in a well-known Anglo-Norman poem, the *Roman de Rou* – the story of the escape at night and alone of William (before he became the Conqueror) from a castle near Cherbourg to a friend at Ries – there is a good description of the country. Of special interest is the account of William's crossing at low tide of Le Grand Gué (now Le Grand Vey), which indicated there was a ridge of rock and gravel which crosses the muddy bay and enables the passer to avoid a detour of some 40 kilometres. Air photographs confirmed the existence of the ridge.

Bernal found, also, differences, which were to prove of great strategic importance, between the country of the plain of Caen and that of Bocage, which began near Port-en-Bassin. The military importance lay in the fact that the geological formation which leads to a large number of small fields and hedges on rocky soil on one side, and the open, treeless plains on the other, made for very different kinds of fighting after the landing. He found some names which intrigued him in the maps. For instance, the village of the Marais, which had disappeared, indicated the existence of a marsh, where today there were just open fields. Nearby, an even more surprising name was given to a small promontory of low-lying land called the Hable de Heurtot. He thought this could be the name of a harbour. He found not only that such a harbour had existed in the Middle Ages,* but also that in the sixteenth century a great storm had so sanded up the harbour mouth that it could never be cleared. The whole area was unreliable ground,

---

* There was extant a law suit in the fourteenth century between the Sieur de Courseulles and the King of France confirming this.

much too soft for tanks. This view was confirmed when he saw during the invasion, a little way down the coast on similar ground, a tank which had sunk right up to its turret, and where tanks had gone across by letting one sink right in and then driving over the top of it.

From such investigations, together with air surveys and studies of comparable formations in England, a pretty accurate map was drawn up. This indicated the nature of the soil and sub-soil, the parts safe to be crossed by wheeled vehicles, and those which would need some kind of road to be built. Mostly, Bernal confessed, in a lecture some twelve years later,* 'The military authorities were naturally a little dubious of all this theoretical reconstruction and wanted confirmation. I knew myself that when you are studying such an extensive field nothing short of a full survey can possibly give adequate information. But it was obviously necessary to provide some sort of tangible results and so some Sappers were sent with instructions to collect samples at various points along the coast which, very fortunately for me, confirmed my predictions and led to the acceptance of these maps.'

Bernal showed his insightful genius in following up Mountbatten's interest in the Baie de la Seine. The German general staff did not consider that a landing in the Baie was likely because of the bad reputation of that coast. The Calvados and Bernieres reefs were regarded as too dangerous for navigation. Bernal made a study of them using existing, and much older, charts. He discovered that those in use were not based on a recent survey, but on charts of the great French hydrographer, Beautemps Beaupré, who had based them on charts prepared by royal command in 1776. Those first charts were fine, but a number of errors had been made when they were copied, the most serious being the omission of a number of submerged rocks.** This had not mattered up to then in practice. Sailors

---

* This was given at the 74th Congress of the Association Française pour, l'Avancement des Sciences, appropriately in Caen, in July 1955. I am indebted to this for the information about Bernal's approach to the problem as detailed above.

** Bernal suggested this was due not necessarily to the laziness of the copyists but to the fact that they were paid by the number of charts they copied, and not by the number of rocks!

kept well away from a well-known rocky coast. Fishermen had experience rather than charts to guide them: it was their knowledge which turned out to be most valuable. The *Proceedings of the Linnaean Society of Caen* provided the information. The Abbé Huc, during the last century, went around with the fishermen, and drew up a map of the rocks, using local names such as the *Dos de l'Âne* and the *Vieille Femme*. Every rock had its name, and the passes between them were found by observing the appearances and disappearances of different rocks in the tide, and taking cross bearings from them. It was possible to construct a pretty accurate chart of the rocks, which enabled the whole landing force to pass over without any losses.

The details he had gathered proved very useful to Bernal on a day after the Normandy landing, when he came in again and found 'our own boats at a bad period of tide floundering among the rocks. I actually took charge of one of them, and from my memory of the rocks managed to get it safely on to the shore, though I committed the frightful solecism of not knowing which was port and which side was starboard (or *bâbord* and *tribord* in French).'

Another problem was presented by the tide: to calculate it there was most difficult. There were no current tables available for Courseulles, but by using the older tables and tide-analysis machines it was possible to predict the tide at all the places of landing to within about 5 cm. The need for such accuracy was challenged, but Bernal pointed out that as the slope of the beach was often as low as one part in 200, an error of 5 cm would mean an error of 10 metres along the beach: for beaches defended by mines and other obstacles the precise point of embarkation was of vital importance. He found, also, that the tides provided a way of measuring the depth of water down to the low water mark. For deeper water the refraction of the waves provided indications: a wave travels more slowly in shallow water, and using appropriate formulae it was possible from an air photograph alone to calculate the depth of water.

Always, for him, the problem was not only the landing, but also the passage over the somewhat marshy strip on to the firm land. He began, therefore, a study of the campaigns fought in that region in the past. He found little information, because the Normandy coast had been a very peaceful place with very little fighting, compared with the plains of Flanders and Picardy. But in the *Archives of the Linnaean Society of Cherbourg* he found a complete report, written by Vauban in 1685, on the defence of the Cotentin Peninsula, in which Vauban expressed alarm at the defencelessness of the region.

As D-Day approached, the Germans began to put up various defences, but they were late and did not move fast enough. Apart from one beach, the real trouble came only after the landing. But many of the difficulties arose from natural causes. For instance, the meteorological records indicated that June would be a good month for the landing. The advice was that the probability of three days of bad weather, with the wind at force 7 or more, was small, about one in thirty, so that it could be ignored. Theoretically, no landings should have been undertaken because the weather experts agreed that to land on an exposed coast with a strong wind blowing straight on to it was to invite disaster. Actually, it was the wind that saved the landing. It gave the Germans false assurance that nothing could take place. It upset, also, a lot of the Allied calculations. The wind blew force 8 for forty-eight hours straight on to the Baie. This caused a lot of water to be piled up there, and the tide predictions were wrong by about 30 cm. However, it helped to carry the boats right over some of the worst obstacles.

'Under the command of General Eisenhower, Allied naval forces, supported by strong air forces, began landing Allied armies this morning on the northern coast of France.' This was the first Overlord communiqué, issued at 09.30 on 6 June 1944. Bernal did not go in with the first assault troops on that historic day. But later, on the afternoon of that day, according to the account he gave C. P. Snow, he was able to get ashore – dressed somewhat improbably in the uniform of an Instructor-Lieutenant, RN[115]* – and to 'see many of the things that had only existed for me before in aerial photographs. I was

---

* Normally, he refused to wear military dress, but was persuaded finally to do so when he agreed that he would be shot as a spy if caught dressed as a civilian.

just in time to see the details of the defences before the occupy-
ing troops had made them unrecognizable.'

How he came to make this claim is not clear. Was there
something of the Walter Mitty in him? I am satisfied that he
did not go over on D-Day. T. A. (Tom) Hussey, a naval
captain who was in command of the division in which Bernal
worked, states quite explicitly, 'Of course, Bernal did *not* go to
Normandy on D-Day. He did go with me on D+4 day.'[116]
Clearly, if he had wandered about the beach on the first day
he would probably have been killed, either shot by our own
troops or by the enemy, or blown up by a mine. It is true that
Bernal was never on the Ultra list (that is, those cleared
to receive the very secret deciphered German coded messages,
Enigma), or on the Bigot list (those concerned with the
actual planning of invasion). In fact, those who knew Bernal
were warned, in the five months of planning for the invasion
beginning on 1 January 1944, not to talk to him. However,
many persons who were not on those lists, but who were involved in command activities, as was Bernal, had a pretty
good idea of what was going on, and could make an accurate
enough guess about invasion developments.

In his own account, he went on, 'I understand only too well
now why there is not a science of war – it is a miserable subject
anyway: it is that the soldiers concerned are much too busy to
examine anything, and they obliterate very quickly all the
traces of the actual fighting.' He pointed out – seemingly with
uncharacteristic immodesty – that the major point he had
made about the unreliability of the sand proved to be right
in almost every place. However, he added, the beds of shingle
stones low down which he thought would be firm, turned out
to be most unreliable for tanks.

A fortnight after D-Day he revisited the coast, but could
not land because of bad weather. He had to stay on the cruiser,
and during three days he watched the smaller craft being
battered to pieces. Finally, the cruiser had to return to England
without any landing. In those circumstances, it was clear that
what had saved the landing was the early establishment of the
artificial harbours, the Mulberries.

Mountbatten was bitter about the opposition expressed to

such devices as the Mulberry. 'No-one can believe what we were up against in trying to introduce these original approaches and these original projects through these unoriginal minds. I was certainly not very popular. For instance, I was accused of taking away needed shipbuilding capacity and resources. Early in June 1944, on the eve of D-Day, Rear-Admiral Cyril Douglas Pennent and the Naval C-in-C Bertie Ramsay could see landing craft everywhere in the mightiest invasion armada ever assembled. Ramsay said that he had come to the conclusion that Mulberry and PLUTO (pipeline under the ocean, for the transmission of oil, dreamed up by me) were a waste of time. Ramsay said, "Well, Cyril, old boy, you must hand it to Dickie Mountbatten that although we were all bitterly opposed to him he has provided this vast armada, which had made the invasion possible. But if God said to me, 'Bertie, if you had one wish what would it be?', I would wish 'Sink PLUTO and Mulberry before we start.' " They could not see the problem. They could not see that without an artificial harbour the moment the gale started the invasion would have to stop.' §

Overlord was remarkable. On D-Day itself 156,000 British and American troops were put ashore; and eleven weeks later when the Battle of Normandy was ended, two million men, three million tons of stores, and 50,000 tanks and vehicles had been landed.[117] An astonishing achievement, to which Bernal, the scientist, contributed in a key manner: no wonder that he found himself whetted with joy at being once more on French soil.

There is a frightening sequel. After the liberation, he visited a friend, Professor Jean Wyart, a geologist at the Sorbonne, who hoped the information on beach gradients and tidal conditions on French coasts he had been sending (at great risk) to London had been of use. Bernal was shaken. He duly found it – docketed and filed away in secret cabinets, all unused.[118]

Bernal was involved, also, in one of the most amazing wartime projects. It was code-named *Habbakuk*,* and was the

* Fergusson stated it was believed to be named from the 5th verse of chapter I of the prophet Habakkuk (note the different spelling: the error was due to a Canadian typist): 'Behold ye among the heathen, and regard, and wonder mar-

brainchild of Geoffrey Pyke. He saw ships of ice sailing the seas, invulnerable to the missiles of destruction. The conception was based on the fact that in the autumn of 1942 the allies lacked air power in distant battlefields. There was a shortage of aircraft, it was difficult to have them operate where they were most needed, and they had a limited range. What was required was an aircraft-carrier able to make aeroplanes operational hundreds of miles from their base. Pyke's idea was to build a giant aircraft-carrier – 2000 feet long with 30-foot-thick hulk – out of reinforced ice. His plans were contained in a huge, tightly wrapped parcel sent by Pyke by diplomatic bag from New York to Mountbatten in London. It consisted of 232 pages of typed foolscap. Mountbatten sighed, and took it home for eventual reading. When, a few days later, he picked it up he was attracted by the opening quotation about the police. It was from a G. K. Chesterton story of Father Brown, called *The Point of a Pin*. It read, 'Father Brown laid down his cigar and said carefully, "It isn't that they can't see the solution. It is that they can't see the problem." ' That decided Mountbatten. 'This was a breakthrough. My action became clear. I summoned all my planners, and insisted that the scientists were to be brought fully into the framing of questions for whose solution their help was needed, and their function was not just to answer questions put by the uniformed staff.' Pyke had enclosed a cover letter with his proposal. It stated, 'It may be gold: it may only glitter. I can't tell. I have been hammering at it too long and am blinded. You promised me half an hour of your time. I don't ask too much to begin with. Read only the first thirty three pages. If you find it no good, so be it. Chuck it away. But if you find the basic ideas new and good and important in the war, *then* you must read on to the end of the half hour. There you will find a note with a practical suggestion for what to do with the rest.'

Mountbatten's imagination was seized by the vast concept: he saw how the great iceberg carriers could provide fighter airfields against the north-west coast of France, in case it was

---

velously: for I will work in your days, which ye will not believe, though it be told you.'[119] However, David Lampe quoted a note written by Pyke that the name was derived from Voltaire's *Candide*, 'Parce qu'il etait capable de tout.'[120]

decided finally to invade the Continent from that direction, and airfields in mid-Atlantic from which aircraft could operate to help in the anti-U-boat war. Pyke believed that Habbakuk would solve not only war problems, but also many of those of the peace. The iceship would be made of a new material called pykrete, and would be unsinkable. It would contain many workshops, freezing plants, aeroplane hangars, and living quarters. It would provide suitable runways to launch any aircraft then in use, or on the drawing board. It would economize, also, in the use of such strategic materials as metals, wood, and concrete. Pyke put forward, also, a proposal for pykrete freighters, each large enough to carry as much cargo as eighty Liberty ships. These giant freighters would not be unloaded by cranes, but holes would be carved in their sides and cargo would be slid off on to ice barges, following which the sides would be frozen solid again.

Mountbatten passed on this astonishing memorandum to his Chief of Staff, Brigadier Wildman-Lushington, asking him to read it and then hand it on to Bernal.* Bernal was not in his office on that day, so it went to Zuckerman, who read it and commented 'that the idea of a vast ice-ship, if it ever could be achieved, was probably more suitable for times of peace than war'.[122] Bernal, however, reported in favour, stating that the building of giant bergships presented no problems which could not be solved. Mountbatten was encouraged to put the scheme to Winston Churchill,** who was intrigued and became highly enthusiastic. In December 1942, Churchill issued a directive giving the highest priority for Habbakuk, a project of great urgency and secrecy. A special committee was set up, of which Bernal and Zuckerman were members. Others, apart

* There had been a request, typical of Pyke, for Mountbatten to read it all before passing it on to 'that damned fool Lushington'.[121]

** In an after-dinner speech years after the war, Mountbatten explained, 'I went to Chequers to see the Prime Minister and was told he was in his bath. I said, "Good, that's exactly where I want him to be." I nipped up the stairs and called out to him, "I have a block of a new material which I would like to put in your bath." After that he suggested that I should take it to the Quebec Conference.' The demonstration in Churchill's steaming tub had been most dramatic. After the outer film or ice on the small pykrete cube had been melted, the freshly exposed wood pulp kept the remainder of the block from thawing.[123]

from serving officers, were Cherwell and Sir Charles Goodeve, deputy controller for R and D at the Admiralty. They both disliked Pyke and the whole project. Goodeve regarded the one million pounds spent on it, that he had to provide from his own research budget, as a waste, and parted company with Bernal over it. Each Saturday morning, a memorandum prepared by Pyke was circulated to a select few. On one memo, which was highly optimistic about pykrete, Cherwell wrote, 'Strongly disagree', to which Goodeve added, 'Concur with Cherwell'. (Goodeve recalled this was an unusual experience, for he and Cherwell were at odds at times.) As a physical chemist, Goodeve thought that Pyke and Bernal were misreading the hydrogen bonds, and the relationship with concrete: also, compared with steel, ice had less than one hundred times the strength. His unfavourable comments annoyed Mountbatten greatly.[124]

In his directive, Churchill had expressed the view that it would be essential 'to let Nature do the job' of making the Bergship to overcome the considerable technical difficulties. He suggested that ice-floes might be towed in from the Arctic to the Atlantic, and used as airfields until they were broken up by melting. However, it was soon discovered that the surface of an iceberg above the water was too small to allow of it to be used as an air-base, and ice-floes were too thin to withstand Atlantic waves. Technically, what was required was a freeboard of at least 50 feet to enable the continuous operation of aircraft from the deck of a carrier; the minimum length of runway for bombers was 2000 feet, and the most desirable width was 200 feet. Also, the vessel had to be sufficiently seaworthy to withstand the waves of the Atlantic and Pacific oceans, must be self-propelled, have a speed sufficient to prevent drifting in the wind, and must be difficult to sink. Such a vessel could not be built without accurate information on the mechanical strength of ice. Bernal, who was in charge of the scientific/technical aspects, brought in Max Perutz, a young Austrian refugee, who had worked with him in the Cavendish Laboratory on molecular structure. Perutz, who had been working on Pyke's 'Plough' project, was now to work full time on the properties of fortified ice.

Pure ice is a typically brittle material: cracks travel through it for distances of many miles. Generally, it is not thought of as a structural material. It is very similar molecularly to pure concrete, although it has a lower tensile strength. In early experiments, an extraordinary thing was discovered: if you had ice with 2 to 4 per cent of reinforcement frozen in – almost anything will do: the Eskimos use moss, Bernal's team used old newspapers – it was converted into virtually a new material, which could not be cracked. Pyke had experiments carried out in the Cold Research Laboratories of New York's Brooklyn Polytechnic Institute. An active collaborator there was the physicist I. Fankuchen, who had worked closely with Bernal in Cambridge and in London. Between 4 and 14 per cent of wood pulp was added to water, and the resultant mixture frozen to form a material which came to be called pykrete.*

By the summer of 1943, the mechanical properties of pykrete had been established well enough to allow of the Bergship design. This was to be a massive undertaking for it would need a draught of 150 feet and a displacement of 2,200,000 tons: that is it would be a ship twenty-six times heavier than the *Queen Elizabeth*. The directive was for the prototype of such a monster to be built in one winter, and for an entire fleet to be ready for the projected invasion of Japan.

However, the priority was taken off the project early in 1944, although the work continued under Perutz. The priority fell because the great floating airfields had to have enormous steel skeletons, round which the pykrete was built, and the demand for steel was so great that it could not be afforded for that; the Portuguese allowed the use of their airfields in the Azores so that a staging post was no longer needed; the addition of long-range tanks to planes made it possible to operate allied fighter across wider stretches of the Channel; and,

---

* In addition, 'the crush resistance of clear ice is between 250 and 1300 pounds per square inch, but pykrete's crush resistance proved to be more than 3000 pounds per square inch. A one-inch column of pykrete was found to be strong enough to support the weight of a medium-sized motor car quite easily. The wood-pulp insulated pykrete remarkably after the material's outer surface thawed, making it considerably more stable at high temperatures than ordinary ice. A relatively small expenditure of energy would keep it frozen.'[125]

althougn *Habbakuk* was supposed to be able to withstand
between seventy and eighty torpedoes before disintegrating,
it was agreed finally that it was much cheaper, simpler, and
quicker to construct large numbers of conventional carriers,
using about the same amount of steel: even if some were sunk,
there would still be enough left to carry on. § Perutz has concluded that 'from the point of view of the war effort the research and planning spent on the Bergship project proved to
have been wasted. Yet, it was only one of several apparently
impossible engineering feats conceived during the war (e.g.
the atomic bomb)', and that 'the question was not so much
one of absolute feasibility but rather of whether the ultimate
strategic advantages were in proportion to the expenditure of
manpower and material involved. In fact, I think that had not
the course of the war and the state of our armaments changed,
the Bergship could have been made, though at prodigious
cost.'[126]

There are some delightful stories involving Bernal and Pyke
during the project. For instance, Pyke sick in bed with jaun-
dice – in a luxury flat in the Albany in Piccadilly owned by
Cyril Ray – held a meeting with Mountbatten, Sir Harold
Wernher, Captain Tom Hussey, Bernal and Zuckerman.
They sat at the foot of the bed, Pyke 'with his strange beard
looking like some jaundiced Christ'. He was not satisfied with
Mountbatten's assurances that work was proceeding as fast as
possible. 'Without faith,' he kept protesting, 'nothing will
come of this project.' 'But I have faith,' replied Mountbatten.
'Yes,' said Pyke, 'but have the others got faith?' He turned and
asked this of Sir Harold. 'Have you got faith, Brigadier?'
Poor Wernher did not know what to say, and Mountbatten
remarked speedily, 'Wernher's on my staff to see that I am
not over-lavish with my own faith.'[127]

I asked Mountbatten whether a story about Winston
Churchill just missing a bullet that ricocheted at a pykrete
demonstration was true. He told me, 'I was trying to sell the
idea of pykrete as a material during the Quebec Conference
in 1943. I sent Des and Pyke to a refrigerator plant to prepare
some blocks of ordinary water ice and of pykrete. One block
of each was placed on a dumb waiter serving the dining room

linked to the Conference Room at the Château Frontenac.
The four British Chiefs of Staff and the American four (one
was Leahy, the President's representative) – eight in all – were
present. We were at cross purposes. Each chief had brought
about six hangers-on, so there were some fifty or sixty people
in that conference room. Alan Brooke was in the chair. He
decided to send out all the advisers, who crowded against the
doors anxious to hear what was going on. Within three minutes the atmosphere changed, and we began to talk commonsense.

'I seized the opportunity to introduce pykrete, the essential
material for *Habbakuk*. The blocks of ice were wheeled in: one
natural, one pykrete. There was a big meat chopper between
the two. I asked for a strong man to use the chopper on the
ice blocks. Arnold said he would. He was a tough character.
He lifted up the chopper, and split the ice in two. He then
prepared to attack the pykrete. I tried to warn him to be
careful. But he swiped away, and jarred his arm so badly that
he shouted, "Oh, oh." The block was hardly affected. The
staff waiting outside said, "They have begun hitting each
other."

'Then, in the excitement, I took out my service revolver and
fired at a second block of ice. The bullet went straight through
and it shattered. I then fired at the pykrete block, and the
bullet ricocheted dangerously. No-one was hurt. Hearing the
shots, the advisers – still outside – said "Now they are shooting
at each other." Desmond was not in the room so he did not
witness this remarkable scene.'§

After that, at Churchill's request, Bernal was asked to
demonstrate to President Roosevelt that pykrete melted far
more slowly than ice when put into hot water.* Despite the

* 'No-one else was there when Professor Bernal was ushered in (to a suite of
the Château Frontenac Hotel), followed by a waiter who carried a silver platter
of boiling water and two large silver punch bowls. "Wait till you see this," the
Prime Minister said excitedly as Bernal placed a small block of ice in one of the
bowls and added water. "See!" smiled Churchill after a few minutes. "The ice
has melted!" Roosevelt nodded and watched Bernal put a cube of pykrete in the
other punch bowl and pour on some more scalding water. Churchill waited
several minutes, then sat down in his chair and said quite happily, "Hasn't
melted at all!"'[128]

President's acceptance, his Chiefs of Staff were unconvinced. They were asked to set out their doubts on paper. Bernal, recognizing that they were not as familiar with the subject as he was, helped them in this exercise. 'Desmond, who was so expert in expounding the points in favour, with his Jesuitical mind produced also all the points against. Incredibly, his arguments turned the scales against the project,' recalled Mountbatten. 'Winston Churchill was not amused. The Prime Minister sent me a telegram, "The next time you come to a Combined Chiefs of Staff conference, you must not bring your scientific advisers with you." '§

After the Quebec meeting, a Joint Anglo-American–Canadian *Habbakuk* Board was created. Dean C. J. Mackenzie, president of the National Research Council of Canada, was put in charge of the North American aspects of the project, and Pyke himself was to supervise the large-scale tests in Canada. However, the Americans had had enough of Pyke, and a message from Mackenzie insisted that Pyke would have to stand down. Bernal, the message went on, had been consulted, and agreed. Pyke was astounded, and concluded Bernal had insinuated himself deliberately 'for the glory'.[129] Of course, that was nonsense: it was entirely untypical of Bernal, the most generous and unselfish of persons.

It was *Habbakuk* that finally broke up the Bernal–Zuckerman partnership. After the Battle of El Alamein at the end of October/beginning of November 1942, many of Rommel's troops had retreated successfully despite intense activity by the Desert Air Force. How did they get away? To see whether there was useful information for Combined Ops in finding the answer, Bernal and Zuckerman were to be sent out to the Middle East. This was suggested early in December 1942 at an informal meeting of 'independent scientific advisers' to the service departments held under the chairmanship of Sir Henry Tizard. They did not leave until 15 January 1943, packed in a small Catalina flying-boat which took off from Bournemouth. Their first stop was at Foynes on the west coast of Ireland in a slight sea-fog. Zuckerman recalled now the Irish-born Bernal 'was all but overcome by sentiment. After looking around he turned to me and said, "I feel like taking off my shoes, tying the laces together, slinging them around my neck, and just walking off into the mist." '130 His birthplace was only a few hours' journey away.

They were grounded for nearly a week, and they found the atmosphere – no blackout, no rationing of food or drink – very pleasant. On long walks, Bernal was in good form talking about the history of Ireland, particularly on the differences between the various ruined abbeys they visited. Finally, they reached Cairo on 30 January, by way of Lisbon, Lagos, Kano, and Khartoum. They were provided with a makeshift uniform, for they were to be treated as RAF officers in case anything went wrong. Zuckerman doubted whether two more awkwardly dressed men existed in Africa, as they looked less like airmen than like commissionaires of some seedy backstreet hotel.[131]

They moved on to Tripoli, where they spent a few days reconnoitring the town and harbour. There it was that they parted, breaking up the extraordinary relationship that existed between the two men, basically so different in outlook and personality. As Mountbatten put it to me, 'I always tried to get Desmond to look more respectable: to do something about his hair, and to wear neater, tidier clothes. He compared so badly with Solly, who was always well turned out. Desmond did not understand that you do not have to express revolutionary views in a revolutionary way, but to be diplomatic, gain people's confidence, then put forward the more extreme views. Solly was very good at this. However, Desmond was one of the most engaging personalities I have ever known. I was really fond of him, and enjoyed my discussions and arguments very much. He was interested in everything. For instance, he was fascinated by the way in which in my book on *Polo* – a sport on which he was not in the least keen – I had analysed hitting, and explained lucidly the details of the game for beginners.'

In Tripoli, Bernal said he had something to tell Zuckerman. In Cairo he had been given an instruction to proceed to Canada as quickly as possible for a meeting on *Habbakuk*. 'Des had kept quiet about this for nearly a week. He had been just as nervous about telling me as he always was when making a break with one of the many women who used to fall in love with him.'[132] Zuckerman was appalled at the thought of the

work he would now be required to do on his own. That evening, by candlelight for there was no electricity in the hotel, he
spent hours pleading with Bernal not to go. He insisted that
Habbakuk was nonsense, and reminded him of many of the
projects which had filled him with enthusiasm and which he
had then dropped because he had recognized he had been
wrong. 'Des became more and more silent as, in desperation,
I added accusation to accusation. But all to no avail. He had
already made arrangements to depart, and the next day I
accompanied him to the airport and sadly saw him fly away.'[133]
Bernal's journey to Ottawa was not easy, or comfortable. He
was marooned three times – on Ascension Island, in Accra,
and in the middle of a forest in Brazil.

Zuckerman has written that, in retrospect, he used to think
that if Bernal had not gone off he, and not Zuckerman, would
have become concerned with strategic planning. However, he
could not fret for too long over Bernal's departure: there was
a war to cope with. That parting was decisive for Zuckerman
in another sense. I believe he would not have gone on in post-
war years to become chief scientific adviser to a number of
British Governments, and a peer, if he had remained in close
working harmony with Bernal.

Mountbatten allows that without Bernal, Zuckerman, and
Pyke 'we could not have produced the key devices, such as
Mulberry, which helped us to win the war'. He felt that Pyke
was 'really a lost soul, and this was shown when I left for south-
east Asia'. I suggested to Mountbatten that without him as
CCO not even Bernal or Zuckerman could have succeeded.
'In the beginning,' I said, 'they needed someone who believed
in them with all their eccentricities and originalities of mind.
You gave them meaning.' He replied, 'I am not a humble
person, and I appreciate very much what you are saying.
They certainly did need my protection and no one else would
have thought of having them at that time.' § This last comment
was justified at all times. For instance, as D-Day approached,
Zuckerman learned that civilian advisers were out of favour:
even distinguished individuals, such as Blackett, the best-
known scientist in the Admiralty and the father of operational
research, were being denied access to the War Room. Blackett

told him that Bernal was unpopular 'since he had raised unnecessary hares about the difficulties of the beaches'. Zuckerman had been warned not to discuss with either of them the planning problems in which he was involved.[134] At an earlier date, late in 1943, Bernal had asked for a pre-war colleague to work with him. There was a long delay in moving him from his war-time work. Bernal pestered Mountbatten, who was told eventually that the transfer had been held up because before the war the man asked for had been 'associated with a notorious Communist, one J. D. Bernal'.[135]

I put the view to Mountbatten that he gave Bernal 'his finest hours, providing him with an environment, and resources within it, which enabled him to express himself fully in the service of what he believed in entirely – the need to destroy Hitler and Nazism, thus to help his country, and also the Soviet Union'. Mountbatten replied: 'You may well be right. But when you write about him do remember his generosity. He never minded slaving away on other people's ideas, helping to decide what could or could not be done, without himself being the originator of any of the major ideas on which he worked. This may be the reason why his great contribution to the war effort has not been appreciated properly. But those of us who really knew him, and who knew what he did, have unbounded admiration for his contribution to our winning the war.' There can be little doubt that Bernal's war work entitles him to be regarded as a major figure. The Americans recognized that in 1945 by awarding him the Medal of Freedom with Palme.

What did Bernal himself think at the time? What was his attitude towards the generals and top brass who dominated people's lives? 'Generals of genius are, in fact, somewhat of a liability. They always imagine that the enemy is going to do the clever things which they would have thought of themselves, whereas the enemy usually does not do anything of the sort, does exactly the stupid things that the ordinary stupid generals think of themselves, and consequently the commands on both sides are fairly reasonably matched.' He found military science very incomplete, and largely a fictitious branch of study. Up to a point, rightly so, because the factors, especially affecting land warfare, were so complex that many of the ways of dealing with them by scientific methods had to be so arbitrary as to be dangerous: crude experience he found to be a better guide. 'Nevertheless, we are able to do something to bring a new type of exact quantitative military science to this subject, only to find, and I think very happily so, that it is a subject that will end almost as soon as it began. The same science that has made it possible to discover how to carry out acts of destruction has so advanced in capacity to produce them, that war has now become a suicide for the whole human race. Let us hope,' he ended his words at the 74th Congress of the French Association for the Advancement of Science at Caen in July 1955, 'that man's ingenuity will be applied to better uses than was mine in those years before 1944.' His post-war years were devoted exactly to that.

8

Science Internationale

Over his coffin, his friend Bernal said, 'Joliot's tragedy was the tragedy of a noble nature.' That night he added, 'It's also the tragedy of science.'

ILYA EHRENBERG[136]

It was some time early in December 1944. Bernal was on his way to India. En route, he had to stop on the island of Djerba, in the Mediterranean, off Tunisia. It was there, sitting in a mosque in the old Spanish fort, that the idea for an international federation of scientific workers came to him. He claimed that the thought was not original, that it was already in the air. At that time, it seemed quite clear that this war would be won by the Allies. Many scientists were expressing the hope that their colleagues in all lands, not only in the victorious group, but also among the defeated, would continue together after the war to ensure the most rapid increase of science, and its application for the benefit of mankind. 'The scientists of the world have already a common language: they have a common purpose', he wrote in 1946. 'They know each other personally, and through their work, more than any comparable body of people in the world. They form, therefore, an essential element in the creation of world unity and world peace. How effective the scientists can be for this purpose will depend very largely on the existence of a live and growing international scientific organization.'[137]

Although Bernal was a strong protagonist of UNESCO in its early days, despite the absence of the Russians, he wanted to see the wheels of international scientific collaboration beginning speedily to turn. He guessed that at some stage the Soviet Union would have to become involved in UNESCO, but he believed that the animating drive would have to come, not from governments, but from scientists themselves. To secure this, he wanted a new organization to express on an international plane the aspiration of the world's scientific workers. He was encouraged by the fact that during the war there had been a marked growth in national bodies representing scientists as 'workers' rather than as specialists. In Britain, the AScW membership in December 1945 was at the high figure of 15,600. There were similar groups in Canada, Australia, New Zealand, and South Africa. Active new bodies had been set up in China and in France. In addition, many politically progressive scientists, who had taken refuge in Britain, had been involved with the AScW through a Foreign Scientists' Committee. When, after the war, a number of them returned to their homelands, they were active in fostering national associations of scientific workers, particularly in the socialist countries. Contact was maintained with the British AScW through the International Relations Committee. This provided a channel for discussion of the ideal of a world federation concerned with the social relations of science and the problems of economic security.

In June 1945, Bernal was in Moscow for the 220th anniversary of the Academy of Sciences. His friend Frédéric Joliot-Curie was also there. As scientists with a social conscience, they had been in close liaison in pre-war days: for instance, from the late 1930s they had been members of a small Anglo-French scientific committee which included Blackett, Zuckerman, Joliot, Biquard, and Rapkine. Both Bernal and Joliot were devoted to Paul Langevin. Bernal first met him in 1924, shortly after he had founded the Comité de Vigilance des Intellectuels Anti-Fascistes, which inspired in Britain a corresponding body, For Intellectual Liberty. Bernal saw him regularly in Paris, and on Langevin's fairly frequent visits to England. He was for Bernal and Joliot the model of the individual who demonstrated that it was possible, and necessary, for the scientist to undertake his social and political responsibilities. Once, returning home with Joliot after one of his regular lectures at the

Collège de France, and speaking partly to Joliot and partly to himself, Langevin asked, 'Was I not wrong in devoting too much of my time to social affairs?' Then, a few moments later, he answered himself, 'After all, I am sure I was right'. To Bernal, on another occasion, he gave a more explicit answer. He said, 'The scientific work which I can do, can be done, and will be done, by others, possibly soon, possibly not for some years; but unless the political work is done there will be no science at all.'[138] Bernal was fond of quoting this, for he regarded it as a basic justification for his own long absences from his laboratory. Langevin had had another significant influence. It was from him that in 1935 Bernal was first made aware of the technical aspect of the terrorization of civilian populations during war, by the threats of bombardment and of gas, and it was that influence which started the Cambridge Scientists' Anti-War Group. Thereafter, according to Bernal, Langevin gave them much help, and made many suggestions for practical work.

In Moscow in 1945, together with Joliot, Bernal began discussion with a few Soviet scientists on a proposed new international body. They had to recognize that if they wanted a federation of purely trade union bodies they would not get very far: for instance, the body Joliot-Curie would represent, the Association des Travailleurs Scientifiques, which had its origin in a resistance group at the Front National Universitaire, was not a trade union, but co-operated with unions which had scientific workers as members. There were further discussions in London in February 1946 at an international conference on 'Science and the welfare of mankind', organized by the AScW. This was a major meeting, the first of its kind after the war to seek to link the application of science to the needs of an impoverished and insecure world. Sir Robert Robinson, President of the Royal Society, was chairman at the opening session; and Sir Julian Huxley, at the final session, made his first public speech after his appointment as UNESCO Executive Secretary. Bernal, with Joliot, took an active part in two private discussions with representatives from other countries: these led to a request to the AScW to prepare a draft constitution and to convene an inaugural meeting. That was held in London on 20 and 21 July 1946. At the meeting, which took advantage of the presence of many overseas scientists at the Newton Tercentenary celebrations organized by the Royal Society, there were delegates and observers from eighteen associations in fourteen countries, and from the UNESCO Natural Sciences Division. It was agreed unanimously to set up a World Federation of Scientific Workers (WFSW), whose aim was 'to work for the fullest utilization of science in promoting peace and the welfare of mankind'. Joliot-Curie was elected president of the provisional executive, and Bernal and the Soviet scientist Semenov, vice-presidents. However, the Russians did not become members until 1952. The WFSW office remained in London until UNESCO moved officially to Paris in September 1946. The WFSW Secretary-General-designate was J. G. Crowther, an eminent British science writer who, as director of the science department of the British Council, had played a notable part in stimulating and maintaining international friendship in science during the war years. He was a Marxist, impatient with those whose 'bourgeois outlook' impeded the unity and advance of the progressive forces.

At two o'clock on the morning of Friday, 24 September 1948, some forty scientists from many countries were singing loudly as they walked hopefully along a country road in Czechoslovakia, a few kilometres from Gottwaldow (then Zlin). They were led by Bernal, Joliot, and Crowther. They were participants in the first assembly of the WFSW, whose bus had broken down about midnight after leaving their meeting place, Castle Dobris, outside Prague. Now they were many hundred kilometres from there, and had to walk to the nearest village to find a telephone. The only visible light was in the pharmacist's shop, and there they drank tea and *aqua vitae*, and continued their song-making. They arrived at Zlin at 7.20 a.m. Reports from that first meeting are filled with such nostalgic memories.

Of significance was the discussion on a charter for scientific workers, presented in draft by Bernal, who had written it, on the afternoon of 22 September. The charter is a remarkable document, a concise statement, original in its expression. It begins, 'During the past century science has become a principal factor in controlling the condition of men's lives throughout the world. From being the vocation of a secluded few it is now the main occupation and livelihood of some half-million men and women. It affects directly those engaged in teaching and research in the universities, industry, and government service, and scarcely less directly millions of others – engineers, doctors, and agriculturalists whose profession involves the application of scientific method and knowledge.' There follow seven sections dealing with the responsibilities of, status of, and opportunities to become, scientific workers, facilities for employment, conditions and organization of work, and the special needs for science in developing countries. The charter, when adopted, was described by the chairman, Professor J. Belehadrek, Rector of Charles University, Prague, as historic. 'It was the first time in the history of science that scientific workers have succeeded in arriving at agreed general rules concerning their duties and rights,' he said. It was seen as 'one of the instruments by which the WFSW can strengthen the mutual understanding and solidarity of scientists in the world, so that they can as far as possible speak in general agreement, and with one voice, on all questions of fundamental importance which affect them as scientists'.[139]

From its first days the WFSW was concerned with charges of political bias. The Federation of American Scientists (FAS), which had two representatives at the inaugural meeting, declined in 1946 to ratify the constitution and articles of affiliation. The FAS director, Jeremy J. Stone, later wrote, 'The cold war had intervened. In the socialist camp, WFSW had been ballyhooed as an organization of considerable weight and importance. But in the West it was almost totally unknown; where it was known, it was considered irrelevant.'[140] The New Zealand AScW, and then the Dutch and South African bodies, objected to what they described as 'political affiliations'. This clamour arose following an accord signed in January 1950 with the World Federation of Trade Unions (WFTU) for the WFSW to do research on military expenditure and workers' living standards, occupational disease, and workers' nutrition. A message of goodwill had been sent to the

Above left: Elizabeth Bernal, *née* Miller, Desmond's mother.
Above right: His father, Samuel George Bernal.
Below: Bernal as a child.

Portrait by Lettice Ramsey, 1932, in Cambridge. Bernal helped Ramsey and Muspratt when they started to experiment with solarization in their photographs.

Above left: Nos. 21 (right) and 22 Torrington Square, with Bernal's private flat in the top left-hand corner of no. 22.
Above right: Drawing of J. D. Bernal by the artist Kapp.
Below: With colleagues in the Cavendish crystallographic sub-laboratory. Standing, left to right: R. C. Evans, W. H. Taylor, Bernal, W. A. (Peter) Wooster. The lady is unidentified, as is the man seated left. Sitting on the right: A. F. Wells.

Above left: Opening of the biomolecular research laboratory by Sir Laurence Bragg in July 1948. With Bernal is Gordon Jackson, Master of Birkbeck College.
Above right: Bernal speaking at a W F S W meeting abroad.

Bernal and his researchers in 1948. Left to right, standing: Sam Levene, James Jeffrey, John Hirsh, Jeff Pitt, Elena Scoloudi; seated: Anita Rimel, W. Ehrenberg, Bernal, Helen Megaw, H. C. Carlisle.

Model for the structure of water, now in the Science Museum in London.

Above: W F S W meeting in Budapest, 1958. Left to right: F. Joliot-Curie, interpreter, Bernal, A. I. Oparin.
Below: With Mao Tse-tung in 1954.

Above: In Moscow with Dorothy Hodgkin and A. V. Shubnikov.

Below: Physics department outing on the Thames about 1957.

Above: The Bernal goniometer.
Below left: Bernal left, Ms Dornberger looking at him, Isadore Fankuchen standing.
Below right: July 1968, with Anita Rimel.

inaugural meeting in 1946 by Louis Saillant, Secretary-General of the WFTU, a Communist and a good friend of Joliot-Curie. But, expressing the cold-war atmosphere, a number of 'Western' trade unions had left the WFTU to form the International Confederation of Free Trade Unions (ICFTU), so that what remained was regarded as a Communist-dominated body.

Joliot-Curie's view, shared by Bernal, was that the questions proposed needed scientific research to help in the raising of human conditions. The internal WFTU changes did not alter his attitude to collaboration, provided the questions remained the same. 'When one tries to be entirely independent of politics, one runs into the danger of becoming politically biased oneself, and under the pretext of being independent, one may make the mistake of doing nothing at all. The WFSW and the WFTU have a common aim – science for the welfare of mankind and for peace – that is why the two bodies should work together.'[141]

However, the criticisms were not stifled. At the council meeting of the British AScW in May 1955 there was much complaint at the left-wing policies of the AScW executive, which, it was alleged, were detrimental to natural recruitment. At the end of 1954, the union membership was only 11,318, a drop of about 4000 compared with a decade before. It was claimed that affiliation to the WFSW was a hindrance to the work of the union for better salaries for scientific workers, and that it was disapproved of by the British TUC. Although the WFSW performed an important function in acting as a bridge between 'West' and 'East' in the difficult post- and cold-war years, it was – and still is – regarded as an instrument of a Moscow-based viewpoint. On each occasion when the federation has sought to have a meeting, this has been made difficult by the national immigration authority. For example, visas to enter France were refused to members from Eastern countries and the Chinese People's Republic to attend the Second Assembly in Paris in April 1951. That assembly was held in parallel in Paris and in Prague, based on constant telephone communication. Again, the British government refused to grant visas or entry into England to non-British members of

E

the executive council for a meeting at Madingley Hall, Cambridge, in March 1952. (The meeting was held later in Vienna in June.) In addition, those who did not require visas were warned that they would not be allowed to land at a UK port.

The Russians did not become members of the WFSW until June 1952, when, at the Vienna Council, the affiliation of the Trade Union of Higher Educational and Scientific Workers of the USSR was accepted. On that occasion, other new members were the Scientists' Section of the Polish Teachers' Union and the Hungarian Association of Scientific and Technical Societies. The new affiliations, which increased membership to 84,000, in effect saved the federation: the desperate financial situation was eased. The Russians offered to pay 20 per cent of a proposed budget of £5000 a year, as the USSR covered one-fifth of the world.

Bernal pointed out that in its early years the federation had had to work in very disadvantageous conditions. It had to fight against an increasing tendency to split the world into two parts. In certain Western countries, that tendency operated on the affiliated organizations, which led them to adopt an ultra-cautious, and negative, attitude to the federation activities. At the same time, those activities were confined to the mere mechanics of meetings, because of the meagre resources. In this regard he gave assurances that his personal secretary, Anita Rimel, would continue to have federation work as her first priority, as British assistant secretary to the WFSW. The federation could only live and grow based on the real services it provided. The adhesion of the Chinese and Soviet associations made it the only organization in the world which had within its ranks representatives of organizations of scientists from all the most important countries. 'Its value to its members derives precisely from this fact,' stated Bernal. 'Those who, for one reason or another, wish to restrict it, or put it into the control of either of the blocs of states or ideologies into which the world is divided unfortunately today, misconstrue the essential purpose of the federation. It can serve now particularly as a means of making scientists in each part of the world aware of the problems and activities of those in the other. It can help in providing a greater exchange of scientists and scientific information.'[142]

The federation has always been concerned with promoting the cause of peace. It was one of the sponsors of the World Peace Congress, the head of which for many years from its inception was the WFSW President, Joliot-Curie. When Joliot died in August 1958, Bernal succeeded him as President of the World Peace Congress. His travels abroad, which were already many, now multiplied so that I recall his telling me, with a smile as he exaggerated, that in the past few days, after leaving London, he had gone to Prague, Copenhagen, Oslo, Stockholm, Berlin, Helsinki, and Vienna, intermingling sleeping and working in day sessions that ended in the early hours, in seemingly measureless committees and sub-committees, in which the boredom fought the excitement of seeking to check the armaments race, and to spread economic and political co-operation. In the large house on the banks of the Vltava in Prague, the headquarters of the World Peace Council, Bernal would sit in a room in which he spent his day, before a council meeting began, reading through masses of documents. If he happened to be there on a Sunday, he might go to the Writers' Club at Castle Dobris with a congenial companion, such as Ilya Ehrenberg.

In Moscow, one day in September 1954, at 4 a.m., he wrote to Ehrenberg: 'I have been given a room in a far too luxurious hotel. My apartments are richly decorated in good academic taste, with pictures printed in real oil-colours, and I know that they might be even worse. To help me to sleep there is a bright streetlamp shining opposite my window, and under it there is a taxi-rank; the drivers start up their engines and talk together loudly; if I could understand the language their conversation would probably entertain me. A programme has been worked out for the few days I can spend in Moscow: a ride in the metro, Gorky Street, and on Sunday to see the architecture of the agricultural exhibition. This is my eighth visit to Moscow; I know a dozen clever, interesting people in this city, but instead of giving me the opportunity to talk to them, when there are so many engrossing things happening in the world, I am being treated like a sacred cow.'[143] It was in that letter that he quoted a line from Villon, 'Je meurs de soif auprès de la source'.

As with the meetings of the WFSW, it was difficult to have World Peace Council gatherings in the Western countries. The second congress was to be held in Sheffield, but about two months before the meeting date, it became clear there would be entry problems for those without British passports. The congress was transferred to Warsaw. There were, also, other forms of discrimination, more personal. Bernal joined the actions of protest when such priests as Abbé Boulier and Dom Gaggero were defrocked, and when a number of academics lost their posts.

In 1958, the year that Joliot died, Bernal set out in a book, *World Without War*, how they might make an ally of the angel of peace. He wrote it at great speed as a contribution to immediate discussion, for he saw every month of drift as increasing the dangers and diminishing hope in the future. Essentially, his is a plea for co-existence in a world in which, he believed, defence, in any ordinary sense of the world, had lost its meaning. But, the very advances of science, which had made the possibility of destruction so absolute, were just those which could transform the whole economic situation of mankind. Bernal's belief in the use of science in the service of humanity was never faltering. 'The wealth that would be available to us now, through the application of the amount of science we know already, is far greater than anything that could be obtained from our conquest of the most fruitful territories, or by winning the most exclusive controls of sources of raw materials, oil, or coal.'[144]

When, on 6 August 1945, the bomb was dropped on Hiroshima, he was still 'working in the centre of the military machine'. He looked around at the uniforms of the allied officers 'that surrounded me in Whitehall, and thought, "You are all finished – as out of date as the Yeomen of the Guard".' He recalled that a Chief of Staff had said to him, 'At the beginning of the war, strategy dictated weapons, but at its end it was weapons that dictated strategy.' He regarded such use of atomic fission as a gross betrayal of science. He had always considered science as a positive factor in human progress. After Hiroshima, it became also a negative factor.

For him, the abolition of war would mean that it would be possible to remedy the gross inequalities of wealth and living standards between the different countries. This could be secured through 'the use and spread of a scientifically directed and controlled productive system'.[145] This was a linked theme to which he returned frequently. He had written into the WSFW charter: 'We must work for the creation in all countries in as short a time as possible of an indigenous body of scientists working in conditions of political as well as economic liberty. This implies the assistance of scientific workers of the more advanced countries to educate the people and more particularly the potential scientific workers of un-developed countries. In the meantime it is the responsibility of scientific workers in industrial countries to help the people of undeveloped countries with their urgent problems.'

In Warsaw in 1959, and in Budapest in 1965, the WFSW organized symposia on this theme. At the former, Bernal asked, 'How can science in the industrialized countries, which are undergoing what is virtually a second industrial revolution – a scientific-industrial revolution – and science in the great areas of Asia, Africa, and Latin America, be linked for the greatest mutual benefit?'

Bernal insisted that a major pre-condition of the use of science was the absence not only of war, but also of war preparations. He stated 'the melancholy fact that something like 80 per cent of the world potential measured in money, or something like 60 per cent of the world scientific potential measured in manpower of all grades', was directly or indirectly occupied in war preparations. However, if Khrushchev's scheme for total disarmament in four years could be accepted, in that period 'we could multiply the useful scientific effort by a factor of at least three'. He saw, arising from the many view-points presented, that 'it should not be impossible to organize a world plan for science, which should in no sense be imposed but arise from the collation of plans of the use of science in different countries'.[146]

To the Budapest Symposium, at which through illness he could not be present, he contributed a paper warning that although they were right in what they hoped for, they were completely wrong in their expectation of achieving it, because they imagined 'that the disinterestedness of those who drew up the principles embodied in the *charter* would be matched by the activities of those charged with assistance to science in the developing countries'. He thought it should be possible now to distinguish between the indicative aspects – the direction of science, which was concerned mainly with economic and political aspects – and the critical aspects – the results of science, which have a built-in check in the form of a tradition of scientific criticism and the test of experiment. The science-of-science should enable those two aspects to be well separated. It would enable science and its application to develop as rapidly as possible, and to avoid exploitation at all stages. He saw no real basis for competition between the needs of science and the needs of one's own country. He was discussing not just a political or scientific question, but one of personal and collective morality: how far the enthusiasm of the newly liberated people could be mobilized to take them through the grave difficulties involved in raising intellectual and cultural standards up to those of the rest of the world within as short a time as possible.[147]

Over the years, Bernal was much concerned, as were others, with the major criticism of the WFSW that, despite its important bridging East-West role, it was essentially 'a tool' of the Soviet Union. In 1964, for instance, in comments in preparation for the Budapest Symposium of 1965, he felt that the federation was liable to be attacked, and to some extent justly, 'for taking a rather superior and neo-colonialist attitude towards science in developing countries'. He then went on to make a critical point with regard to 'our Soviet colleagues', to whom it had to be made clear that unless means were provided for doing that, they might just as well organize a political conference, 'which will be largely concerned with blackguarding the Soviet Union'.

In November 1967, he seemed disillusioned and unusually bitter. The whole function, even the existence, of the WSFW had to be reconsidered. At one time there was a possibility of building up a strong, united federation covering the whole world, but due basically to the Sino-Soviet and Middle East (Arab-Israeli) 'quarrels' this had been hampered. Originally, science was limited largely to the industrialized sector, which included the Soviet Union and the other socialist countries, and now China and Cuba. In the rest of the world, science effectively was completely under American influence. 'It implies the domination of explicit anti-Communism under the detailed control of the CIA.' He saw the struggle in the WFSW as not so much to improve the conditions of scientists in the industrialized countries, but to see that its aims were possible of achievement throughout the third world. In that regard it came into conflict with China, with those Chinese 'who refuse to recognize all international organizations which do not follow their lines, and naturally oppose their activities'.

What was the best way of achieving a world science approximating to the federation charter? The methods they had used thus far were of limited value. The world conferences they had called had revealed major deficiencies: the delegates represented mainly 'the old guard' of European scientists; the US scientists were the relics of the American AScW. The third world nations were hardly represented, and they were in no position to call conferences in their own countries. The Chinese had called a scientific conference, but that, he wrote, was 'more of propaganda than science, and concerned largely with the denunciation of the Soviet Government'. He was doubtful whether more positive action would meet the wishes of the European members: for instance, of the British AScW, composed mainly of technicians, 'who have not yet seen the relation between scientific and political factors'. By contrast, the Chinese solution of armed resistance, in the slightly different form put forward by Castro and Che Guevara, had yet to gain any adequate support, even in the most favourable countries of Latin America. 'The struggle between these different views presents for the moment a choice of almost unacceptable alternatives, yet is of ultimate importance. In the meantime, it may serve to split the progressive scientific movement throughout the world.' He advised, therefore, that for at least the next two years the WFSW should concentrate on developing and increasing national organizations of scientists whatever their character, rather than to attempt to create an international unity which would remain largely illusory.

Bernal's comments were an expression of wider dissatisfaction. One of the key British representatives on the federation council wrote in 1972 to a friend of 'the colossally inept role WFSW has assumed over the past decade', and suggested that it 'plods on having meetings about a charter of scientists, a conference for youth with everything controlled by inflexible old men mostly over sixty . . .'. Bernal himself was highly aware of the importance of securing younger members. He saw the federation grinding to a halt under the weight of years.

The WFSW still exists and is active, under its president, Eric Burhop. However, it has never been able to meet Bernal's criticisms. It continues, regrettably, to be regarded as 'a Soviet front organization'. On the occasion of the first Pugwash meeting in 1957, the key role of the WFSW in helping to bring that about was not made public. It was because there were too many attempts to discredit that gathering on the ground that it was Communist-inspired. On the other hand, the affiliated organizations in Eastern Europe found it difficult to understand why the important part played by the WFSW could not be referred to. That dilemma has never been resolved. It was seen again in the fact that no public protest has been made about the scandalous treatment of a former honorary secretary of the federation, a distinguished Czech biologist, Academician Ivan Malek, who was dismissed from his institute after 1968 for his support of Dubcek. Certainly, much protest has been made in private, but to no avail. Bernal was aware of his, and loathed 'the dilatory and feeble activity' by the WFSW and its Czech affiliated organization in that affair. By then, his illness made action by him impossible. He saw that the charter of the WFSW in this regard was in danger of becoming meaningless.* He, who was looked on as a sentinel on guard for the future, felt himself betrayed by the petty temporary monarchs who surrounded him with their intolerant bureaucratic visions.

---

* e.g. '5. Conditions of work for Scientists. f. 36. Freedom to discuss work freely with other scientists, and to join and participate in the activities of scientific societies at home and abroad without restriction or prohibitive expenditure.'

9
Science in Policy

But there is also a sense in which he was a voice crying in the wilderness. What he wanted done with system and foresight was happening at haphazard and blindly. What he vaguely hoped might be an act of planned philanthropy under government direction and royal patronage was being carried out by individuals actuated by selfishness and in fulfilment of no plan.

BENJAMIN FARRINGTON[148]

In discussion with German scientists, Bernal learned how they were cut off from the military side of things under Hitler, and unlike Allied scientists could not make any effective contribution. Although the Germans began the war with a technical lead, the scientists were given questions and were expected to answer without knowing what it was all for. Fortunately for the Allies, this was disastrous behaviour. By contrast, towards the end of the war the British had built up a definitely organized system in which technical scientific work ran parallel with operational scientific work. In each service, there were two sections: a large production section made up of those concerned with the scientific and technical development of inventions, and an operational research section of those concerned with the use of weapons and the general study of operations.

Bernal wanted to have that approach applied to peacetime industrial processes. It would further the integration of science into productive activity. His picture of an industrial process was that of a cycle which began with the discovery of a need, and ended with satisfying it. He insisted that science should enter into every stage of that cycle: in determining the need, in finding out the devices to satisfy it, in their design and production, and in following up their performance in practice. And that process applied not purely to single industries, but to the whole interlocking network of human productivity. The integration of production was as important as its detailed efficiency. For example, at the outbreak of war many items of equipment for each of the three services were designed without consideration for the other services, so that when the services had to work together the items did not fit. In time, every item of equipment came to be designed so that it could be sea- or air-borne, and the ships and planes were designed reciprocally to take them.

Bernal wanted Britain to develop 'a scientific industry'. He saw no intrinsic reason why British industry should be inefficient. But this would require enough trained men, and the abolition of industry's anti-scientific practices. The latter were due in part to traditional conservatism, but mainly to vested interest and monopoly. The cost of modernization on the scientific side was not heavy. It was, however, large compared with what had gone to science in the past, and it did mean a very rapid expansion of science itself. Estimates made in mid-1945 by the Association of Scientific Workers indicated that £25 million a year would need to be spent on research and development, about three times the sum then spent. Of that amount, about £2 million would be required for fundamental research. The national income was about £8000 million, so the total for science was well under 1 per cent. However, the difficulty was not the money, but the lack of trained people. There was a yearly output from the universities of 3000 scientifically trained students, most of whom, however, went into education. To get anything like the numbers needed, the output would have to be about 20,000 a year. And increases of that order were needed, also, in technical staff such as laboratory assistants and draughtsmen. Bernal warned that the country could not go on producing a learned elite and a few professional technicians. A modern state could not be run without raising the scientific level of the whole population.[149]

In 1945, as chairman of the Scientific Advisory Committee of the Ministry of Works (he was involved with the committee until 1956), he was concerned primarily with organizing research and widening its scope. His impact was important. He sought constantly to make clear that the only difference between doing anything scientifically and doing it technically was in the organization and the measurement: in bringing those together, in reducing them to some common standard, and then, from that common standard, going back to the technician and into practice. Consider his approach to pre-fabricated houses. Bernal explained that one day in November 1954, the Minister of Health 'threw on to me at very short notice this terrible task, which has baffled all architects for years, and which it is certain will get me down also'.[150] It was to study 'every kind of the 1300 varieties of pre-fabricated house which have been put forward, deciding which seems the best, and putting all the ideas together'. Despite the fact that for him the function of a house was to prevent his papers from being blown around, he argued that the approach of a scientist was of some value. For instance, he pointed out, scientists had found classificatory ways of dealing with some 20 million species of insects: 'so that a mere 1300 pre-fabricated houses is a comparatively simple business'.

Classification could be based on a number of relatively independent features. 'You can separate the classification of main structure, wall structure, from that of floors and roofs and foundations. You can go still further, and this is perhaps the most important distinction, and classify by construction. Essentially the same type of house, with the same materials and the same type of frame, can be put up by putting up the frame first and then fixing the cladding on to it, or can be made up and cladded either on one side or on both in the factory. That, of course, does not exhaust the varieties, because when you put them up you can put them up in small pieces which can be handled, or in larger pieces which can be handled by two men or a light crane, or in whole wall slabs handled by a heavy crane or a gantry.' When all the varieties were considered, it was clear that every single variety was a solution so that none could be the best solution. It was fairly easy to find a house which could stand up, keep warm and comfortable, and last. The problem became complicated because they were not working in a technical vacuum. That meant there would never be an ideal pre-fabricated house, but there would be a sufficient variety, each belonging to the class of best solutions in their own field. The example of the war was always with him. 'We shall try to do with housing exactly what we did with weapons of war. We had to have a tank at once, even though we knew that it was a pretty poor tank, but we were always working on Mark II and Mark III while Mark I was out. I think that the Spitfire got up to Mark XXV by the end of the war.'[151]

In the *Journal* of the Royal Institute of British Architects (RIBA) there appeared in the issue of March 1946 the text of a lecture he had given on 'Science in Architecture'. It was his first paper to an architectural body, and arose from the attempt, begun before the war, by Bobby Carter, then librarian at the RIBA, to have Bernal influence architectural thinking. Although, as Carter put it, the lecture showed 'marvellously his capacity to shoot an arrow of original thought into a stuffy old body', he was not entirely successful beyond impressing a small, politically progressive group. However, he was involved in the formation of a RIBA Architectural Science Group, of which he became a (not-very-active) member.

In succeeding years, he was involved in a variety of organizations, and sat on many committees and *ad hoc* bodies seeking to help the country advance into productive wealth by the use of science. He even penetrated the topmost circles of the Labour Party, despite the fact that he was known as a Communist or Marxist activist. On the evening of 16 November 1962, for instance, he was a guest at a private dinner party at Brown's Hotel in Albemarle Street, London. The other guests were Harold Wilson, asked to attend by Hugh Gaitskell, then Labour Party leader, Sir Howard Florey, president of the Royal Society, and Frank Cousins, secretary of the important Transport and General Workers Union. Wilson, shortly to be named as deputy leader of the Labour Party, of course had been given a list of the guests in advance. He had approved. His attitude towards Bernal was different from that of some

Labour leaders, who would avoid contact with 'the Red Scientist'. The host was Marcus Brumwell, head of a successful advertising agency, and a devoted member of the Labour Party. He had been responsible for over six years for organizing, at his own expense, a number of 'top scientists' – men such as Blackett, Snow, Zuckerman, and Bronowski – to meet regularly to advise the Labour Party on scientific policy. Bernal, of course, could not be involved in any matters concerning Labour Party administration and organization, but his ideas on general policy matters were expressed clearly. Brumwell was an admirer of his, and they maintained a strong personal relationship. He invited Bernal to a number of these discussion-dinners organized by him. Bernal was, in fact, a member of 'the VIP Group' which met occasionally to give advice or policy guidance. There was, also, a broader working group to which he might be invited.

Bernal's influence was apparent in papers entitled 'A Labour Government and Science' presented in July 1959, which would have been the basis for a science policy if Labour had been returned to office. These were six short papers to help ministers to make decisions on such questions as scientific and technical manpower, fundamental science, science and industry, civil research and development, government machinery to co-ordinate scientific resources and activities. Some of the key points raised dealt with 'the great single bottleneck, the shortage of trained manpower'; government machinery 'to give adequate guidance and co-ordination to the national scientific effort'; and the problem of defence. ('Research and development work on weapons absorbs at present 60 per cent of all scientists and technologists engaged on research and development, so that civil research is handicapped. The questions arise, to what extent does this imbalance weaken the whole economy; would a stronger economy be a better form of defence; and can this question itself be investigated scientifically?')* These papers were sent to Gaitskell on 16 March 1960, with the advice that they had

---

* Many of the proposals in one form or another have been put into practice. The papers are a tribute to the original thinking Brumwell's group was responsible for.

been 'produced by a VIP party of extremely distinguished scientists, probably the most influential group of the size that could be gathered together in this country'. The Labour leader accepted them. They provided the basis for the Labour Party policy statement, 'A new deal for science', released to the press immediately before the 1960 general election.

Bernal's ideas were put forward, also, through the AScW of which the VIP scientists, and Brumwell, were members. In May 1960, the Association issued 'A Policy Statement on Science and Education', largely the work of its secretary, Roy Innes, whose arguments in essence were the same as those in the Gaitskell papers. In the following month the AScW Central London Branch held a meeting in the House of Commons at which Alf Robens, MP, shadow minister for science, spoke on 'Science and Government', with Arthur Skeffington, MP, then acting as the Party's special liaison on science, in the chair.

Despite the fervent anti-Communist attitude of the party leadership, there was no doubt that Bernal's views were inseminated into all Labour Party behaviour. He, and those who thought like him, were everywhere. Although he was a loyal friend of the Soviet Union, he recognized that the Kremlin's way of life was alienating an increasing number of left intellectuals, who were his colleagues. The 1930s atmosphere was gone. His tragedy was that he stood at the foot of a slanting stairway, but saw it only as straight. Hessen's 'vulgar Marxism', which had come to be seen as an example of crude economic determinism, was under critical examination, particularly by Marxists who rejected the direct linear approach between economic needs and scientific developments. Bernal's political influence domestically began to wane in the 1950s and 1960s, but his ideas for the rational use of science in the development of national wellbeing always had an audience. It was accepted that science had a social function, even by staunch supporters of the capitalist system. But it was becoming more apparent – even to good friends of Bernal's such as Needham and Hogben – that a centralized bureaucratic, planned society on the Russian model was not a good thing. The domination by the British Communist Party of the intellectual left had vanished.

Discontented scientists were no longer becoming Communists as they had in the 1930s. 'By 1950 only a tiny minority led by the faithful and stoical Bernal were to be heard publicly defending with all the old accustomed vigour science as practised under Stalin.'[152] But Bernal was never really a propagandist for the Soviet way of life, only for a scientific way of life. That is why his views were acceptable to the social democratic Labour Party leadership. He was the leader of an intellectual, not a political, revolution. I have yet to meet any of his laboratory colleagues – for example, Carlisle, Perutz, Klug, or Mackay – who complained that he tried to involve them in party political activity. Each one has denied this unequivocally to me.

It was felt that some kind of publication would provide a necessary tribute for the 25th anniversary of the publication of *The Social Function of Science*. During the process of gathering manuscripts I was greatly impressed by the warmth of the response to requests for contributions.* The book, *The Science of Science*, appeared in April 1964. It was a great success, and there were translations into Russian, Spanish, Japanese, Hungarian: also an American edition and a Penguin paperback. Following various discussions, the Science of Science Foundation was launched in 1964, with Bernal as an Honorary Fellow.**

Bernal's attitude to the need for the development of a science of science followed directly from the attitude expressed in his first book. In an interview*** I had with him early in 1965, he said he was concerned that the one place where science was not used was in studying the processes of science itself. Because science was a major human activity, it needed to be studied, as were other human activities, by sociologists and economists. He was critical of the fact that although a

* Professor John Maynard Smith, for instance, handed to me J. B. S. Haldane's last article. It was handwritten in an Indian school notebook, done whilst he was in hospital, dying from a form of cancer. His personal note to me was typical. He wrote that the cancerous cells were multiplying more rapidly than his words. Would I, in future, not ask old men to write last-minute articles?
** The name was changed to the Science Policy Foundation in 1967.
*** Published in *Science Journal*, April 1965. The magazine had a short life, and was absorbed in the *New Scientist*.

scientific paper was a kind of sketch map to the truth, what the reader rarely discovered was how or why the scientist did his work, 'because the logical steps described in his paper are quite different from the steps which he actually took'. In a science of science, these activities would be just as much an object of study as would the formal logical research presented in the scientific paper. I asked him about the role of chance in discovery, and whether we had reached the stage at which first class scientists, given enough money and the best equipment, might achieve a required result without fail. He replied, 'By no means have we got as far as this, but it is one of the hopes of the science of science that, by careful analysis of past discovery, we shall find a way of separating the effects of good organization from those of pure luck, and enabling us to operate on calculated risks rather than on blind chance.' The frequency and range of scientific discoveries could be much increased by more intensive studies of several fields of science. 'There is no difficulty in investigating nature. To understand it means more a conquest of our own limitations of thought and of the limitations to scientific advance.'

Science was a human enterprise, he went on, and as such it was concerned at least as much with its uses as with its intrinsic developments. But as far as our lives were affected, the most important discovery had been in the field of the science of science. 'Essentially it is this: science pays.' It was now necessary to develop a new branch of activity, the economics of scientific research. Because science was essentially a gamble, that had been a serious limiting factor. 'Even with a considerable effort in men and money, it is still impossible to guarantee scientific or technical success, but the converse is absolutely clear: given no men and no money the absence of scientific discovery can be predicted with certainty.' But no proper theory of the finance of science had yet been evolved. So far the application of science was something that had occurred in answer to whatever human, business, or military needs had happened to be referred to the scientist. No scientist, collectively or individually, had been able to plan the advance of his subject. His intrinsic dual role was to find out something about nature, and to find the money to do so. That money had to be obtained from a patron – a state – which could not be expected to know or understand what it was being used for.* Bernal thought that a national policy for science was a necessity. It did not need to impair the freedom of science if it was made by scientists to guarantee its internal consistency and harmony with the principles of science, and by representatives of the public to ensure it served the needs of the community. In a paper for the Science of Science Foundation, he argued that as the costs of such social consequences of technical change as unemployment and the wrecking of communities, and secondary consequences, such as the destruction of amenity, all of which emphasized the disutility of technical progress, were not paid for by its makers but by the community, we might have to alter our whole system of costing. 'An invention that alters the social pattern especially to create new needs cannot be borne in any equity by the public, directly or indirectly.' To minimize social losses, alternatives should be considered and cared for. That implied 'a careful phasing', something which had never been attempted because we had not the means to carry it out. There was, for example the changeover in transport methods between road and rail, or between rail and plane; these were known to be taking place, but at a rate which could not be predicted. That affected, for instance, the siting and planning of airports, which were always too small and inaccessible, so the advantages of air travel were largely lost. It had become possible to use computers to examine a number of alternatives to achieve the minimum social dislocation. But that needed an integral approach involving planning in space and time simultaneously.

He warned that such planning could not be precise without a danger of rigidity and loss of opportunity, and that in a capitalist society profits to monopolies would have to be balanced against national interests. For instance, in the choice between oil and coal, planners had to balance short-term against long-term interest, in which the former had enormous

* Sometimes Bernal got down to his final argument for the finance of research. It was that pure science was still in credit with society for the discovery of electromagnetic induction. Thus, a small national royalty on electricity would pay for all past, present, and future research.

pull, which led in many cases to permanent wrecking of equipment and areas of dispersal of labour force. He stressed that the interaction of different aspects of the economy had to be followed out as a decisive factor in any particular situation. 'In the age of computers, it should be possible for international organizations to draw up a matrix of the major features of variation to be expected, and to indicate the kind of social implications that follow them.' His plea was that 'we should look forward as well as we can, and issue warnings which may be heeded in time'.

In another paper, Bernal proposed planning, in two quite different directions, for needs (using the new tool of computers, and mixed teams of experts to cover the technical and economic aspects of improvement in productivity and the secondary, social effects), and for possibilities. The strategy would consist in combining these two approaches in the most economical way. Planning for possibilities was really free scientific research without regard for immediate economic benefits. It was there that new methods would emerge, as they had done already, in, for instance, transistors, computers, lasers, antibiotics, and insecticides. The motive for the discovery of possibilities was intrinsic to science: so it might be sufficient 'to let the scientist have his head and not to worry too much about whether it is likely to be useful or not'. But that should not be so with the application and general direction of his work. 'The actual solution is to trust to luck and hope that some application will be jumped on by firms intelligent enough to see which side their bread is buttered on. This does not work, however, without the most irritating and unnecessary delays.

'Another, and apparently more rational solution, is to look periodically at the progress of science and to recommend relevant research in the most promising fields.' There was an essential difficulty, however. 'Development is only effectually pushed by the original inventor, and he may not have the necessary business, or personal, character to cope with the inevitable obstructions and jealousies. For instance, the development of the jet engine was very soon taken out of the hands of the original inventor, Captain Whittle.' Nevertheless, he felt that they needed to look for a solution along those lines.

'Already trends in invention and development have been set up and are becoming apparent, but not sufficiently in industrial circles. It is evident that very small communities composed of persons with the real interest of increasing productivity at heart, must be set up on a virtually whole-time basis to reorganize, if necessary, the whole pattern of industry and services.'

Bernal was much taken by the computer as a tool for general use. It made possible as never before the examination of a matrix of possibilities and the preparation of a grid of hope. He had distinguished in the pre-computer period two forms of development. There was the divergent, which consisted in noting any novel discovery or invention in any field of science, and seeking in what other fields of industry or science it could be used. The idea or notion was the central point. Examples were, in Renaissance times, the various uses of gunpowder or printing; in modern times, the uses of lasers or paper chromatography. Divergent research made use of any techniques, therefore it involved scientists of many different disciplines. In the other system, convergent research, the central point was the practical problem, that is why it had come to be called problem-oriented. For example, in Renaissance times, the finding of the longitude, or the prevention of sinking; in modern times, the development of heavier-than-air flying machines or space vehicles. Many disciplines might be involved, but principally the one in which the solution was found ultimately.

These two forms of development usually were carried out quite separately and casually. With computers it should be possible to combine both methods, and 'by a back and forth process of successive approximations, deduce a poly-dimensional network of development with both divergent and convergent limits'. The approach would work in the following way. Once a new effect was observed it would be examined to ascertain its sphere of applications, and from that would arise a number of new problems, previously not envisaged because there would seem no means of solving them. 'This first stage of exploration ideally would have to be exhaustive: that is, all possibilities would have to be examined, even those which did not appear to lead to any soluble problem. Of particular importance are the breaking-off points or impossibilities.' He knew that many promising lines of investigation had never developed fully because they came up against deficiencies or insuperable obstacles in materials or processes. Subsequently, in no connection with the original work, those difficulties disappeared, but there was really no way of notifying that a number of years had to go by before the original idea was taken up again. For example, the laser principle to produce controlled-phase monochromatic light was all that was needed to make holography possible.

The computer would enable a very large number of 'block removers' to be discovered without the labour of developing them. After selecting the major 'breakthroughs', the less promising possibilities could be stored to be extracted according to relevant developments, such as new materials. In this way a matrix of potential, and partly available, developments would accumulate, and could be the basis of development planning. Bernal went on to provide an interesting analysis of the 'breakthroughs'. He saw them as a measure of two things: the ability of the attack, and the weakness of the defences, and as depending on the existence of substances, or processes, with properties developing from the normal by many orders of magnitude.* 'We know that our knowledge is so imperfect, and there are so many possibilities of breakthroughs, that

---

* He gave as examples: 'there are in nature a number of substances which have altogether exceptional properties: for instance, calcite (Iceland spar) has the anomalous property of double refraction, which, when studied in the seventeenth century, gave rise to the understanding of the nature of polarization of light (light has sides). Most of the valuable types of crystals, used as jewels or as magic stones, have such properties; for instance, diamond amber (electron) which attracts bits of straw, and was the stepping-off point for the study of electricity. Iron, or its oxide (the lodestone, the black stone from magnesia in Asia Minor) is magnetic, and is the basis of magnetism. Incidentally, the discovery that the energy levels of this iron isotope Fe^{57} are so close with resonant absorption from sensitive to slow mutual velocities, was a basis of the Mossbauer effect, which was discovered in 1958, and has proved of great value in verifying Einstein's principle of special relativity, as well has having many future applications that remain to be followed out.

'Selenium conducts electricity when illuminated, and is the basis of photo-electric cells. Quartz (rock crystal) has many such properties: it turns the plane of polarized light, and is the basis of the polarimeter for testing sugar content of

merely plugging on with work on known substances or methods may be rendered useless on account of the breakthroughs we are missing.' Even without knowing where they were it should be possible to compute how much effort should be devoted to looking for breakthroughs. It should not be so much as to hinder the general flow of research, but certainly more than at present. He guessed at not more than 5 per cent.

The other factor of importance was the intensity and character of the attack. Not even scientists could look for or discover relatively new facts, and still fewer had the sense to appreciate the potential value of such discoveries. He recalled how he had once asked a distinguished physicist whether he would care to look for new and better semiconductors. The physicist replied he had enough to do already studying the properties of the ones he knew. The selection of scientists with original qualities was an important factor in the general advance of science in industry.

Bernal's comments on the first report (1946) of the new body, The Advisory Council on Science Policy, which had replaced the Advisory Committee, a body he had helped to set up, were strongly critical because it revealed an attitude which he believed likely to be very damaging to the future of scientific research. For instance, there was the committee's view that the advance of scientific knowledge could not be directed from any centre. He objected that that admission very largely destroyed the object of the report, because nothing

---

solutions; it gives electrical charges when compressed sideways (piezoelectricity), and is the basis of echo-sounding (sonar). White tin has no resistance near zero degrees absolute, and is the basis of superconductivity, which, in turn, has many recent applications, particularly to high-field, permanent magnets. Similarly, the properties of the rare earths, particularly gadolinium, have been vitally important in constructing lasers.

'To summarize, these are all what used to be called the virtues of substances, to which were added many of a purely magical character, such as the taming of unicorns by virgins, and the breaking of diamonds by goat's blood. Actually, they are all important not only in themselves, but also because they are all lead-ins to whole fields of new knowledge. The examples I have chosen are all examples of *substances* with extreme properties, yet the same applies to radically new *methods*. For instance, the discovery of the method of paper chromatography, which makes use of an effect of the spread of coloured material in rings around an initial spot, something which has been observed for thousands of years with blood or ink stains, but only used effectively in 1945.'

else was put in place of central direction by way of qualified support for scientific research. Generally, he considered the report gave evidence of inadequate study of the principles upon which the policy of science should be based, and of the economics of scientific research.

Of course, for Bernal, what was happening nationally was related to the international scene: as a social institution science was intrinsically international. He had been critical, as were others, of the International Research Council (IRC) formed in 1919, which for a long time excluded German scientists from its activities. But its gravest weakness was the passive way in which it sought to implement the concept of scientific union. It was a name without reality, for it had no staff and no funds. Its successor, the International Council of Scientific Unions (ICSU), which the IRC became in 1931, was more positive: it enabled those scientists who had to work together on account of the intrinsic nature of their science to secure a mechanism for their collaboration, and it helped in the foundation of such vigorous unions as those of astronomy and meteorology. The International Union of Crystallography was yet to be added.

During the 1930s, in the years of uneasy peace, scientific congresses were being turned into ideological battlefields, and over all were the twin shadows of military and industrial secrecy. The general atmosphere did not favour international scientific collaboration. And during the war, apart from some continuing activity by the astronomers, the existing forms of international scientific organizations were suspended. The break between scientists of the Allied powers and those of the Axis was almost complete.[153] But in the former countries there grew up a new type of scientific organization of a positive character, concerned not only with immediate war problems, such as weapons and tactics, but also with secondary ones, such as health and agriculture. He regretted that in the beginning the countries involved were only the UK, the USA, and the British dominions. The USSR was excluded.

The needs of war, he saw, had caused to be developed a type of organization far more efficient than anything seen before: largely because in each country the extremely limited number of available scientists had to be used economically, and with priorities spelled out clearly. War science had to be planned, and the plans of the Allies had to be co-ordinated. That meant an exchange of information and personnel on a scale, and with facilities, that was entirely new. In effect, the war had provided the experimental trials of the type of organization which the post-war world would need to bring into being.

Bernal was clear about the tasks that required to be undertaken by a world scientific organization. First, it would need to even out the inequality arising from the lopsided distribution of research throughout the world. In the mid-1940s, he guessed, some 90 per cent of fundamental research was being done in the highly industrialized countries. To exploit to the full the available human potential of intelligence, more effective use should be made not only of trained people in the highly developed countries, but also of the untouched reserves in the undeveloped regions. Further, only an intense and immediate application of scientific techniques could help to meet the crises of lack of food, poor health, rising population, and low efficiency. But the people themselves would have to apply those techniques. He saw in 1945 that an answer was the development of self-reliance, and that relief in kind could be only a most temporary palliative.

Bernal was involved in the discussions and activity leading to the creation of U N E S C O (the United Nations Educational, Scientific and Cultural Organization). The foundation for this was laid during the war at a conference of allied educational ministers in London.* Bernal, when consulted, would stress that the tendencies which had existed for some decades were pointing to a common pattern for the organization of science inside modern national states, or federations. In industrially advanced countries, scientific activities were carried on in university laboratories or independent institutions, which did mainly fundamental research: in industrial laboratories, con-

---

* Originally, there was no 'S' in the conception, but the conference had a scientific mission, of which J. G. Crowther was secretary, and through his efforts, and those of Joseph Needham, the very successful director of the Sino-British Science Co-operation Office at Chungking, science came to be included.

cerned with applied research; and in government laboratories, which bridged the gap and overlapped. During the war, that situation had hardened, and, increasingly, would become the pattern. He was concerned that encouragement of a closer integration of national science without similar effort in international science would aggravate the tendency to split science on national lines. He saw that whilst national science was organized through independent scientific societies it was possible, and likely, that there were closer links between scientific workers in similar fields in different countries than between workers in one field with scientists in another field within their own country. He was ardently in favour of international collaboration: the rate of advance of science as a whole, and as a consequence, also nationally, depended on effective international communication.

Although the 'white-hot technological revolution' of the Wilson government turned out to be rather tepid,* the activities in planning it did not pass unnoticed in Eastern Europe, where there was more commitment to a planned economy. The activities and publications of the Science Policy Foundation were followed with attention and used by the East European planners of science in argument for support by their own governments.

---

* The intellectuals of the Labour Party and its supporters were convinced of the importance of science, but the implementation foundered because of inability to carry the Trade Unions along. Jam today was preferred to jam tomorrow.

10
Pursuit of the Possible

The formulation of a problem is often more essential
than its solution, which may be merely a matter of
mathematical or experimental skill. To raise new
questions, new possibilities, to regard old problems
from a new angle, requires creative imagination and
works real advance in science.

EINSTEIN AND INFELD[154]

Bernal was chosen, without knowing it, to perform a
special role in the development of science. He touched both
earth and stars in the process, and could not find true tran-
quillity. I refer to his work in the laboratory, where his genius
was first made apparent, and his weaknesses as a very human
being: a tendency to ascribe a reality to a fanciful interpretation of events seen by hindsight; a hurting, yet non-deliberate
blindness about key work done by members of his staff.

About his genius there was never any doubt. For instance,
Zuckerman could not understand why Bernal did not get a
Nobel prize for work he did in the late 1920s on the sex hor-
mones (oestrone and oestriol).* He was able to resolve the
chemical makeup of some minute crystals he had been given
by the biochemist, G. P. Marrian, who, at University College,
London, was working on the identification of a female sex-
hormone. Zuckerman recalled walking with Bernal from the

---

* Crowther reported the same comment, when he was being entertained by
some French scientists in Paris early in 1940, just before the German occupation.
One scientist said Bernal should have been awarded a Nobel prize for his demonstration that the accepted chemical structure of steroids was wrong.[155]

college to Euston Station which was nearby and where, to his surprise, he had to lend Bernal 10 shillings to get back to Cambridge. Within a few days, Bernal, using purely physical techniques of preliminary X-ray measurements and optical investigations, was able to make an important contribution to an understanding of the dimension of the sterol skeleton, by showing that its proposed structure could not fit his X-ray measurements. Not long afterwards, his colleagues, Dorothy Crowfoot and Harry Carlisle, by a detailed X-ray analysis not only confirmed Bernal's measurements, but also the chemical structure for a sterol skeleton.

From his first days in X-ray crystallography Bernal saw how it had distanced itself from geology to become 'a branch, or sub-division, of chemistry, and like it, followed directly from fundamental physics'. He saw that 'the new methods were synthetic: there were now means of saying *a priori* that such an arrangement of atoms was possible and would produce a crystal of such and such properties. That was very different from the old descriptive side of mineralogy.'[156] He saw how the unification of physics and chemistry, that had taken place since the beginning of the century, was to lead to a similar unification of biology. He had been in close contact with biology in the excitement of the twenties and thirties in Cambrige, when the biological and physiological laboratories under Hopkins and Adrian were doing key work, preliminary to the tremendous biological breakthrough in the 50s and 60s, uncovering basic mechanisms such as movement and reproduction. He understood that the study of the structure of dead matter was almost ended, and that of living matter was beginning. His contribution was outstanding, although, unlike Rutherford or the Braggs, he did not come to found a school. His strength lay in causing other minds to light up. This he was able to do throughout his life, but his own major, purely scientific contributions were made before 1939.

In 1930, during his first academic appointment in Cambridge, Bernal was involved, together with Sir William Bragg, Arthur Hutchinson, and W. A. Wooster, in urging the development of the 'new crystallography', which would require a remodelled teaching for producing the new research workers. The outcome of their efforts, pessimistically foreseen by them, was the creation of a chair in mineralogy and petrology, with crystallography associated with that department. The position so far as Bernal was concerned was unchanged, although the ever-leaking roof of his miserable hut (which he shared with Wooster) was repaired. In the summer, the heat in it drove them out; in winter, the cold froze the gas meter, turning off the gas fires and freezing the solvent benzene. They conceded, 'The petrologists had won the day.'[157] The next attempt to introduce the 'new crystallography' was made by Joseph Needham, who in a letter to council dated 12 January 1935, proposed unsuccessfully that the Jacksonian Chair of Experimental Philosophy should be given to a crystal physicist interested in biological implications. Together with Bernal and Dorothy Wrinch, Needham sought also to have set up a research institute bridging the three basic disciplines of physics, chemistry, and biology. This proposal arose following a visit to Needham in 1934 by W. E. Tisdale representing the Rockefeller Foundation.

In May 1935, Tisdale paid another visit to Cambridge, this time accompanied by Warren Weaver, who since 1932 had been responsible for the foundation's natural science programme. Weaver believed ardently that the future of physical science lay in its application to biology. His programme was based on the 'new biology', a biology inspired by the methods of physical science. In 1938, he coined the term, 'molecular biology'.*[158] Twelve years later, W. H. Astbury commented, 'The name "molecular biology" seems to be passing now into fairly common usage, and I am glad of that because, though it is unlikely I invented it first, I am fond of it and have long tried to propagate it. It implies not so much a technique as an approach, an approach from the viewpoint of the so-called basic sciences with the leading idea of

---

* Pages 203–19 of the 1938 Annual Report of the Rockefeller Foundation were devoted to the 'natural science' section. It was headed 'Molecular Biology', and began, 'Among the studies to which the foundation is giving support is a series in a relatively new field, which may be called molecular biology, in which delicate modern techniques are being used to investigate ever more minute details of certain life processes.'[159]

searching below large-scale manifestations of classical biology
for the corresponding molecular plan. It is concerned particularly with the *forms* of biological molecules, and with the
evolution, exploitation and ramification of those forms in the
ascent to higher and higher levels of organization. Molecular
biology is predominantly three-dimensional and structural –
which does not mean, however, that it is merely a refinement
of morphology. It must of necessity inquire, at the same time,
into genesis and function.'[160]

Tisdale and Weaver would not support proposals by
Needham for an institute either of experimental embryology,
or of physico-chemical morphology (in which Bernal was
suggested as director of a crystal physics division, and Dorothy
Crowfoot as his research assistant). In the following year,
Needham failed again when the university would not give
support to his scheme, despite the Rockefeller Foundation's
conditional agreement.

Bernal was a member of an informal – but influential –
group which called itself the Theoretical Biology Club. Its
leader was H. H. Woodger, a cytologist at the Middlesex
Hospital Medical School, known as Socrates. Other members
included J. Needham, C. H. Waddington, E. S. Russell,
G. C. Robson, Nevill Mott, L. L. Lancelot Whyte, and A. A.
Ritchie. The club met usually in Woodger's home – Tanhurst,
Epsom Downs – or in Cambridge. Bernal became involved
through Needham, and attended his first meeting on Saturday
13 August 1932.[161] In 1934, he produced a memorandum on
the importance of crystal physics in biology. This was another
expression of his abiding interest in the phenomena of life.
Even as a schoolboy he had rejected the traditional differenti-
ation between the physical and biological sciences. At Cambridge, he was struck by 'the precise way in which all
biological phenomena, when carefully investigated, turned
out to be in accordance with physical laws, including
those of chemistry, and not to involve any special vital
principles'.[162]

This view was reinforced by such friends as C. H. Waddington, who in his geological studies pondered over the extreme
persistence of complex patterns in fossils, or Joseph Needham,

concerned with the sequential evolution in chemical processes.*

Bernal believed there was a radical, fundamentally philosophical, difference between biology and the 'exact' or inorganic sciences. In physics, for example, the search was for elementary particles necessary to the structure of the universe: the laws controlling their movements and transformations were intrinsically necessary, and were valid over the whole universe. Biology, however, was primarily a descriptive science, more like geography, dealing with the structure and working of a number of peculiarly organized entities, at a particular moment on a particular planet. He argued that full and true biology was yet to come: it would be concerned with the study of the nature and activity of all organized objects wherever they were to be found – on this planet, on others in the solar system, in other solar systems, in other galaxies – and at all times, future and past.[164]

Bernal had a vision of a biological science based on known molecular structures.[165] He argued that among the problems of biological structure, that of the structure of molecules occupied a central position and tied together the different disciplines from chemistry to histology that made up modern biology. He was himself involved intimately in the development of molecular biology through his work in the X-ray structural analyses of fibres, sterols, proteins, and viruses. C. P. Snow pointed out how from his first days at Cambridge Bernal 'had equipped himself, through crystallography, with a powerful technique for probing into the structure of materials: how he began to use that technique on materials of biological significance, in the first place amino-acids, sterols, and vitamins. Then he went on to water, since most organisms are made of it. . . . Then to proteins and viruses.'[166] He claimed to have popularized Ewald's conception of the reciprocal lattice, and drawn attention to its heuristic value.

* That is, 'with the different ways that organisms, as they evolved, got rid of their nitrogen products successively as ammonia, urea, and uric acid, for biological reasons that were quite clear in themselves, but depended, essentially, on teleological considerations on how far the process helped the organism in its way of life on land or sea.'[163]

But members of his team did hear him remark on a number of occasions that he was unaware of Ewald's paper describing the reciprocal lattice at a time when he was developing his own method of interpreting X-ray oscillation photographs, which depended on the use of the lattice to make interpretation easier. In fact, he seems to have come across Ewald's paper only during the course of his work.

In 1925, he applied space group theory to the deduction of the crystal structure of graphite, and in 1926 he provided a systematic account of rotation methods, and printed the Bernal charts for plotting the layer lines. These charts are still used. He was much taken by the work of V. M. Goldschmidt, a genius not generally recognized, the father of modern geochemistry and crystal chemistry. When he first met him in 1928 in Bad Ems, Goldschmidt was recovering from a bad attack of fish poisoning: he had been 'too enthusiastic in watching an analysis. This may condemn him from the point of view of chemists,' commented Bernal, tongue in cheek.[167] Goldschmidt became involved in crystal chemistry, he told Bernal, through a lawsuit, engaged in at the end of the First World War, between the Norwegian and British Governments. To protect her chemical industry, Britain had introduced a tariff on the import of organic chemicals. Calcium carbide was referred to: if it was an organic chemical it would be taxed. There was to be a test case in London.

Goldschmidt was selected as the Norwegian expert, although he was not an organic chemist. When he heard in London that he would be opposed by Sir William Pope, an internationally recognized expert, he decided on another approach. He took a crystal of calcium carbide to Sir William Bragg, and asked him to work out the structure. (Sir William got it wrong, Bernal recalled, but no one could know that at the time.) Goldschmidt then fought the case on the basis that it was the structure of an inorganic crystal, and won. When the Norwegian government asked him how he had succeeded, he attributed it to X-rays; he was then provided with an X-ray tube and a powder camera. He did very well with the camera, and produced the table of ionic radii.

In the spring of 1934, Bernal made a major contribution to the study of the structure of proteins by X-ray crystallographic analysis. He took the first X-ray photographs of a wet protein crystal. As with many great discoveries, it was made possible by the chance of coincidences. John Philpot was then working in Uppsala on the purification of pepsin. While he was away skiing, a preparation he had left standing in a refrigerator produced some beautiful, large crystals, 2 mm long. Glen Millikan, a friend of Bernal's, who was passing through, happened to see them. He was aware of Bernal's urgent need of crystals, and obtained a tube of them in their mother liquor, which he took back to Cambridge. Bernal, using a 3 cm radius cylindrical camera in a series of 5° oscillations, in collaboration with Dorothy Crowfoot, obtained photographs showing hundreds of X-ray reflections, rather large, corresponding with the size of the crystals, and with an even distribution of intensity.[168] That night, 'full of excitement, he wandered about the streets thinking of the future and of how much it might be possible to know about the structure of proteins if the photographs he had just taken could be interpreted in every detail'.[169] This led him to propose to the Theoretical Biology Club in 1934 the systematic examination of a series of typical proteins to discover the main lines of their architecture, and an investigation of the internal structure of the protein molecule by intensity analysis. But Bernal's small team could not undertake that: they were already heavily committed. Others, however, were greatly stimulated. From Vienna came Hermann Mark, who was so excited when he saw the photographs that he forgot to mention Max Perutz to F. Gowland Hopkins, with consequences of some significance to come later.

It was J. B. S. Haldane who gave Bernal his first real interest in the origin of life. The problem, as they saw it, was as follows: at one time there existed nothing more complex than an ordinary inorganic chemical, subject to a possible heating to several thousand degrees Centigrade; at the end, there was the whole panorama of the multiplicity of living organisms covering the world, and spreading possibly to other planets. The first state turned into the second by no other external agents than were contained in itself. In discussions, they had considered often, and agreed, that they knew of life only in connection with certain arrangements of matter. The question was, How did the first such system on this planet originate? In an essay in *The Rationalist Annual* in 1929, Haldane provided a tentative answer in 'the not unreasonable hypothesis that a thousand million years ago matter obeyed the same laws that it does today'. Bernal had not then read the essay, but he was familiar with the argument. Another great influence on Bernal was provided by the Soviet biologist, A. J. Oparin, whom he met first on his visits to the Soviet Union in the 1930s, and with whom he was to collaborate intimately in the development of international scientific worker activities. In a classic paper, published in 1924, Oparin provided a starting-point, based on the idea of chemical evolution, for other researchers on the origin of life.

But Bernal had to be circumspect. Rutherford, when in control of the Cavendish Laboratory, dominated an atmosphere in which speculation was frowned upon. Not only did he dislike Bernal's politics, he warned with great vigour, 'Don't let me catch anyone talking about the universe in my laboratory.' In 1946, whilst on a visit to Princeton, Bernal met Einstein, and in a discussion with him was left with what he regarded as 'the essential clue': namely, 'that life involved another element logically different from those occurring in physics at that time, by no means a mystical one, but an element of history'.[170] As the phenomena of biology were contingent on events, the unity of life was part of the history of life, therefore was involved in its origin. In 1947, he lectured to the Physical Society in London on 'The physical basis of life'.[171] He wrote it up two years later for publication, and to clear his own ideas in working out a more rational programme for biophysics. N. W. Pirie commented, 'It ought to be called "A physicist's approach to Biology". Only one page seems to have anything novel to say about the ostensible subject of the paper.'[172] The title of the lecture, Bernal wrote, was 'an unconscious echo of the once celebrated lecture of T. H. Huxley delivered in Edinburgh in 1868'.[173] He stated that he did not read that lecture until long after he gave his own. The positive part of Huxley's lecture – that life had *one* physical basis – was as valid in the mid-twentieth century as when he first stated it. What Bernal found curious was that Huxley had not attempted to explain the unity of life in terms of a common history. It was that search for origins which was his excuse for his lecture. He took advantage of the growing interest in the problem, expressed particularly by the chemists, H. C. Urey and S. L. Miller,* to suggest that the mechanism whereby chemicals suspended in a primitive ocean eventually become definite organisms was through absorption of the active chemicals on fine clay particles derived from earlier rocks and deposited in estuarine waters.

N. W. Pirie was caustically critical of Bernal's view. In a review of the lecture, under the title, 'Vital Blarney',[174] he argued against what he described as Bernal's 'dogma that proteins are essential'. He went on: 'Life is not a property of a system: it is a statement about our attitude of mind towards the system.' He charged him with dogmatizing not only about the physics of the original environment ('that he would be qualified to do and in any case it is traditional'), but also about biochemistry, where his generalizations were surprising because he was unaware of the limited range of organisms on which the biochemists had worked. Pirie found Bernal's little book unsatisfactory, 'although not as bad as Schrödinger's *What is Life?*': but 'there are so many subjects – crystallography, politics, building, bomb-damage, ethics, housing, etc. – on which he writes authoritatively and convincingly that we must put down to pure Irish whimsy his decision to write a book on life. So much has already been written on the subject that impatience is justified at a contribution made up so largely of blarney.' But Bernal and Pirie were such different personalities, that the resultant controversy was not very productive. Bernal recognized that what Pirie was implying was that what was true was not new, and what was new was not true. Pirie maintains that viewpoint even today.

* They carried out the first experiments on the synthesis of pre-organismal chemicals by means of ultra-violet acting on the composition of the *presumed* earliest Earth's atmosphere of methane and ammonia.

F

On 12 November 1946, Bernal was in Paris. He was due to read a paper at a congress to commemorate the fiftieth anniversary of the death of Pasteur, a scientist whom he respected as one of the greatest of the century. He had arrived with his lecture prepared to be given the following day, but his good friend, Jean Wyart, with whom he had spent many a bohemian night, had a great surprise awaiting him: it was Pasteur's original and unpublished notebooks, detailing his discovery of molecular asymmetry. That was the theme of Bernal's paper. Delighted by his good fortune – 'rare in a lifetime', as he put it – he recast his lecture hurriedly, and never re-wrote it for publication as he wished to preserve his immediate reactions to the authentic record of a great discovery, buried for nearly a century.[175] Pasteur's discovery was for him a classical case of the convergence of ideas from chemical, crystallographic, and physical fields to reveal a new property of matter, molecular asymmetry (*dissymétrie moleculaire*). It had many effects of great importance, particularly in the development of the physical method of X-rays, which supplemented and came to replace the chemical methods of arriving at molecular structure. This was because it was a direct method which considered substances as they were, and not as a result of their transformation into other substances. The work of Bernal, and of his students, in using crystallography to find not only the structure, but also the composition, of a molecule in advance of chemical analysis justified Pasteur's premonitions that the crystalline form carried within itself the secret of the molecular structure.

Linked with his interest in the origin of life was his curiosity about the structure of liquids. This was a study of obvious interest for him. The liquid state was the least understood of all the states of matter, yet the belief that the universe was created out of water was the beginning of modern science and philosophy.

He liked to tell of how in 1933, as he sat talking with the physicist, R. H. Fowler (Rutherford's son in law), in the early hours of the morning at Moscow Central airport during a long period of fog, they discussed water and agreed that the more it was studied the more anomalous did its physical properties appear.* They felt the explanation of the physical properties of a liquid, as of a crystal, had to be found in the geometrical and physical relations between the molecules, atoms or ions of which it was made. From this resulted a stimulating paper on the hydrogen bond and the liquid state.[177] Aspects of this were developed years later.

In addition, because the study of liquids was so difficult a field, it was challenging. Bernal could indulge himself in a certain amount of speculation and possibly find escape from the detailed computations, successful but so tedious, for the other state of matter. His reference to the 'tedious' is revealing, for I have seen him engaged in what has seemed to me the most tedious of tasks: his efforts in making a model of a liquid structure. He began by trying to work out from first principles what should be the structure of the simplest liquids – the molten metals and liquefied rare gases such as argon, in which the basic units are atoms rather than molecules, as is the case with water. He made two assumptions: first, that a liquid is made up essentially of a set of molecules similarly, but never identically, placed with respect to one another; second, that a liquid is roughly homogeneous, varying only slightly in density from place to place, but not in general structure. The arrangements were quite irregular. The problem was the difficulty of imagining complete irregularity, and to describe it in some kind of geometrical way. He was convinced, however, about order in disorder: the trouble was to find it. He spent a great deal of time and energy building physical models to initiate that kind of irregularity. During my visits to his office in Birkbeck College in the late 1950s, I was one of many who interrupted him – 'every five minutes or so', he would say – in building up an array of balls joined by stiff wires of various lengths. He did not resent the interruptions because they enabled him to achieve almost perfect randomness: by the time he got back to his model, he insisted, he had forgotten what he had been doing last.

* According to Ilya Ehrenberg, it was raining hard. There was no waiting room. Bernal stood under an awning, and it was there that interest in the structure of water was aroused. He told Fowler, and on the plane discussed it with the other members of the science delegation who had been with him in Moscow.[176]

Another model he had constructed, which for many years stood boldly like a ship's figurehead in a central courtyard in the college, and is today in the Science Museum in London, had the right kind of disorder, and roughly the right density. However, when he checked it against randomized arrangements of spheres to see whether he might not unconsciously have introduced some order, he found to his great surprise that often five-fold arrangements prevailed among the balls surrounding any one of the arrangements. This was almost incredible to a crystallographer who had been taught that molecules could be arranged two-fold, three-fold, four-fold, or six-fold symmetry, but not five-fold. The solution lay in understanding that five-fold symmetry makes filling space with a regular array impossible: like trying to pave a floor with five-sided tiles. This was a definition of crystals, not of a non-crystalline, irregular structure. To treat a liquid as a *heap* of molecules in contradiction to the regular *pile* characteristic of a crystal structure was only a beginning. He found that there was not much known about heaps, therefore a new subject he called statistical geometry had to be developed: it had so far been avoided, he thought, because of its ugliness and difficulty. It was intensely unfashionable, for the study of polyhedra in three dimensions had gone out with the Greeks. But it was needed to answer the question of what is the structure of a liquid. Why it had structure was a question of statistical mechanics, and one which he did not try to answer.

Historically, the first measure was that of a heap of corn, arrived at by filling it into baskets. In fact, the measurement of volume preceded those of length and weight. Geometry could measure a regular pile of objects, but not irregular heaps. But what was the difference between a heap and a pile? He found, during a lecture he gave at the Royal Institution in 1958, the clue that set him on the track of how to analyse the nature of the heap, and what was its geometrical origin. He saw that whereas in the regular pile the arrangement was always one in layers of six-fold symmetry; in the heap it was quite as often five-fold as six-fold. At a later stage, with the help of his son, Dr Michael Bernal, and the use of the London University computer, he was able to produce another random model. But even that was not satisfactory, and, finally, he fell back on the study of a model of a large number of ball-bearings. By 1962, he had established that the original concept of a liquid as essentially a heap of molecules, that is, being homogeneous and continuous, had been well substantiated (at least for monatomic liquids). This meant the absence of long-range order. He had succeeded in presenting an approach which linked a way of treating liquids with that of crystalline solids. He was able to provide a material representation in space of the instantaneous positions of the molecules in a liquid. As he said, 'All I hope is that I have made a beginning at a new way of looking at liquids, and what comes of it will lie on whether this beginning is something that can be built on or remains a scientific curiosity.'[178] The interaction of the experimental and theoretical work on liquids has been a beautiful example of how understanding advances. Sometimes Bernal would ask his assistant, John Mason, to build him a particular model; John Mason, an independent New Zealander, would reply, 'Oh no Prof – you don't want it like that, you want it like this,' and built it his way. Bernal, then, would often have some new insight from the style of model he had not thought of.

At 4 p.m. on Thursday, 1 July 1948, Sir Laurence Bragg declared open the Biomolecular Research Laboratory at Birkbeck College, made possible through the generosity of the Nuffield Foundation. Typically, given his strong feeling for the importance of an historical approach to problems, and his genuine liking for the key figures in science, he approved of the proposal by Carlisle to name a number of rooms after them: Wallaston, William Bragg, Coolidge, Muller, Westgren, Pasteur, Federov, and Goldschmidt. However, the new laboratory was hardly Bernal's dream of an institute for protein structure to be developed as a centre of excellence:*

---

* See C. P. Snow, *The Search*, in which the planning of such an institute is a key theme. Bernal was the starting point for the character of Constantine in that novel. 'As a general rule, though there are exceptions, novelists like a living original to get them going, though they often depart from it or fuse it with other originals before they have finished', Snow wrote to A. L. Mackay on 3 November 1972. 'In this case, though I departed from Bernal in many respects, I didn't take as many liberties as usual. It certainly is not a portrait, but some of it might be said to be something of a rough sketch.'

but it was a necessary step to an independent crystallography department. However, that was still some seventeen years away. The laboratory was two old houses, numbers 21 and 22 Torrington Square, built in 1835, bombed during the recent war, and patched up roughly. But Bernal was accustomed to working in old buildings; in fact, he had always had to do his research in 'slum-like' rooms. Certainly, his former dreadfully inadequate research laboratory at Breams Buildings in Chancery Lane would not have done. Fortunately, it had been destroyed by enemy action, and Bernal's unit was given shelter in the Royal Institution. 'I am back where I started', he wrote to Fankuchen on 27 November 1945, 'on the top floor of the Davy-Faraday, with one X-ray tube which works about one day a fortnight between breakdowns, and vague prospects of getting three more and a few of my old cameras . . .' Then, for a year (1946–47) before moving into Torrington Square, part of his research laboratory with Carlisle and a few others was in a house in Hendon, shared with C. H. Waddington.

He was concerned with the application of physical methods to the understanding of the structures and reactions of molecules in biological systems: in particular, with molecules intermediate in size between those of active metabolites, such as sugar, and those of fibrous or other tissues, such as muscle or skin. This meant emphasis on the proteins varying in size between the smaller molecules, such as ribonuclease with a molecular weight of 13,000, to the large virus molecules with molecular weights of several million. The main method of attack on the central problem of protein structure was X-ray analysis, a direct continuation of the work he had begun in Cambridge in 1935. But as this was at the very limit of existing techniques, to improve the experimental and theoretical tools electronics and electronic computer sections had been added. The former, under the direction of Dr W. Ehrenberg, would provide better sources of X-rays to study minute crystals, and develop new methods of studying small angle X-ray diffraction. The latter section, led by Dr A. D. Booth, would seek to develop a computing machine of such speed that it could carry out the necessary enormous calculations required for protein analysis. Basically, the problem was that, although methods of great power were being evolved for the determination of the structure of molecules within a large number of atoms, and these were to be used with success in the case of molecules of up to about forty atoms, there was a fundamental difficulty, partly physical and experimental, with molecules of the order of 1000 atoms. This was due to the limitations in the resolving power. There was another, more serious, theoretical difficulty concerning phase determination. Booth had completed the design of such a machine, and the plan was that after assembly at Imperial College it would be transferred to a building adjoining Birkbeck College. Booth invented the magnetic memory, and various other vital steps in the development of the computer, but never provided a computer, because other parts of the field, such as numerical analysis and language translation, were so interesting. Paradoxically, this held up crystallographic computing at Birkbeck for several years. In getting Booth and a computer section, Bernal had stolen a march on most of world science, but, sadly, the gain was frittered away.

Jim Jeffery, after the departure of Helen Megaw and Stefan Peiser, was made director of the Cement Section which, funded by the Department of Scientific and Industrial Research, was working on the structure of Portland cement and other cementive materials, and on the nature of their reactions with water. Bernal believed the properties of hydrated cements were probably closely related to those of many hydrated proteins, and were influenced strongly by the same long-range forces. Later, it became an agreed tenet that the best place to look for topics for pure research was in applied science. Cement alone provided many PhD topics.

By special arrangement, a large part of one of the houses was given over to the chemical research work of Birkbeck College, under Professor Wardlaw and Dr Rydon. But there were separate facilities for chemical preparative and analytic work for the crystallography laboratory. Although the research laboratory officially was part of the college physics department, it was *de facto* run independently.

The central problem of the internal structure of the proteins was attacked along converging lines, through direct X-ray analysis of native proteins, and of protein constituents working from simple amino acids to peptides. Harry Carlisle, director of the X-ray analysis section, first met Bernal in October 1938. He had come to England from Burma, where he was born, and India, where he was educated, to continue his studies. He was interested in the magnetic properties of crystals, and Bernal accepted him as a research student. Within a short while he found himself picking up the subject of crystallo-graphy so rapidly that he began to get a liking for it. He remembers, also, reading *The Social Function of Science*, which impressed him greatly. 'In 1939, we all knew that war was imminent. In September, I went to Bernal to get his signature on my application for a post in the R A F. He said, "Hold that application. Wait until you hear from me." Within a fortnight he had made arrangements for me to take the X-ray equip-ment to Oxford to Dorothy Hodgkin.'[179] Carlisle remained in Oxford throughout the war, and through Bernal was soon in-volved in some war work, later aiding in the survey of photo-graphs of aerial bombing in Britain and in Germany. With Dorothy Hodgkin as supervisor, he provided the first detailed three-dimentional determination of a complex structure (cholesterol iodide). Bernal supported the presentation of the paper in 1944 in the *Proceedings of the Royal Society*. In early 1945 he was offered a place by Bernal in the Birkbeck College research team. Dorothy Hodgkin advised him to accept. 'I did, and, along with others, I was appointed an Assistant Director of Research.'

There were hopes that Isadore Fankuchen, then a professor of physics at the Polytechnic Institute of Brooklyn, might be induced to return to London. He had joined Bernal in Cambridge at that exciting time in the mid-1930s when the first protein crystals were being examined by X-rays. He re-mained always a physicist interested in crystallography, because he found that in X-ray investigations he was able to apply physics in more and more refined ways to problems of interest in industry and biology. Fankuchen arrived shortly after Dorothy Crowfoot, Bernal's research assistant from 1932, had gone back to Oxford. This was a great loss for Bernal, for she was the only one available with sufficient experience to prepare protein crystals. Fankuchen provided consolation in another aspect. He began research with Bernal on an examination of the sterols which, in the form of vitamin D and its analogues, had just come into biological and pharmacological interest.

But very soon they were diverted from the main line of protein crystallography to the first examination of tobacco mosaic virus (TMV) solutions, based on preparations by Bawden and Pirie in 1936. These turned out to be quite different from anything examined before. They are composed of long particles with a strong tendency to parallel packing, typical of the rod-shaped viruses. At that time, before the development of the electron microscope, this had to be worked out by X-ray and optical methods. Bernal could not have wished for a better collaborator. As he wrote, 'Fankuchen threw himself into this examination. He excelled in the devising of apparatus specially tailored for the purpose.' For example, with his original invention, an X-ray monochromator, he studied the long-range forces which operate in gels; that is not only with the long-range forces between virus-like particles, but also any kind of colloidal particles in solution.

Fankuchen continued his virus investigations in 1938 at Birkbeck College at Bernal's invitation. This led to an absolutely key paper – 'X-ray and crystallographic studies of a plant virus' – which dealt, among other matters, with internal structure. Even in solution virus particles 'have an inner regularity like that of a crystal. Virus preparations are thus in a sense doubly crystalline.'[180] Olby has pointed out that it is not easy today 'to appreciate just how striking was the discovery that TMV rods were some 2000 Å in length, and yet they were rigid structures displaying a remarkable degree of order, so much so that when these TMV rods were oriented in solution in a capillary tube and given a 400 hour exposure to X-rays, the resulting diffraction pattern was so like that of a single crystal that Bernal and Fankuchen went on trying to index the diagram and derive the unit cell when the data contained too many ambiguities. And yet Bernal was aware that he was dealing with material which was *almost* a single crystal, *but not quite* – that was what intrigued him, this biological world of the almost 3-dimensional crystal!'[181]

On the eve of the war, Bernal was on a lecture tour in the USA, during which he seized the opportunity to talk with Edwin Cohn, of Woods Hole, about how Fankuchen might be helped to carry on the X-ray protein research. He did not complete his tour, but rushed back to England, and by September 1939 he was working at Princes Risborough in the technical department of Civil Defence. In a letter to Cohn dated 12 September 1939, he wrote: 'Events seem to have decided things and any co-operation in the protein field will have to count out most if not all Europe from now on. I am sorry because it seemed as if we might have contributed something to the solution of the war problems. It is particularly unfortunate with regard to X-ray work. I shall not be able to touch it for a long time, and I do not think anyone else here will either. My only hope is that it may be possible to get it well started in the States through Fankuchen, who I am sending over with all my materials to carry on if he can find some means of doing so.'[182]

To Felix Haurowitz, he wrote on the same date, urging support for Fankuchen 'because the work was in a promising stage and unless it takes roots in America I am afraid it may be forgotten altogether in the stress of events'.[183] Fankuchen returned to the United States, and Bernal was plunged into a world of new activities in which time had begun to change its meaning. 'I am right out of science', he wrote to Fankuchen on 1 December, 'so I cannot do any more myself.' He was concerned with publication of their joint virus particles paper. Fankuchen was slow in completing it, and the final preparation of the text and the drawing of some of the illustrations were done by Dorothy Crowfoot Hodgkin at Bernal's special request. The Royal Society found the paper too long for publication. After much urgent and sad prodding from Bernal – in early 1940, he wrote to Fankuchen, 'I hope you have been able to do something about the virus paper,' and again on 25 July, 'How are things going? I have not heard from you for a very long time, and am anxious to know how you are getting on with the proteins. . . . Have you been able to do anything about the virus paper?' – it appeared ultimately in 1941 in the *Journal of General Physiology*, a publication which had nothing to do with X-ray diffraction. It was, however, a recognized scientific journal, and upset as Bernal might have been, the paper was out, and the research moved on. It was most fortunate that Fankuchen finally wrote up that important paper, because Bernal would never have done so.

Fankuchen died of cancer in 1964. He was fifty-nine. Bernal mourned the passing of 'Fan', who was one of a very small group, which included Carlisle, Hodgkin, and Perutz, who extended Bernal's ideas. Fan played a large part in spreading the ideas of crystallography, and promoting understanding in industry of its benefits. 'He will be remembered not so much for his scientific achievements as for his personality and inspiration. His ebullient good humour, friendliness, and helpfulness, and his zest for life', wrote Bernal in an obituary tribute.[184]

When I was speaking to Dr Max Perutz about Bernal, I was startled with the manner in which his eyes lit up as he remembered. It was as if he had fallen into a well of happiness, and was content to float in it knowing he would never drown. On the wall behind his chair there was a studio portrait of Bernal when a young man. He fell under Bernal's spell from the first moment he met him in late 1936. 'I knew I was in the presence of a real intellectual. I had never met anyone like him before', he told me.[185] Perutz, Austrian-born, had graduated as an organic chemist in Vienna in 1936. He was not greatly excited by that field, but responded keenly to what a young lecturer had told him of the biochemical research being carried on under F. Gowland Hopkins in Cambridge. When, in the autumn of 1935, he learned that Hermann Mark and Fritz Eirich were to take part in a Faraday Society meeting in Cambridge, he asked them to negotiate a post for him with Hopkins. Fortunately, as it turned out, they forgot all about it. Bernal's first X-ray pepsin crystal photographs had made a great stir, so that when Bernal told Mark he was looking for a worker to carry on research on those first single crystal pictures, Mark, on his return to Vienna, suggested to Perutz he should work with Bernal. 'I protested that I knew nothing about X-ray crystallography. Mark replied, "You will learn it, my dear boy." ' In September 1936, Perutz entered the crystallography laboratory in Cambridge, and he found himself in 'a few ill-lit and dirty rooms on the ground floor of a stark, dilapidated grey building'. Bernal, typically, was abroad, and he was received by Wooster, who helped him to be admitted to Peterhouse College. 'I asked for work of biological interest, but no protein crystals were available so I worked on iron rhodonite (a silicate) from slag. It was a terrible task; the apparatus was crude and did not work.' However, 'those dingy quarters were turned into a fairy castle by Bernal's brilliance and his boundless optimism about the powers of the X-ray methods. He gave inspiring lectures to those in the know, but I am afraid they were incomprehensible to undergraduates.'[186]

Perutz made a short visit to Vienna, then went on to Prague in the summer of 1937 to see the husband of a cousin of his, Felix Haurowitz, who advised him to contact Gilbert Adair, in the physiology department in Cambridge, about some haemoglobin crystals. 'I did, and obtained some beautiful 0·5 mm crystals of horse haemoglobin. I was lucky, because they were of methaemoglobin of the horse, and these proved to have the simplest crystal structure of any protein of comparable molecular weight, with features so favourable that they make a crystallographer's heart leap with joy.' However, there was great hesitation because there was no direct method for obtaining atomic positions: 'it was as promising as a journey to the moon', Perutz commented at the time. On the structure of haemoglobin, 'we all floundered hopelessly. They were long, lean years.' In a lecture to the Royal Institution on 27 January 1939, Bernal stated that one way of solving the structure of crystalline proteins might be through some physical artifice, such as the introduction of a heavy atom. This was the germ of an idea which led to success twenty years later. Interpretation was so difficult because the diffraction pattern of a crystal gave only half the information needed to solve its structure: it revealed the amplitudes but not the phases of the diffracted rays. 'In classical X-ray analysis a start is often made by guessing the approximate structure – with luck, this is accurate enough to calculate the phases of some of the diffracted rays with their help and with the measured amplitudes more is found out about the structure, and this knowledge in an iterative process leads to the determination of more phases. In this way the structure is gradually refined until the positions of all the atoms are determined. In crystalline proteins this method breaks down', wrote Perutz in November 1955, 'because we have no certain knowledge of what even the approximate structure is likely to be.'[187]

However, before the war, single crystal X-ray photographs had been taken of five different protein crystals, including insulin for the first time in 1935. When Bernal heard about this, he looked up a 1934 paper by D. A. Scott, and wrote 'a quick letter' to Dorothy Crowfoot, undated, but earlier than March 1935,* noting that cadmium as well as zinc could be used in the crystallization of insulin, 'and promising to get cadmium insulin from one of his Cambridge friends (? Chibnall) – which he did'.[188] However, the result was disappointing: Dorothy Hodgkin could find no difference between the X-ray diffraction patterns of the cadmium and zinc insulin crystals because the difference in weight between these two atoms was too small.

Very early in the 1950s, Bernal's 1939 suggestion was taken up again, and it did help to solve the phase problem. Perutz and his colleagues prepared two kinds of crystals of the haemoglobin, identical in all respects but one. In one kind, a mercury atom, which is much heavier than a cadmium atom, was attached to the haemoglobin molecule in a position filled by a hydrogen atom, the lightest of all, in the other kind. That altered the diffraction pattern in a measurable way, and allowed Perutz to determine the positions taken up by the heavy atoms, enabling him to calculate the phase of the diffracted rays. That method provided the first pictures of haemoglobin to be seen and to be worked out. The principle was established that the structure of proteins could be solved by X-ray analysis, despite the complexity of the problem.[189]

The work which Perutz had begun with Bernal was interrupted for a while when, in June 1940, Perutz was detained

* Before 15 March 1935, because that was the date of her first letter to Bernal about her difficulties in growing cadmium insulin crystals.

as an enemy alien – he was still an Austrian citizen – and sent to Canada, where he was interned in the Citadel of Quebec. Bernal protested strongly, intervened in the right quarters, and by Christmas of that year Perutz was released, and within a month, January 1941, was back in England. When he went again to North America, it was as a privileged scientist, to work on the high priority *Habbakuk* project.

The 'centre of excellence' that Bernal had always longed for was the MRC Laboratory of Molecular Biology set up under the direction of Perutz in Cambridge in 1969.* There it was, on the occasion of another visit in May 1978, that I met again Dr Aaron Klug. The last time I had seen him was in 1953 when he was a member of Bernal's department at Torrington Square. He recalled how as a student in South Africa in the early 1940s, he had come across a copy of *The Social Function of Science*, and, despite reservations about its analyses, had been greatly impressed by the sweep of its attempt to express 'the laws of social behaviour'. The first time he saw Bernal was at a university board meeting at which Klug was a candidate for a Nuffield Fellowship. This was some time in 1952 or 1953. 'I remember how Bernal prompted me during the interview.' He began research at Torrington Square working with Carlisle. He found Bernal 'terribly clever, with great enthusiasm, but not involved in the detailed research. He never would look very closely at what was happening. He was, when I first met him, not a field commander, but a good strategist.'

For Klug, matters changed greatly when in 1954 he met Rosalind Franklin at Torrington Square, in an attic, where she had earlier taken up research on virus structure. The next year he published a first paper on TMV with Franklin. Now he began to see much more of Bernal, who was always 'Professor' to him, never 'Sage'. (It was only Bernal's own Cambridge generation who called him that.) He and Rosalind would hear Bernal running up the stairs, wait for him to burst into the room, and to ask 'What's new?' Although they were

* It was the successor to the Unit for Research on the Molecular Structure of Biological Systems opened originally in Cambridge in 1947. The name was changed in 1968 to the Molecular Biology Research Laboratory, and again a year later.

very much heartened by his support, nevertheless they both found this somewhat exacting, because the question could not be answered afresh each day. 'We asked each other what he would do if nothing was happening. But, scientifically, he was very forward with his ideas. He was never possessive.'

Bernal had the highest regard for Rosalind Franklin. 'I had come to know and respect her and to admire her, too, as a very intelligent and brave woman.'[190] He thought her work was distinguished by its extreme clarity and perfection in everything she did; her photographs as among the most beautiful of any substance ever taken. He attributed their excellence to extreme care in preparation and mounting of the specimens, as well as in the taking of the photographs. All this she did almost entirely herself. He mourned her early death a few months before her thirty-eighth birthday. She worked to within a week or two of her death, which she must have known for many months to be inevitable.

Bernal inspired others. That was his role. Olby wrote, 'The reputation he established in the 1930s lived on, and when Sven Furberg, Rosalind Franklin, and Francis Crick turned to biology, it was to Birkbeck that they went, in search of a place in Bernal's laboratory. In this sense, too, Bernal did succeed in achieving his ambition, for it was at Birkbeck that Furberg established the structure of DNA, and Franklin established the structure of TMV.'[191] Why did he not receive a Nobel prize? I cannot establish that his name was put forward, and I have asked intimates of his who were themselves Nobel laureates, men such as C. H. Powell and F. Joliot-Curie. Somehow there was something missing: there was enthusiasm, but not obsessiveness: there was nothing to fix on which could proclaim, 'I, and I alone, am the product clearly of J. D. Bernal's brain and work.' Of course, he knew himself that he would not get a Nobel prize. At a Ciba Foundation Symposium on 'Principles of Biomolecular Organization' in 1966, he said, 'I have spent my time, when I wasn't doing things even more vague than molecular biology – things like the structure of liquids which have no proper structure at all – speculating on the meaning of those aspects of molecular biology which are run now by other people. I still have the delight in my memory of seeing some of the beginnings of these discoveries myself. But these days are over for me.' Alan Mackay's comment, 'Diffuse contributions receive diffuse awards', is apt.

Equally revealing, was Bernal's review of the book, *The Double Helix*, by James Watson. This was a curious statement. Most scientists probably would not have read it, because it appeared in the *Labour Monthly*, a Communist political, and non-scientific, magazine. It embarrassed Bernal's intimate colleagues, because it overstated his case, and ignored the essential contributions made by some of them to the discovery of DNA. The review appeared in July 1968: yet in 1953 Bernal had written of Pasteur what he might later have said of himself, 'It is an odd fact that in the excitement of the subsequent discovery Pasteur seems to have overlooked entirely his debt to Hankel. . . . What is even odder is that Hankel himself . . . seems never to have claimed priority . . .' Then followed a revealing sentence, 'Published papers may omit important steps and the memory of men of science, even the greatest, is sadly fallible.'[192]

In his book review, he wrote, 'I should say here that the distinction between the fully and partially crystalline structures was fully recognized in practice between Astbury and myself. I took the crystalline substances and he the amorphous or messy ones: first it seemed that I must have the best of it but it was to prove otherwise. My name does not appear, and rightly, in the double helix story. Actually the distinction is a vital one. The picture of a helical structure contains far fewer spots than does that of a regular three-dimensional crystalline structure and thus far less detailed information on atomic positions, but it is easier to interpret roughly and therefore gives a good clue to the whole. No nucleic acid structure is well known. It may be paradoxical that the more information-carrying methods should be deemed the less useful to examine a really complex molecule, but this is so as a matter of analytical strategy rather than accuracy.'

He went on, 'A strategic mistake may be as bad as a factual error. So it turned to be with me. Faithful to my gentlemen's agreement with Astbury, I turned from the study of the amorphous nucleic acids to their crystalline components, the nucleosides. The easiest to prepare of these was cytidine. Very fortunately, there came to my laboratory at that time a young crystallographer from Oslo in Norway, Sven Furberg, who had been working under Professor Hassel. He undertook the study of the structure of cytidine. He worked very quickly and well and the structure he found proved to have wide implications.' They did not realize how wide, Bernal confessed. 'In fact, had we realized it, it contained the key to the whole double helix story. But this key was never used because as far as we know neither Watson nor any of his friends knew of it or realized its relevance.' In a sense, it was like Wyart's reports on the invasion beaches over again. This was due, in part, to a lack of communication between men who knew each other, and often worked in the same laboratories. He confessed, 'I, myself, should have noticed it, but I was too preoccupied with other things, and let the opportunity slip. This may stand as yet another example of a missed chance of an almost simultaneous discovery.' He would not make any claim for it himself, but he thought that 'for historic justice' Furberg's contribution had been grossly overlooked. When Crick gave him 'a nearly accurate account of the genetic code', Bernal 'fully recognized the importance of base order, I should have tried to work it into the X-ray picture of cytidine – another example of missed opportunity'. Simultaneously, Franklin had recognized and measured the phosphorus atoms in the helix, 'which proves to be the outer one, thus showing Pauling to be wrong, and the helix to be a double one, though this inference is not drawn. Thus, all the elements of the structure of the full solution had been given, though it remained to fit in the genetic evidence. This proved quite easy . . .'[193]

Those on the inside could not regard this as an accurate, or fair, statement. It attributed too much to Bernal himself, and he, after 1945, was absent increasingly from the laboratory. For instance, one member of his staff who was 'supervised' by him saw him only twice in three years. The facts are that Furberg came to Birkbeck in 1947 on a two-year British Council scholarship. He was not concerned with molecular biology, but with extending his crystallographic experience. He had just obtained his Cand:Real: degree (roughly equivalent to an MSc), and Bernal asked Carlisle to supervise him. 'Consequently,' Carlisle told me, 'I was left with a tall order to supervise someone to carry out research and write up a thesis in two years.' Carlisle had the original idea to have Furberg work out the structure of cytidine. He encouraged and guided him so well that Furberg, a willing and intelligent person, was able to gain his PhD in two years.

Carlisle received little or no recognition for his key guidance in what was an important contribution to the later model-building studies of Watson and Crick, who put forward a plausible structure for DNA in 1953. Furberg, in fact, had built the first helix, some two years before Pauling came out with his α-helix, and showed that the helix could be a natural structural system for biological macromolecules. It was through the excellent X-ray photographs taken by Franklin, and from Chargaff's chemical evidence, that the final confirmation was obtained that DNA was a helical structure, a double helix as proposed by Watson and Crick.

However, no one disagreed with Bernal's conclusion that 'such a decisive breakthrough in human thought is not necessarily the work of an individual genius, but only of a pack of bright and well-financed research workers following a good well-laid trail'.[194]

From 1945 until the early 1960s he was at the height of his international activities, 'burning the candle at both ends', as Carlisle put it. But, he was thinking also of the future of crystallography. Within Birkbeck, his own position was under challenge. Sir John Lockwood, then Master of the College, had little sympathy for him. When, in 1952, the Nuffield grant ended, Bernal and his staff were paid by the Physics Department. Up to 1960, Bernal had been building up a strong physics element in his laboratory: for example, he appointed Furth, a good theoretical physicist, who, unfortunately, was never given a personal chair, despite Bernal's strenuous efforts. By 1960, the internal dog-fights had become more open. The battle was joined to prevent Bernal from having a separate department of crystallography.

His argument in favour was direct, expressing a view he had long held. He had felt for many years that crystallography had not played anything like the part it should play in university teaching. That was largely a result of the very slow rate at which new knowledge penetrated into universities. Indeed, it had become so much slower than the rate of advance of knowledge itself that it had become a serious brake on it. The limitation, he argued, was essentially a biological one. It was clear that new ideas could only enter universities at the rate that new appointments were made, and that meant, generally, at the rate at which professors retired. That restriction applied most forcibly at the introduction of a new scientific discipline: then, it was not a matter of replacing old ideas by new, but of finding new places for them.

It was clear, he insisted, that professors trained in the older disciplines did not yet appreciate the contributions of crystallography. Many of them never would, although the subject was already fifty years old. However, the great advances in structural crystallography had made the subject more than ever necessary as a basis for other sciences. How could that be done without overloading syllabuses? He felt sure the ultimate answer was a radical revision of syllabuses in chemistry and physics. He wanted a general course in chemistry based from the beginning on such concepts as ionic size, the length of the valence bonds, packing considerations, etc. This would give the subject a logical system of ideas. In physics, there was no need for so thorough a revolution. The subject was moving towards the study of the solid state. Thus, not only normal structural crystallography, but also abnormal crystallography, the study of imperfect crystals and distortions, needed to be introduced at a fairly early level. What was required in physics teaching was more a matter of a rational internal arrangement by which subjects with the same essential interrelation of parts were brought together: for instance, in that of X-ray, electron, and ordinary optics as special examples of the extended behaviour of wave particles. In mineralogy, the importance of structural work was very clear. In biology, a short course on the elements of structural crystallography, particularly that of polymers and fibres, needed to be linked with the ultra-histology being produced by the electron microscope.

He thought it would be a mistake to introduce full-scale

crystallographic courses as an undergraduate study. More was to be gained, he felt, by bringing someone with a fair knowledge of chemistry, physics, metallurgy, or mineralogy into contact with the more advanced parts of crystallography. 'We want to build crystallography into every stage of the teaching of physical science, so that the concept of the spatial array of atoms and their physical consequences becomes second nature to physicists and chemists alike. The concept of the crystal and its regularity must become as familiar as that of the molecule. At the same time we must not lose sight of the attraction of the methods of study which through the phenomena of diffraction can reveal these structures, as by a most powerful but sophisticated microscope. We must hope even at the undergraduate level to attract a naturally gifted group of students by the beauty and interest of crystallographic studies so that we can maintain and increase the number of those who will advance our subject in the future.'[195]

These were the ideas he expressed at the first meeting on the teaching of crystallography in 1959. They were, also, the arguments he used at Birkbeck, which resulted finally in his being appointed to a chair of crystallography in 1963. It was specially established for him. The current joke was that he was a professor without a department. The joke came to an end a year later, when the Department of Crystallography was recognized. It was in 1963 that he was delighted with the great honour of election as president of the International Union of Crystallography for a three-year term at its congress in Rome. He recalled, in his presidential address, how in 1928 he had visited the centres of crystallographic research in Europe, and how enchanted he was, when in Stuttgart, to meet Ewald and Hermann. They had had discussions on the possibilities of some international organization of research in crystallography, which took form in 1947 in London under the hospitality of the Institute of Physics. Here was another social structure to foster the study of the structures of 'the living fossils', which were the actual organic substances, and it was in that study that he believed we would discover, in time, the means of controlling the living world, and of understanding its origin. But mankind had to survive to ensure that: and

the struggle against the betrayal of science that was represented
for him by the atomic bomb was to tax him plentifully in the
coming years. This was, I believe, to speed the arrival of his
barren days of enforced withdrawal.

I I

Sordid Affairs

It is a commonplace story enough much of the time,
sometimes sordid and shameful, sometimes heroic,
and one in which, like it or not, many of us today are
personally involved.
Book jacket blurb for Margot Heinemann novel[196]

Even during his most creative years, Bernal existed on
sufferance: he was never acceptable to the inner power groups
in Britain, neither in the major political parties, nor in the
scientific establishment. Because of his intellectual brilliance
he could not be rejected, but his presence, always forceful and
effective, was resented. Those who opposed him philosophi-
cally and politically were frequently lesser beings, but they
had an astuteness which he lacked. Crowther's view that he
was naive politically is supported by his maltreatment by the
British Association for the Advancement of Science (BA, or
BAAS), and in his attitude to Lysenkoism. In the former,
an excessive patriotism by the officers of the BA made them
blindly stupid in their assault on him; in the latter, Bernal's
own lack of real intimacy with the Russian people and un-
swerving support for the Soviet Union led him into ignorant
complicity with Stalinist corruption.

1. The British Association

At their meeting on the afternoon of 4 November 1949, the
Council of the British Association for the Advancement of
Science (BAAS) decided by a majority not to re-elect Bernal

as a member. Thus ended a shabby little episode in the history of a body then in its 188th year, and visibly in decline. Its first years, when pronouncements at its annual gatherings had the effect of lions roaring with certainty and vigour, had long gone. Its president, enthroned for a year, was still a scientist of reputation, but the death-making weight of tradition over-shadowed all. The officers, to maintain themselves, were obliged to eat air.

No one could deny that Bernal had been an active council member. In the preparation of the meetings of Section A (Physics) since the resumption of post-war activities he had played a most useful part, probably more than most of that section's committee members. Professor Neville insisted that Bernal 'had thrown himself quite wholeheartedly into the work of the Association, and the success of Section A's meet-ings had been due more to him than to anybody else'.[197] But such arguments counted for little, such considerations were described as irrelevant. Certain council members were out to get Bernal, not for himself but as a leading protagonist of a viewpoint they detested, and they were determined to take advantage of what, at worst, can be described as a loose formulation by him of a long-held, and often-expressed, view.

On 27 August 1949, Bernal spoke at a conference of the Soviet Partisans for Peace in Moscow, bringing greetings as a representative of the World Federation of Scientific Workers. He said that scientists had a particular responsibility for peace; the evil use of science had been developed as never before, for in the decay of the capitalist system war remained the last and most profitable investment of the monopolists. The direction of scientific research – radar, long-range rockets, the atomic bomb, radioactive poisons, bacterial warfare – was increasingly turned to war uses. 'For now in capitalist countries the direc-tion of science is in the hands of those who hate peace, whose only aim is to destroy and torture people so that their own profits may be secured for some years longer.' He provided figures to show how 'the perversion of science for war' had reached 'fantastic dimensions' in Britain and in the USA, where 'it will soon be the case that no one who is not, and has not always been, an enemy of the Soviet Union will be allowed to teach or research in science, and Britain will obediently follow suit.'

He went on to insist that in the hands of decaying capitalism science could be used only for increased exploitation, unemployment, crises, and war. He was not astonished that that produced a reactionary attitude to science, not only outside, but also inside, science itself. There was a revival of the concept of pure, objective science removed from all practical social utility, an attempt to divorce science from its responsibility. That did not restrain its advocates from virulent anti-Soviet propaganda. Outside the scientific world, there was a move to reject science altogether, and to replace it with a mysticism that could easily again turn to the perversion of the Nazis. The call from America to reduce the world's population could lead logically to an even more scientific variety of Hitler's gas chambers. The greed and cruelty of capitalism had made the world not fit to live in. In the hands of the people there would be room and food for all. For capitalists and their social democratic supporters, there was no future to look forward to: but it was capitalism that was doomed, not civilization. 'Only under capitalism is it true that science can bring no happiness but only destruction. The scientist has no freedom – he is a slave to masters who have lost their senses.' He ended with a tribute to 'the Great Soviet people, who by their heroism have saved science and secured its future for mankind, and with them their great leader and protector of peace and science, Comrade Stalin'.

On Monday, 29 August, *The Times* carried a story consisting of two brief paragraphs based on a Reuter report. It was headed: Prof. Bernal Praises Mr Stalin, 'Protector of Science'. The first paragraph quoted him as saying that 'direction of science in "the capitalist world" was in the hands of those who hated peace and wanted war', and the second that 'science in the hands of capitalists could never be employed usefully'. The Council of the BAAS was meeting on 31 August at the annual talk-fest in that year in Newcastle. I am reasonably convinced that if it were not for that coincidence Bernal would have been re-elected. But a certain hysteria had already been built up nationally; some key BA officers insisted that the association had to present itself as loyal citizens, rejecting in those cold war, McCarthyite days any who would describe Stalin in praising terms. In March of that year, Bernal had been one of four British delegates – another was the actress, Patricia Burke – to a world peace conference in New York whose visa had been revoked by the State Department. It was not only Bernal who was to be 'exposed'. In France, within a twelvemonth, his friend, Frédéric Joliot-Curie, member of the French Communist Party, president of the World Federation of Scientific Workers and of the World Peace Movement, was to be dismissed by Prime Minister Bidault from his post as High Commissioner of the French Atomic Energy Commission for his pro-Soviet utterances. Bernal was to use that incident as a strong justification for the correctness of his assertions in Moscow.

The council agreed that Bernal should be invited 'to substantiate or otherwise' the statements represented to have been made by him, and until then his nomination for council should not be proceeded with, and a vacancy would be maintained. The BAAS secretary on 9 September wrote accordingly to Bernal. He added that the council recognized 'in discussion that it was necessary to distinguish between political statements of members of the council (which did not concern the council), and statements on the direction and use of science in this country (on which the council, representing the Association, might be expected to have views). The press reports of your speech in Moscow contained statements on the direction and use of science to which the Council could not subscribe.' The statements to which exception was taken were two: that concerned with the direction of science as in the hands of peace-haters, and that with science under capitalism as bringing only destruction.

On 13 September, Bernal replied he had learned with surprise while still in Moscow of the council action, and regretted that the press had been informed before he had been contacted. He enclosed the full text of his Msocow speech. If exception was taken to the general nature of the speech, 'I may be justified in feeling that political rather than scientific considerations were allowed to enter into the discussion. The views in the speech are essentially those which I have expounded many times in public meetings at home and abroad, and are to be found in many of my published writings. Never before have they been considered to justify action by any scientific body. They represent conclusions honestly arrived at which I am prepared to sustain by arguments based on verifiable facts.'

He went on, 'I have nothing to withdraw of what I have said'. He knew that many persons on the council would not agree with his sentiments, but political statements were no official concern of the council. However, there was one passage in the reports of his speech on which a genuine misunderstanding might have arisen. 'I can assure the Council that it was never my intention either to state or to imply that the scientists responsible for the detailed direction of research in this or any country were haters of peace. Such a statement would be palpably absurd, and I am surprised that my colleagues should ever imagine that I should make it. I had never supposed that unanimity on questions of general politics was either required or desirable in such a body as the British Association.'

Also, on 13 September, a leading columnist, A. J. Cummings, in the daily newspaper, *The News Chronicle* (now defunct), commented in a bitter piece on how strange it was 'that a man with such a background as Bernal's should swallow so gullibly every tale that he hears in the propagandist chambers of the Russian capital'. In a lengthy reply published the following day, Bernal compared the Moscow he had lived in fifteen years ago – this was his first visit since 1934 – with the great reconstruction he was witnessing. 'There are plenty of difficult problems today in the Soviet Union, but they are problems that are being tackled and will be tackled successfully if there is no war. That was the single question and doubt put to me insistently by almost everyone I talked to while I was there. It was the burden of the speeches at the peace conference. The best guarantee of peace is that the people of the Soviet Union need it. Our own people need it no less.'

The BAAS Council meeting was to be held on 4 November. By that date many letters of support for Bernal had been sent in: from such scientists as Kathleen Lonsdale, Dorothy and Joseph Needham, W. A. Wooster, V. Gordon Childe, J. B. S. Haldane, L. S. Penrose, F. Yates, and N. W. Pirie. But these could make no difference to the outcome. In a letter to *The Times* published on 8 October, Bernal, replying to Sir Edward Appleton, stressed that in speaking of the direction of science in capitalist countries he was clearly referring not to administrators such as Sir Edward, but to politicians and business men, mostly in the USA. 'They have decided that 60 per cent or more of the total national expenditure in research and development should be spent on war science. The latest available figures are £300 million out of £500 million in the United States and £57 million out of £110 million in Great Britain. These are the figures for 1947: the proportion is certainly greater now.' He went on, 'Further, as the financial interests of these men are closely linked with war industries, as the press and political figures allied to them openly treat of war as a method of containing or destroying Communism, I do not feel that I went too far in describing them as enemies of peace. Even now, in our desperate financial situation, we are not only maintaining but actually increasing the number of scientists in war service, and thus holding back indefinitely the possibility of technical improvements in our industry which alone would enable us to survive as a trading nation. I would not criticize the civil section of Britain's scientific effort or suggest that in detail it is not perfectly free. On the other hand, I consider it grossly inadequate in scale and in effective co-ordination. That people like myself benefit from it to the extent of being allowed to pursue fundamental research is beside the point. Such work is not a favour to individuals but a national necessity. Any country, private enterprise or socialist, which failed to carry on fundamental research to the extent of providing a continuous flow of new ideas and trained minds would soon lose its technical and economic independence. As we are spending today, at most, £6 million, that is, less than 10 per cent of our military science expenditure, on such research, we have little enough on which to congratulate ourselves. Complacency rather than criticism is the real danger in British science today.'

The council discussion reflected how the scientific community, facing a critical reappraisal of the nature of science and of its place in society, could do nothing but insist on the maintenance of a traditional outlook. There was another, unmentioned, fact of importance: on 23 September the Soviet Union had exploded its first nuclear device. In the event, the decision of council was not to re-elect Bernal.

A week after the council meeting, on 12 November, Critic in *The New Statesman & Nation* commented, 'In brief, my view is that a silly utterance is penalized in a rather silly way.' He missed the point. There was much more to the affair than that. Certain members of the council felt they were helping to kill a Communist conspiracy, to counter a threat to democracy in Britain, and 'that the time had come for evil lies to be nailed to the mast' (as the Headmaster of Blundell's School declared in a letter to the BA).

Six months later – on 5 April 1950 – Kathleen Lonsdale wrote to the secretary of the BAAS that several members of the council had expressed surprise that she could have 'defended' Bernal, and had commented also on 'the questionable company' in which she found herself in doing so. She insisted that however greatly she detested a scientist's views on morals or religion or politics, 'if in the field of science they are outstandingly brilliant (as Professor Bernal admittedly is) then I do not consider that their behaviour or their thoughts outside the field is the concern *of a scientific society*. That is one of the principles on which the election to the Royal Society, for instance, has been based in the past.' She thought that Bernal's speech 'was stupid, although I believe him to have been sincere in making it. I do not agree with him. But I am convinced that it is *much* more important that the British Association should set its face against witch-hunting and purges of all kinds, than that they should register public disapproval of a particular speech, which would soon have sunk into oblivion if so much attention had not been called to it in the first place.' She ended by asking that her letter be shown to 'Dr Hindle on his return from Pakistan. He spoke to me recently on an occasion on which it was impossible for me to reply adequately to him.'

A statement signed by 244 scientists working in university

and industrial laboratories was sent to the BA on 23 March. The signatories declared that they deplored the Council's action in depriving itself of the services of Professor Bernal for expressions of his political attitude – expressions with which many of them disagreed. 'The aim of the British Association is the advancement of science. To the furtherance of that aim Professor Bernal has made signal contribution.' The collection of signatures was sponsored by a group which included two scientists – Dorothy Crowfoot-Hodgkin and Kathleen Lonsdale who were to become presidents of the BA.

Dr Edward Hindle, FRS, director of the Zoological Society of London, was senior general scretary of the BA. He felt it might be in the national interest for that department in the Government concerned with security to have a complete list of the signatories. Accordingly, on 29 March he wrote on Zoo notepaper 'strictly confidentially' to the War Office, emphasizing that the list of Bernal's supporters which had appeared in *The Times* on 27 March included well-known Communists and a number of fellow-travellers. In reply, he received thanks, assuring him that the list had served a very useful purpose, and that he would be grateful for such information at any time.

Dr Hindle later provided the same information and comments confidentially to Professor R. Douglas Laurie, honorary secretary of the Association of University Teachers, in response to his request.

2 *The case of Lysenko*

I have told the story of the BA affair in some detail, because its significance lay not only in the false pettiness of those who proclaimed a non-political approach to Bernal, but who were themselves highly motivated politically, but also in the seemingly ritual, political naïveté of Bernal himself. He was of the generation of Marxists who sought to purify science by removing it from a decadent capitalist environment. For him science was a progressive force, to be cherished and adorned. That was how it was being treated in the Soviet Union. At first, it was not so much the psychology of the Soviet scientists that attracted him, but their material conditions – freedom from laboratory want in a planned society. Later, his monochromatic vision was to broaden, but essentially his pro-Soviet affirmation was never to change.

On 20 September 1949, the *Evening Star*, of Ipswich, Suffolk, published an interview with Bernal given at his country home, the Old Rectory, Combs, near Stowmarket. It was a long statement covering well-trodden ground. What was of particular interest were his comments on Russian agriculture and horticulture. He said that many amazing experiments in growing methods were being tried successfully. 'I saw carrots grafted on to parsley, cabbages grafted on to turnips, and beetroot on to mangolds. By using an old scion in this way you can influence a young stock. Many things are being altered to suit unusual climates by these grafting methods.' He told of how one farmer by planting in a particular way had transformed spring wheat into winter wheat, and had obtained a hybrid which could be grown quite well even in Siberia. This same farmer, who had expressed admiration of the achievements of the British cattle breeders, was now obtaining, in vastly different climatic conditions, milk yields comparable with those in Britain.

Bernal was referring to the work of Soviet Academician T. D. Lysenko, then President of the Lenin Academy of Agricultural Sciences, and newly invested with authority as the autocrat of Soviet agriculture. In the summer of 1948 Lysenko had won a notable victory, for as the result of a special conference in Moscow, which began on 21 July and ended on 7 August, a letter of greetings was sent to Stalin, and a resolution adopted which ensured that teaching of, and research in, what was described loosely as 'bourgeois' genetics – that is the school of Darwin–Mendel–Morgan – was outlawed for fifteen years, and the 'new genetics' of Michurin–Lysenko became the official orthodoxy. When Bernal met Lysenko they both got on very well, according to J. G. Crowther, who was present. He overheard Bernal say, 'I'm a farmer, too.'[198] Bernal was impressed by Lysenko's practical achievements. Lysenko struck Crowther as an honest, but fanatical, man, impatient of any opposition, but with a definite feel for plants and soil. Bernal never denounced the 'new genetics', despite his respect for such colleagues as J. B. S. Haldane, who felt obliged to resign from the British Communist Party in part because of his distaste for Lysenkoism.

Lysenko himself cannot be dismissed purely as a phoney, or as a scientific hatchetman for Stalin, and later Khrushchev. It is true that he set back seriously the study of genetics in the Soviet Union, and in gaining power was responsible for the destruction, among others, of the distinguished biologist, N. I. Vavilov, a friend of Lenin.* However, Lysenko had been active as an agriculturalist for over twenty years. He had been brought to official notice in 1927 when an article in *Pravda* told how he had turned 'the barren fields of the Transcaucasus green in winter'. Lysenko claimed that his particular discovery was the technique of 'vernalization', details of which he gave first in 1928.**

From this followed his theory of 'the phasic development of plants', which led him to the anti-Mendelian claim that 'hereditary' characteristics were not biologically determined, but could be moulded by surroundings: once a plant's heredity had been 'de-stabilized', its heredity could be directed as wished. He presented himself as continuing the work of the gifted Russian gardener, Ivan Michurin. A turning point came for Lysenko in 1935 when, with the intimate collaboration of J. I. Prezent, a Communist who specialized in the methodology and pedagogy of the sciences, he was able to link his Michurinist theory of heredity, his anti-Mendelian thesis, with dialectical materialism. It was Prezent who developed Lysenkoism as a philosophical system which was used to attack classical genetics, not for being unable to help Soviet agriculture, but as an expression of 'bourgeois science'.

In Lysenko's *Bulletin of Vernalization* (*Byulleten' Yarovizatsii*), Prezent was responsible for charging the geneticists with being

* Vavilov was founder of the Lenin Academy of Agricultural Sciences, director of the Institute of Genetics of the USSR Academy of Sciences and of the All-Union Institute of Plant Breeding.
** In essence, this technique consisted of maintaining at a low temperature the previously moistened seed of a winter variety of a given plant. By this means, it would be transformed into a spring plant.'[199]

'Trotskyite saboteurs fawning on the latest reactionary pro-posals of foreign scientists'. Those were accusations with the most dreadful implications in those days, especially as that issue of the *Bulletin* carried also the text of a Stalin statement on 'measures for liquidating Trotskyite and other double-dealers'. In 1938, Lysenko became president of the Lenin Academy of Agricultural Sciences, and proclaimed it was 'necessary to expel from the institutes and stations the methods of bourgeois science which were cultivated in every possible way by enemies of the people, the Trotskyite-Bukharinist diversionists who operated in the All-Union Academy of Agricultural Sciences'.[200] Vavilov's fate was settled. He had described the 'new genetics' as 'an outbreak of medieval obscurantism'. He was arrested on 6 August 1940 whilst on a botanical expedition in the Western Ukraine. Mark Popovsky, a Soviet science writer who left the USSR in 1977, has des-cribed the dreadful suffering of that innocent man before his five-minute 'trial' on 9 July 1941, at which he was sentenced to death by firing squad.[201] For some reason he was not shot immediately, but in July 1942 his sentence was changed to twenty years in a prison camp. He died there miserably of starvation at 7 a.m. on 26 January 1943, at the age of fifty-five.

However, it took about ten years before Lysenkoism secured its ultimate seal of orthodoxy. In 1948, the Mendelian geneti-cists were routed as sterile practitioners and scholastic theorists.

The botanist, Eric Ashby, began in 1944 a year as a scientist at the Australian legation in Moscow. He came to have no illusions then about Lysenko and his 'new genetics'. He found Lysenko's views on heredity not only novel, but also opposed diametrically to the views of scientists in every country outside Russia. 'His theories are not only astonishing; they are unten-able unless the accumulated experience of most other geneti-cists is to be disregarded', he wrote. He had found that Lysenko justified his work by appeal to dialectical materialism, and condemned the work of his opponents in that it was in-consistent with dialectical materialism. The work of Mendel and Morgan was condemned as 'fascist, bourgeois – capital-istic, and inspired by clerics'. Ashby was bewildered by 'talks about the "souls" of plants and their "love marriages" when fertilized by mixtures of pollen, happily referred to as "the lads" '.[202] For Ashby, Lysenko was the peasants' demagogue.

Bernal saw Lysenkoism otherwise, although his attitude changed over the years. In 1949, he regarded the criticisms of Lysenko as 'a major intellectual weapon in the cold war'. He explained that after twenty years of controversy, the direction of field work, research, and teaching in biology had been altered radically along the lines of the Michurin school. That implied a definite break with the accepted view of the outside world in genetics, and marked 'for the first time the assertion of the independence of science in the Soviet Union from the previously universal community of world science'. It was, also, the first occasion on which the Central Committee of the CPSU had declared itself on a scientific issue. Bernal asked four questions: was it competent to do so; was its judgement right; what would be the results on Soviet agricultural practice; and what would be the world repercussions?

The Lysenko doctrines made up 'an agrobiological theory, the first of its kind because until the advent of socialist agriculture the evidence for biological theories . . . had to be picked up piecemeal from farmers, travellers, and breeders'. The new views differed from the old because they were less concerned with the structures, individual characters, and mechanisms, which could be described in a language borrowed ultimately from physics, and more 'with the integral totality of soil, plant, and animal, an approach intellectually more difficult as it is practically more rewarding'. Lysenko asserted, he went on, that desired heritable changes could be produced by direct action, and that acquired characters could be inherited. He added, in what might be regarded as a cautionary phrase, 'and claims to show by experiment'.

Bernal was reviewing the verbatim account of the important discussion at the Lenin Academy of Agricultural Sciences in August 1948.[203] This was available in London in English as *The Situation in Biological Science in 1949*. In this review he presented Lysenko's views with a kind of favourable neutrality. But this was damaging to Bernal. For example, he recognized that the most persistent objection was to the isolation and autonomy of the gene. He stated, 'No one has actually isolated

G

194 SAGE: A LIFE OF J. D. BERNAL

the genes'. A rather defeatist comment at a time when the material basis of the operation of the chromosome was to come under increasing study in his own laboratory. He argued that Lysenko's theories were easy to distort and ridicule if taken out of the context of the practice of Soviet agriculture. He expressed enthusiasm for such 'outstanding contributions' by Lysenko as vernalization and the Michurin-Williams forest shelter belts. These were unfortunate examples as their miserable inadequacy was made clear within a few years. He likened the method of the Lysenko school to operational research, a wartime development with many peacetime applications, and he saw Lysenko prevailing against 'the entrenched forces of scientific orthodoxy'. The Michurinists were more than the believers in a new or heretical theory: 'they represented a movement in science paralleled only by that of the Stakhanovites in industry'.

Read now with hindsight, his earnest defence has a high note of tragedy. For instance, 'There is nothing either in the resolutions of the Agricultural Academy or those of the Academy of Sciences, to give any ground to charges of exile or imprisonment. Though some scientists have been transferred to posts of less importance, there is no indication of any cessation of research work . . .' he wrote. Yet, as Zhores Medvedev pointed out, most of the prominent human geneticists were arrested, and when Khrushchev broke up the special prison-camp system in 1956 not one was found alive.[204] Further, Bernal believed the net result of the changes would be 'an enormous increase of biological research in the Soviet Union'. He foresaw that 'for some time to come there will be in the world two radically different theories of genetics and more widely of evolution'. Again, Medvedev claimed that the liquidation during the pre-war period caused Soviet medical and human genetics to lag behind the rapid development of genetics after 1965.[205]

It is painful and embarrassing to continue this summary of Bernal's 1949 statement. Its sole redeeming feature is its urgent concluding plea that 'we in this country' should hold back 'the drive to war so that the workers, the farmers, and the scientists in the Soviet Union and in the whole world can continue their work in peace'. It is doubly tragic because the whole later course of work on the material basis of genetics has been to confirm the attitude formed by the Theoretical Biology Club, and much of the work was done by Bernal's students.

This article by Bernal in *Modern Quarterly* did his reputation as an independent thinker a great deal of harm amongst many left-wing admirers. Because of Lysenko's known intimate links with Khrushchev, and Bernal's expressed admiration for Khrushchev, whom he met on a number of occasions, it was assumed that Bernal had become an apologist for the current political bosses in the Kremlin. Of course, this was not true. This can be demonstrated by examining his references to Lysenko (or as he called it, 'the great genetics controversy') in the four editions of his book, *Science in History*, published between 1954 and 1969. In the first edition (1954), there was a major section of eight pages devoted to the subject (p. 666 f). This was basically a restatement of his *Modern Quarterly* article which I have summarized above. The second edition expressed the impact of the great changes ('the thaw') immediately following the death of Stalin. The genetics controversy was dealt with in fewer pages than formerly, and the attitude expressed was more circumspect (p. 667 f). He explained that although the ban on Mendelian ideas and genetic research had been lifted, the work of those in 'the apparently opposed school of Michurin and Lysenko' was still being pursued actively. He used the phrase 'apparently opposed' because he believed they had been talking at cross purposes. Lysenko had scored some successes in practice, but there were 'some dubious ones owing to lack of adequate statistical controls and some downright failures'. He added that some of Lysenko's followers had even been accused of faking, but the whole story had still to be written.

It is interesting that Bernal, as a Marxist, never suggested that a full Marxist analysis of the genetics controversy should be undertaken. He does admit (p. 287) that because of the cold war atmosphere he was led to pass over the inadmissible way in which the controversy was conducted in the Soviet Union. He was impressed, also, that immediately after the war, Lysenko's ideas fitted the popular mood and government policy. 'Here, it was felt, was a genuinely Russian theory, Michurin's, taken over by a product of young Soviet science, Lysenko. Through it the hostile outer world could be shown the errors of its boasted science, and at the same time the thesis that nothing is impossible to the new Soviet man could be vindicated.' He insisted that he had been 'formally correct' when he said that the discussion was initiated and carried out among scientists, with whom the final decision rested: at that stage, neither government nor Party was concerned. Lysenko was not a Party member, and the theory had the support only of one or two, not highly influential, Marxist philosophers. But enthusiasm, mostly ill-informed, carried the day, leading to 'unjustifiable' demotions and transfers of scientists, and alterations in teaching methods. 'I accepted them at the time with regret, but I should not have attempted to defend them.' He continued his confessional by stating that the state could intervene when concerned with teaching and research in science, 'but only on the best scientific advice and never in such a way that only one view in a controversial question is presented. That is now recognized in the Soviet Union.' It is sad to read, 'All of the Mendelian geneticists are, as far as I know, back in positions of equal importance to those from which they were removed. The case of N. I. Vavilov is still not cleared up, but his great scientific services have now once again been officially recognized.'

In the third edition (1965), reference to the genetics controversy by contrast was scanty: a mere one page (p. 702). He felt there was little point in continuing to present a detailed account of the controversy 'because the genetic approach to heredity has become fairly uniform all over the world'. He repeated, 'At its height the contestants were mostly talking at cross-purposes'.

Unfortunately, so far as Bernal is concerned his door on the history of the great genetics controversy cannot be closed. His reputation is still involved. It was sad that Bernal should have allowed himself to be misled by the pseudo-revolutionary doctrines of Lysenko and his ideological supporters just at the time when the components of the solution to the problem of heredity were being developed in his own laboratory, which he neglected for political work. As it was, Stalin died early in 1953, and at almost the same time Crick and Watson wrote their letter to *Nature* on the structure of DNA, which showed the answer to be more materialist and revolutionary than anyone could have expected. After that event, the world was different. The Lysenko affair is more than a distant memory. It continues to disturb the ease of the complacent, of those who are obliged to reject the agonies of disillusion.

1 2

Science in History

Though all her parts be not in their usual place
She hath yet an Anagram of a good face
DONNE*206

On 11 and 12 November 1957, an occasion unique in Bernal's life took place in Moscow. It was organized by the Academy of Sciences to discuss one work: his book, *Science in History*. There were over 400 people present, including probably all the seniors in the field of the history of science. He was greatly moved. 'It is a very rare event,' he said to them. 'It is something absolutely unknown in my country, to have a conference called specially to discuss a work of any living writer.' He hastened to add, 'I know in this case that it is not really on account of my book that this conference is called, but on account of the subject with which the book deals. Nevertheless, the fact that my book has been chosen as a suitable example of a study of the relations of science and social progress, makes me feel that the labour spent in producing it was not in vain.'

Science in History was born in 1948. Bernal in that year gave the Charles Beard Lectures at Ruskin College, Oxford, on 'Science in social history'. It was a subject that had been of special interest to him for some years, and he thought he

---

* This was quoted by Bernal in his paper, 'The use of Fourier transforms in protein crystal analysis' (*Proc. R.S.B.* Vol. 141.1, 1953), p. 83. '. . . Though it cannot be claimed for a moment that this *is* the projection of the protein molecules, it is not unreasonable to suppose that it *contains* the essential parts of the projection. As in Donne's second elegy, describing an ugly woman.'

would have no great difficulty in lecturing on it to what he described as 'an intelligent, but unspecialized, audience'. When he came to prepare his material for publication, he began to realize that it would require far more study and time than he had envisaged. He had planned to have the manuscript ready in three weeks. It took him six years, mainly because he never had longer than ten days at a time to work on it. He persevered because he found it far too fascinating to stop. He admitted that it lacked the polish, the care, and the accuracy that a work on history should have. He wanted it published, however, to stimulate controversy and discussion. In that, he succeeded. The book was a popular success. It was published first in 1954. This was followed by a second edition in 1957, a third in 1965, and a four-volume illustrated edition published in the UK in 1969, and in the USA in 1971. Why it should have achieved 'popular, illustrated, schoolboy's-gift status through a boxed, illustrated edition' puzzled the academics. The historian, J. R. Ravetz, for instance, regarded it as presenting 'the paradox of a most unlikely amateur eclipsing the established professionals in the popularization of their subject'. He thought it was likely to be the general history of science that an educated lay public would rely on for a decade* by which time its insights would be half a century old, because Bernal's assumption of what was real in history was 'the natural one for our time: it fitted the experience of the age of industrialized science, of "science policy", and "mission-oriented research" ', while only a minority of professional historians in the West would mention it in their reading bibliographies.[207]

Bernal's seminal book, *The Social Function of Science*, was never published in Russian. *Science in History* was, in 1956. In that year, Bernal, who was in Moscow at Oparin's invitation, giving a series of lectures on the origin of life at the Institute of Biochemistry, had a meeting with the Soviet publisher. The Russian translators had worked from the first edition, but,

---

* The correctness of this comment may be judged by a review in *The Port of London Authority Monthly*, by A. L., May 1969: 'In fact it would have to be a very prejudiced and reactionary mind which did not find this Bernal survey absorbing, interesting, and, above all, splendidly written.'

following the historic 20th Congress of the CPSU, were required to repeat much of the work from the revised second
edition, because it was less pro-Stalin in its views: as Bernal
put it, 'on account of the great changes that have occurred
since the death of Stalin I have largely rewritten the section
dealing with the Soviet Union and neighbouring countries,
correcting as far as information is available, errors in the first
edition'. The Soviet dictator had died in February 1953, and
Khrushchev's revelations to the 20th Party Congress in
February 1956, although not yet made public, were being
talked about. There were some leaks. This was a good period
in which to have basic discussions in the USSR: the ventila-
tion was fine.

Bernal was speaking in Moscow a few weeks after the
Russians had put the first *Sputnik* into orbit around the Earth;
the first point at which, he commented, both the atmospheric
and the gravitational barriers that had kept man to this planet
had been broken. Now, more than ever, was the time to
examine the relations of science and society. He was pleased,
he said looking around, that there was a consciousness that
they could not understand how to organize science without
studying its past, and in a new way. He made clear that in his
book he was trying to study the effects of the developments of
science and technology on the general course of history. He
had had to include a great deal of simple history and some
account of the advances in science because he was writing for
readers who were ignorant in those fields. That was why he
had not gone more deeply into theoretical problems in the
history of natural science and technology.

His general outlook, based on historical materialism, was
that science and technology were progressive and expanding
tendencies in human social history: they interacted with varying social forms (e.g. from primitive clan society to capitalism
and socialism), and were both the products and producers of
further changes. But his thesis was more than that: it was that
technology, and later science, were not constant features of
human social development, but acquired a greater and
changed importance with human progress. 'If I stress this
obvious point it is because I want to make it absolutely clear

that I have at no time wished to set up science and technology as independent idealistic social entities which in some mysterious way acquire the controlling force of society. They are human products used for human ends. But like other institutions in the past, such as religion or law, they have their own history, and as civilization progresses the part of history concerned with science and technology is growing relatively and absolutely.'

Before the meeting, Bernal had been sent an agenda detailing the topics for discussion, and various critical papers.[208] Topics for discussion werc: (1) the significance of the history of natural science and technology, and its place among other branches of knowledge; (2) principles governing the division into periods of the history of natural science and technology; (3) natural sciences and technology under capitalism and socialism; (4) the role of individuality in the development of natural science and technology; (5) the mutual interactions of scientific and technical ideas with the *Weltanschauung* (general world outlook); (6) the effect of technical and scientific traditions on the development of natural science and technology; (7) the role of the working inventor in development of science and technology; (8) the geographical routes along which scientific and technical progress took place; (9) the illumination of the history of science and technology in the book of Bernal; and (10) perspectives of the future development of science and technology.

He was pleased to have criticisms from Professor Kolman, whom he remembered from the delegation to the History of Science Congress in London in 1931, an occasion 'which may be said to have marked an era not only in British, but also in Western, appreciation of the new application of Marxism to scientific and technical development, particularly to the history of science. It was the principles of planning, the principles of conscious integration between science and technology which struck us young progressive British scientists most, and we, perhaps, exaggerated what was being donc, and identified it too closely with the picture of what should be done. Nevertheless,' he went on, 'I do not think we were so far wrong. Even if we had known in more detail the difficulties and failures, and the discrepancies between the ideal and the real picture, particularly in the difficult periods that preceded and followed the Second World War, we would not have lost the clear picture of what was being attempted, and what, in the end, succeeded. It is all more honour to Soviet authorities and technicians that they did have success in face of all these difficulties, and in the face of certain distortions of theory which may have hindered their work.'

Bernal denied Professor Kolman's criticism that he (Bernal) was mistaken in treating science as part of the productive forces of society. He claimed he had tried to separate science from the means of production themselves: science was only one aspect of the activity that produced goods and services. He referred to another criticism by Professor Kolman. It was true that in various parts of the book he brought out the point that scientific progress occurred when the directing class in society was in close contact with working craftsmen. But he did not make that the basic cause: it was the change of class relations involved in the revolutionary trends in history that determined that very contact between the different classes which immediately provoked scientific and technological changes. They were living in a period of the most decisive changes in society, and in science and technology, in which the union between theory and practice was most necessary. It was, however, difficult to achieve, because of growing complexity and the rapid rate of change. They had to think more consciously of what they were doing. Because they could not expect to control those relations within the sphere of natural science and technology alone, they had to call in the social sciences. That was why he had devoted so much space to them in his book.

Characteristically, his comments on each topic were detailed and bold. From a purely pedagogical point of view, the history of science and technology required to be integrated from the very beginning in general history.* It had a place, also, in the teaching of each branch of science. Although he

---

* He commended H. Butterfield's *The Origins of Modern Science* (London 1957) as 'a very good, though somewhat idealistic, history of the scientific revolution'.

did not mention it then, he had begun in 1946 to give each autumn term a set of eleven lectures to first-year students in physics at Birkbeck College on the history and nature of experimental physics before 1900. His aim was to help young physicists to understand how the subject had grown as a result of the interplay of necessities of navigation and gunnery, on the one hand, and the developments of philosophical and religious ideas, on the other.*

He went on to tell the Moscow meeting that he regretted that it was difficult to preserve the contemporary history of science. For instance, modern industry was particularly unkind to its history. It was easier to find out about the technology of a 6000-year-old Babylonian city than that of a twenty-year-old steel works. Again, the 'where' of scientific discovery was as important as the 'when'. For instance, the period of the dark ages from 150 to 1450 AD was represented as a simple retrogression, but looking more widely geographically that was not so outside Western Europe, for there were several periods of advance of the essentially Hellenistic tradition of science in Islamic countries. Chinese science stood apart: it took little and gave back practically nothing to Hellenistic science in theory. But all the major innovations in Western techniques – gunpowder, the clock, printing, and the compass – came from China. He confessed, however, that one of the weaker parts of his book was his comparative ignorance of the facts of the rise of science in Russia. He urged more detailed studies of the lives of the great men of science, who were simultaneously conservative and revolutionary. They were men of their time, holding to the traditions that had formed them: Copernicus remained a devout Catholic, Newton a pious deist, yet their doctrines upset the religious-philosophical world picture. What was needed was to find out more clearly the impact of their society on the great scientists. For instance, Linnaeus was usually represented as a pietistic son of a Swedish pastor, but Bernal had learned that the great majority of his writings remained unpublished because he was violently

* The verbatim transcript of his 1962 lectures was published in the year after his death (together with an additional twelfth chapter written by him after 1962) in the book, *The Extension of Man*.

critical of his extremely reactionary, obscurantist, Swedish society. The impact of scientific discoveries on ideas was slow, so that they were usually out of phase with the scientific discoveries of the day. He wanted to speed up the process, to make people more aware of what was going on in science and technology, and to lead it to influence their actions more rapidly.

A thorough theoretical investigation was needed to distinguish the fundamental differences between technical and scientific advance. The characteristic of the former was the solid base of previous practice. In the construction of a ship there was a continuity, without any notable break, between the earliest hollowed log and the present steel ship, although there had been enormous change in materials used. That reliance on past success was the great strength of the traditional mode of development: by making changes small, it could ensure that only useful changes would be retained, and no major disasters would result. On the other hand, the scientific mode of progress involved reasoning, and depended on abstract theories and mathematics. That could give radically new things. But because no reasoning could of itself include all the factors in real life, but only those selected for calculation, there might be serious, if unsuspected, dangers. That was shown in the development of flight, where the problems of stability and strength of wing structures could be discovered only after a series of painful, often fatal, accidents. The scientific and technical modes were interdependent, and both had to be preserved. In the past, they had been too separate, and were so still, especially in engineering education. Today, every technical construction should be also a scientific experiment giving rise to new facts and new ideas. Every technician should be a scientist: and the scientist's work should help in the advancement of technique.

He went on to deal with another criticism made by Kolman: that he had overstressed the role of craft and technology, and underestimated that of science. 'This may be true, but, if so, I am only redressing a gross error in previous histories of science.' He was impressed with the enormous importance of working craftsmen. Their practical acquaintance with materials, and methods of working them, together with the tradition of observation and trial absorbed in training, led to possibilities of making valid improvements, not only in technique, but also in knowledge. He cited Robert Norman, seaman and compass maker, who discovered the dip of the magnetized needle, and largely inspired Gilbert's *De Magnete*. Interestingly, the line of advance to modern machine tools was not through the fine turners and craftsmen of the seventeenth and eighteenth centuries, whose activities were limited not by their lack of ingenuity, but because they worked for aristocratic masters and on trivial tasks.

Now he had arrived at the last topic, the prospect for further development of natural sciences and technology, with which he linked an earlier topic of their position under capitalism and under socialism. The essential difference was the Marxist-Leninist approach of organized, planned science in relation to industry, agriculture, and medicine for human welfare. In capitalist countries science remained, theoretically, a free occupation without regard to its consequences, and a practical means of earning profits. 'We must not entirely despise the profit motive in its technical aspect, because one of the essential features required for something that pays is that it works: the development, for instance, of the automobile was following a purely capitalist technique, and very largely, in the first place, independent of military considerations.' He felt that the Soviet Union with its concentration on basic requirements, heavy industry, and a scientifically educated population would have the advantage in the long run.

He went on to make some critical comments to his Soviet friends. Those outside the USSR badly needed to understand the economics underlying the industrial and agricultural developments of the past few years and of future plans. They needed to know how the alternative to the profit system worked; what determined wage rates and investment; what was the equivalent of the rate of interest in deciding the relative effort to be placed behind short- or long-term enterprises. As a scientist, although he saw very clearly the qualitative justification for the Academy's plan, he found it difficult to judge how the priorities were assessed. Was it a matter of administrative judgement, or some kind of calculation? Perhaps there had not been any precise theories in those fields of decision. In that case it seemed all the more important to discover the reasons for the overall success of the employment of science in the Soviet Union, as well as of its occasional failures, and the fact that it still contained weak sectors. And a question of that type applied also to its other aspects – social, legal, and pedagogical. The Webbs had written their prophetic book, *The Soviet Union – A New Civilization*, over twenty years ago. Why, he asked, when so much more had been accomplished, was there no comprehensive and simple account, not merely of the factual history, but of an analysis which would make that history comprehensible?

His final point concerned the fact that man's environment was changing 'ever more rapidly towards a man-made environment superseding that of crude nature. And here we face a problem of a different order of magnitude, because it is no longer a matter of blindly constructing things, and then finding out what we have done, but of realizing the consequence, and often the most remote and indirect consequences of each action, before it is taken.' This was an interesting example of his forward thinking, for he was then – thirty years ago – making out a case for what today we call technology assessment. 'All this points to the projection into the future of the results of the study of the history of pure science and technology. I remember sitting next to a Soviet historian at a dinner many years ago, who said to me, "Oh well, you are a scientist, you only deal with the present; now I am an historian and I deal with the future." I hope that the historians of science and technology will be able to combine both these facilities.' He ended, and sat down to a tremendous burst of applause, having spoken wisely, powerfully, openly for an hour and a half.

Bernal thought of Stalin not only as the greatest figure of contemporary history, but also as 'a great scientist, not only in his direct contribution to social science, but, even more, in the impetus and in the creation of the new, expanding and popular science of the Soviet Union'. He may have been influenced, too, by Academician Oparin, his host in 1956, who was not only a devout supporter of Stalin, but also of Lysenko.[209]

I read his article, 'Stalin as scientist', in an issue of *Modern Quarterly* in 1953, with the astonishment of hindsight. I find it hard to accept that he wrote word for word such cliché-ridden, uncritical, personality-cult balderdash: for example, 'Shallow thinkers, philosophic defenders of "Western Civilization", have accused Stalin of being motivated by love of power, but to those who have followed his thoughts and works, the accusation is only a revelation of utter ignorance.'[210]

And 'Stalin's concern for men and women also found expression in his concern for the advancement of oppressed people and nationalities. . . . In the world as a whole it will be Stalin's solution to the nationalities question that has made the most lasting impact.' And, 'Stalin's . . . thought and his example is now embodied in the lives and thoughts of hundreds of millions of men, women, and children . . . it has become an indissoluble part of the great human tradition.'[211] No, it is difficult to accept that that was written by Bernal, even in 1953 and before the 20th Congress. I can only believe that it is the work of a hack, probably in his entourage. Bernal read the prepared article, which may have been needed urgently, changed a word or two, and allowed his name to be used. He did that occasionally for scientific papers: why not for a political piece for which he may not have had a real appetite?

Yet, immediately the Kremlin line changed, Bernal's Stalin Prize for the strengthening of peace between peoples was retrospectively renamed a Lenin Prize. He did not protest. He is believed to have used the money quietly to support scholarships to the West for scientists from socialist countries.

13
Speculation and Holism

Discovery consists of seeing what everybody has
seen and thinking what nobody has thought.
A. SZENT-GYORGYI[212]

In studying Bernal's life and thought I came to
understand, and admire, the way in which he could escape
from the rigid framework in which a problem was posed, and
provide a fresh insight by, as it were, slipping round the side.
He had usually the discipline to make this serve the main
argument, but he could easily go off in any direction – and
would. He was, for instance, asked to contribute a paper to a
book described as 'an anthology of partly baked ideas'.[213]
This, of course, appealed to him, it provided an opportunity
to 'unload some hypothetical and unfinished business'. In June
1961 the editor, I. J. Good, received from him a paper entitled, 'The place of speculation in modern technology and
science'. It was a beautiful example of his highly original
approach which combined the historical, the imaginative, and
the practical. He began by pointing out that as the scientist
was trained not to say anything on which he had no evidence,
it was almost impossible, and certainly most unusual these
days for him to produce an article on untested ideas. A contribution on speculative ideas was basically intensely personal.
Yet, when modern science was born, it was common practice.
Newton filled the greater part of the end of his *Opticks* with
queries which were really speculations. Those queries were to
have the greatest effect on the development of physics, for it
was what Newton did not know that stimulated other people

to work; what he could prove had 'a sterilizing effect'. Bernal argued that 'speculation, disguised as legitimate hypothesis, even if subsequently proved false, still has its use in science – much of science actually grows in this way'.[214] However, even though to go forward with speculation and publish would reflect unfavourably on the scientist, he regarded himself as lucky that he had been in the field for so long that he could not really do much damage to his reputation by going on producing 'crazy ideas'. He recalled how, two years earlier (1959), he had asked his son to add his name 'to a paper of mine in which he had helped considerably'. Michael said, 'It is all right for you, but I have my reputation to consider.'[214]

Revealingly, he went on to say that he imagined most scientists for many years carried on 'a kind of internal dialogue', but could not act on their intuitions because they were too numerous, or too vague, or too impracticable. The experimental scientist had daydreams, but unlike those of the writer, they were about things rather than people. 'Although started by fancy, they tend to be controlled by experience and knowledge. I know myself, as I have kept a certain number of notes of these over the years, although there is a tendency to lack continuity, I have developed only a relatively small number of ideas but have gone on working on them on and off for a long time.* Purely speculative work went on entirely in the interior, and appeared occasionally in a note or a drawing, but was hardly ever realized in practice. For him, as a scientist, the pleasure lay in seeing how far he could go in making a self-consistent, though continually changing, picture of what might work. But, he would not carry it further into practice, because 'you cannot do everything and, especially when you are older, you realize what an enormous effort it would be to get the thing done, and effort which could duly be at the expense of other occupations and of other ideas which, if not so grandiose, at any event are more immediately reliable'.

---

* A few years after he wrote that, he said to me on some forgotten occasion, 'Dream work ought to be paid by the hour.' He daydreamed himself during boring meetings. He kept also a list of what he called 'legacies', described as 'problems not solutions'. These included, in mid-1967, water problems, the origin of life and of meteorites, and science policy.

He chose for his contribution to the book two speculations covering as wide a range as possible – from engineering and from pure science. These were revealed later as having some logical connection, but he was not consciously aware of it when he chose them. He had spent most of his 'idle time' for thirty years on the engineering speculation. The forms it dealt with he could visualize immediately. 'I can build the models of my ideas in my head, I can see how they go, I can do an occasional calculation to see that it is not nonsense, and I can always rely on the fact that I am under no obligation to do anything practical which might spoil them. In pure science such an obligation does exist for a scientist like myself. Ideas ought to be checked by experiment and calculation. Speculation is therefore only permissible in regions far away or long ago where one man's guess is as good as another's.' That was why he had chosen his in the field of the origin of life.

To devise something that would work in practice it was necessary either to consider what was needed, which implied a survey of industry, or what was possible, that is a considera- tion of the properties of matter, leading from pure science to application. In practice, these approaches were followed usually by different kinds of people, but he had tried them both. 'When the requirement is immediate and not very far removed from actual practice, the problem is not a very difficult one and it usually happens that if you are lucky enough to get the answer you get it at once and it works.'

Let us now follow Bernal's advance into speculative sweet- ness. He described his first example as a relatively easy one because it involved nothing more elaborate than ordinary elementary physics, but it did tie a trivial observation in physics to a great human need, which was for water. Through- out the world, most regions with good sunshine were chroni- cally short of water. His thoughts on how to irrigate the desert regions antedated the atomic era, and were inspired by a significant, but forgotten, book, *The Great God Waste*, by J. L. Hodgson.[215] The clue as to how to go ahead came when he was visiting a research station on Lake Windermere. A scien- tist who was studying the behaviour of newts, particularly their habit of crawling under stones in the daytime and coming out at night, associated this with the dangers of loss of water vapour through their thin skins. In an experiment he had done, which Bernal described but which I must omit here, he was puzzled by his findings. Bernal said, however, that he had made a rather childish error in thinking of oxygen as O instead of O_2. 'This brought to my mind the obvious fact, which I must have known since my first few chemistry lessons, that water vapour is just half as heavy as ordinary air, and therefore will go up of itself. It was only then that I realized that I had made the same mistake in my childhood. I had believed the reason why water vapour went up from the sea was that it was heated, whereas that has nothing to do with it: it goes up because it is light.'

He developed his fantasy on the basis of that principle. Why bother to lift up water when it will lift itself in the form of vapour? The appropriate apparatus was readily available in the form of the chimney, which takes up light air automatically and maintains a draught. Once a steady stream of water vapour was available, all that was necessary was to reverse the process and condense the vapour to water again in the desert. Bernal described and drew the kind of arrangement that might work. At a technical level, he believed the scheme could be made to work. The basic snag was whether it could be made to pay.

Characteristically, before leaving the subject, he went on to throw out some further stimulating ideas. He pointed out that although productivity per man hour was increasing rapidly, productivity per kilowatt-hour was going down almost as rapidly. His speculative invention, for what it was worth, was of interest in the long term because it lay in the direction of economy, of doing things which did not use, as most did, the maximum, but the minimum, amount of power by making more use of engineering processes The machining, pressing, forging, and so on that went into the fabrication of metal components were admissions that we did not know how to persuade the ore or the metal to get itself into the shapes we needed without great expenditure of energy and waste of material. He concluded, 'A rationalized industry would attempt to get the ultimately desired effects tending to human welfare by modifying as little as possible the play of human forces.'

His other speculation concerned with the origin of life provided little chance for decisive and unambiguous observations or experiments. But it gave all the more scope for imagination controlled by a rigorous logic, making use of indirect evidence to reconstruct a sequence of more and more plausible images of the past. It might not matter much if those pictures were wrong: sometimes that even helped the process of the discovery of truth. Here followed another insightful comment. The fact that the older scientists (that is, those of the late nineteenth century) took up a sceptical attitude to the question of the origin of life might be considered as another demonstration of the *provisional* character of all scientific knowledge. Owing to the rapid march of science, that might become a major limiting factor to scientific advance. It was becoming more probable that what was said today would be proved wrong in a relatively short time, say one or two years. So why bother? Why not wait until the thing was found out? But such an attitude, if adopted by all, would lead to a complete stop of science itself. Nevertheless, the philosophy of *provisionalism* might become a real factor in the scientific method of the near future. It was already a good corrective to over-confidence, and a training for people to take leaps of imagination without having to believe they had discovered the ultimate truth, or at least a fundamental improvement on the truth held at the particular time.

His two unchecked speculations – on means of raising water from the sea, thus providing for the food needs of an impoverished population, and on the steps in the chemical origins of life – might seem unconnected, except that they occurred within the one brain. They reflected current economic and scientific concerns. But he had seen recently that they had an internal logical connection which might have guided him unconsciously to them. Both had one common material aspect: they dealt with the production of food, more precisely, with that of simple nitrogenous and carbohydrate compounds. The argument could have been: 'If life originated spontaneously on a hitherto inorganic earth, the first steps, which could not have needed complicated enzyme and co-enzyme systems, must have been very simple. Therefore, they should be very easy to carry out, and that not only in the laboratory, but also as industrial processes.' He concluded, 'The way to food production can be found through a study of the chemistry of the origins of life.' In fact, he did not argue that way. He was given the answer first, and he found the question afterwards.

It was clear to him that in speculations of such a kind, the main value lay in having a sufficiently wide appreciation of needs and possibilities. For that, all aspects needed to be kept in focus at the same time, but because of specialization that was becoming increasingly difficult. The idea of the solitary speculator would have to be replaced by collective speculation. They would have to return to that old form of scientific thought, the dialectic, the conversation-discussion-dialogue. He had been stressing the qualitative aspects: to bring in the quantitative, they would have to rely on the radically new factor in thought processes, the utilization of electronic machines. The new partnership of machines with men should enlarge and transform human thought and its range of application. 'The speculations of the future may then be speculations, not of one man or of many men, but of all humanity and their machines.'

Bernal's distinctive quality, his ability to see general linking principles arising from contributions from people from separate disciplines, was an expression of his speculative creativity. A good example was his concluding remark on 7 June 1963 at a discussion on new materials, which he helped to organize for the Royal Society.[216] For two days, he listened to metallurgists, ceramic and glass experts, polymer chemists, and solid-state physicists. He explained that the organizers of the meeting had had to be very restrictive to keep the scope within practical bounds. They had to stick to a very limited field of the key mechanical properties common to all the new or improved substances. What struck him most was that the approach to novelty had been along two distinct lines, very characteristic of the science, pure and applied, of their time. One was to tackle the problem from basic principles, from the properties of the atoms, and then see what kind of substances could be deduced from them, and how the observed properties were related to those fundamental concepts. 'This is the main road, let us say, in physics, the penetration deliberately aimed at trying to get a true understanding of these substances, and not particularly concerned with giving immediate improvements. Yet, ultimately, we all have to live and even the most theoretical metallurgist has to produce something that some untheoretical engineer may find useful.'

The other way was the steady improvement of the traditional methods of making particular substances: metals, glasses, or polymers. He found that the two approaches were converging in the sense that the theoretical research worker was coming much closer to practical utility. He imagined that in a few years the kind of discussion they had been having would not be held any more because the theorist would be fully acquainted with the practice, and the practitioners would understand the theory.

Now that they knew how complicated metals are, they wondered how the primitive blacksmiths ever managed to do anything with steel at all. They knew how to temper and forge without any idea of what was happening, but they got the results to such an extent that until 1930 or 1940 there was very little any theorist could tell a ferrous metallurgist. 'They knew what to do: they did not know why it worked, but they had the same kind of knack that the old chemists had – a nose for it. They had a feeling that if they put a bit of cobalt in here or a bit of tungsten in there, they would produce just the properties the customer wanted. This was, of course, merely based on experience, but it was based on intuitively rationalized experience. Any theories that were made, and all the work based on these theories, are now seen to be complete nonsense. Yet the bad theories did not prevent traditional practice. Here we shall be able to pull these two together and have good new practice based on good theories.'

Bernal then pointed out how matters were quite different with polymers, which were chemical *creations*, and whose rise illustrated a complete comeback of an earlier stage in scientific history. Finally, he came to the central question – the real excitement of the *composite* materials, 'the excitement outside our meeting of what we are doing'. What was happening was the coming into practical use of a class of what had been thought of as useless engineering materials, the hard ionic and semi-ionic compounds, oxides, nitrides, and so forth.

The theme of their discussion in a sense had been 'back to the Stone Age', because that was where they had started. He explained that the academic study of mineralogy in England started with the professorship in Cambridge given to a Reverend Dr Clark on account of a lecture he gave on the jewels in the high priest's breastplate. That was a technical use of gems which was extremely good.

Bernal's summary breathes an excitement which emerges vividly from the staid pages of the final printed record. There are fascinating historical items, and personal stories. For instance, on *whiskers*, fine mineral fibres, which mineralogists have seen for centuries, but whose mechanical properties they have ignored. He gave this as an example of how long it took to discover something useful, and how easy it was not to discover anything. He had made an observation, thirty years ago, which should have given the whole show away, but it did not. 'I was looking at a glass – an organic glass, luckily, or I would not otherwise have examined it under the microscope – and I was trying by heat treatment to make it crystallize. Now glass on breaking down, or devitrifying, contains little, beautifully curled, very thin hair-like crystals, trichites. I was looking at one of these when, accidentally, the preparation got a little too warm under the microscope, and I saw in a flash the little curled trichites suddenly spring out straight. I saw at once that this proved that the hairs must have been bent elastically, and not plastically; that there must have been considerable tensions in the crystals. There in front of my eyes there was evidence of about 5 per cent elastic tension. However, I did not take in what this meant; I could not see that a 5 per cent elastic tension was really extraordinary.'

Commenting on the use of composite materials for great strength, he pointed out how nature already provided some: for instance, bamboo. And for centuries, the bow has contained composite materials: for example, the Mongol bow is a composite bow using materials such as horn, bone, and wood together and making use of their mutual properties. 'But we can go even further back – into our own bodies. One of the greatest biochemical discoveries in evolution, which we have not really caught up with yet industrially, are the hard materials of organisms.' Keratin – the substance of the outer skin, hairs, horns, and claws – is a coiled chain polypeptide, which in the course of evolution has been very much improved by the incorporation of mineral crystals.

He referred to the work he had been involved in during the war to turn ice into a structural material. He had learnt recently how the Eskimos knew the difference between thin sea ice and thin lake ice. The former cracked with much greater difficulty, and they could run a sledge over an inch thick or less of sea ice: because of the included salt crystals, the whole ice bends down and provides a hydrostatic lift. It can only do that if it will not crack as freshwater ice does.

Bernal then drew attention to the fact that glass differed from crystals in that it has no definite melting point. The softening point for the practical glass maker was not an intrinsic property of the material itself: it always involved time, so did the point of crystallization. Glasses could be made out of substances that were not glasses normally if you worked quickly enough. He had in his laboratory some reasonably small spheres of glass from meteorites about 5000 million years old: they were still glass, they had not crystallized. They were made out of magnesium silicate, which was not normally a glass-forming silicate. That implied the spheres were formed and cooled very quickly – in outer space. They were presumably dust from an asteroid, or even from the original formation of the sun which had never got itself properly annealed: that is, shot out and cooled before it could crystallize.

He thought that the general purpose of the meeting had been well met. It was the *use* of new materials that really mattered in the long run. 'We, academic scientists, move within a certain sphere, we can go on being useless up to a point, in the confidence that sooner or later some use will be found for our studies. The mathematician, of course, prides himself on being totally useless, but usually turns out to be the most useful of the lot. He finds the solution, but he is not interested in what the problem is: sooner or later, someone will find the problem to which his solution is the answer.'

His concluding words merit fuller consideration: they are filled with a practical wisdom. They were talking about new materials, but ultimately they were interested in the structures in which they had to function. Their question was the practical requirement and its satisfaction. But how could they know what a requirement was until they knew it could be met? 'We would like all kinds of things which we cannot have; on the other hand, how do we know that anyone wants the stuff that we have got?' It was fifty years, from 1831 to 1881, before electric currents came into serious use: 'no one wanted electric current in large quantities because there seemed to be no way of getting it. No one bothered to make electric current because it seemed that no one wanted it.' Today, we ought to be able 'to think up all kinds of crazy things, and then to find uses for them'. 'By finding out from those working on new materials what is likely to come, the engineering users can begin to think of structures which might make use of them, and at the same time find a market for them, and help to subsidize the research. Conversely, knowledge of what properties are really required will stimulate those working on the production of new materials.' He insisted, however, that to be *practically* useful, the new materials depended on the economic factor, whether they could be produced at the price which would make them a paying proposition. But, although they would need to follow that criterion for as long as it would go, they would need, also, to take account of 'social usefulness'. In conclusion, he said, they could all go away and think how the different ideas could be combined together in a logical and scientific way to provide them with the basic theory and practice of consciously evolved materials, to take the place of those – bone, wood, and stone – that nature had given to early man.

The conviction that research could be thus planned rationally and its results applied for the good of people was with him always. It led him naturally to consider the problem of 'scientific communication' (as he called it, but which has come to be known as 'documentation'). Although an 'outsider', as he declared himself, in this field he was as a scientist a pioneer, with most original suggestions. He had grasped its importance in the 1930s when most working scientists, although victims of 'the literature explosion', had not begun to recognize the problem. In *The Social Function of Science*, he wrote, for example, 'The very bulk of scientific publications is itself delusive. It is of very unequal value; a large proportion of it, possibly as much as three-quarters, does not deserve to be published at all, and is only published for economic reasons which have nothing to do with the real interests of science.'[217] He wanted an organization which would make available to the research worker all the relevant information he needed, and that without his having to do anything to get hold of it.

During the war, he was so irritated by the variety of over-lapping information services he was supplied with, and which took him a long time to scan, that he suggested one central information service for all the military departments. The proposal was taken up, and one of the first things revealed by a census was that there were three separate information services on tanks, none of which knew of the existence of the other two. The meeting which was to set up the unified service was chaired by the Admiralty librarian. He closed all discussion effectively by saying that in his forty years of experience 'he had never found that anyone had any difficulty in obtaining the information he wanted, provided he knew the right person to ask for'. Bernal confessed many years later that although the statement made him sad at the time, the more he thought of it the more right it seemed. 'How often do pieces of information for which we have sought for years, using all the facilities of information services in vain, turn up at last in the head of someone who is accidentally seated next to us at a dinner table or in a railway train.'

In 1947, Bernal presented to the Royal Society Information Conference in London a remarkable proposal for the abolition of all existing scientific periodicals, and for single papers to be distributed by central agencies, all tied in with a system of abstracts on cards, to subscribers in particular fields. Scientists and publishers were infuriated. A *Times* leader castigated the scheme as 'Professor Bernal's insidious and cavalier proposals'. There was so much opposition that he carried out a pilot survey. He found that most scientists did not work the way he did: that 80 per cent of all scientific literature read by scientists was obtained from libraries, where the disadvantages of the bound periodicals largely disappeared. Accordingly, he dropped his proposals, and withdrew them publicly at the conference.

A decade later he was involved in the International Conference on Scientific Information held in Washington in 1958, although he had found time only marginally in the interval to concern himself with the problem. The main point of his contribution was that a knowledge of the requirements of the different users of scientific information, and the uses to which they wish to put the information they secure, should be the ultimate determining factor in the design of methods of storage and retrieval of scientific information.[218]

By the early 1960s, he was declaring that what he had foreseen in 1946 had come to pass. 'The flood of material, mostly unregulated, has surpassed all the means of dealing with it, with the result that the channels of communication of science are choked, and there is a very great actual wastage of scientific information. Beyond a certain point, if the information is lost, it might just as well never have been found in the first place', he stated in a introductory lecture, which he could not deliver in person, to a meeting of the Crystallographic Society of Japan in 1962. He urged that the problem of scientific information in crystallography and solid state physics should be treated as one in communication engineering. 'We should clearly define what we want. We do not necessarily want journals, papers, or data compilations, or any of the traditional forms of information, but we do want to get the best information in the minimum quantity in the shortest time, from the people who are producing the information to the people who want it, whether they know they want it or not.' He put this another way in discussing the changing function of the information officers. Where they were going wrong was not in dealing with unanswered questions, but with unasked questions. What they had to find out was what people really wanted to know.

In 1964, he was optimistic that despite 'the chaos of scientific information', the new means of communication and of computing made it possible to deal rationally with the problem for the first time. He admitted that where he went wrong in his 1947 proposal was not in the direction in which improvement would come, but in overestimating the ease with which it would happen, and underestimating the prejudices that were holding it back. Or, as Herbert Coblans put it, 'When he has had to retract it has often been a case of the logical and rational having to bow down to subjective and prestige considerations. Perhaps in an essentially individualistic setting he has sometimes not given enough weight to the irrational elements. But that is the fate of all pioneers, and his consolation can be that, if his views may have been premature, they are gradually becoming accepted.'[219] His consolation in practice was that his proposal for a scientific information institute, as detailed in his *Social Function of Science*, was the prototype for the influential Institute for Scientific Information in Philadelphia and VINITI (the State Institute for Scientific and Technological Information) in Moscow.

14
Endings

Or else, tomorrow, workers, kings and crooks
Will all have aeroplanes and be fast friends,
In a world no longer divided by dividends,
Where love will be almost as simple as it looks.
FRANCIS SCARFE[220]

Secretaries have no illusions about those they serve. Bernal obtained always great loyalty and high respect from them, without any deliberate seeking on his part. Brenda Swann, who collaborated with him in the mid-1950s in obtaining data for *The Social Function* in the squalor of Breams Buildings where Birkbeck College was then housed, was much moved by his consideration in asking during her first week whether she would like an advance in salary, as her uneasy financial situation had been pointed out to him. She found him 'tough, but fair, a delightful companion, especially for a woman'.[221] One secretary, Kathleen Watkins, in 1940 compiled some 'guidance to an understanding of Bernal for a new secretary'. She advised:

1. There is no need to be afraid of him, though many people are. In spite of all appearance he is really good tempered, kind-hearted, and exceptionally reasonable.
2. He will frequently appear to be utterly unreasonable. This is due merely to thoughtlessness, and a protest will always be effective.
3. He will usually treat you as an equal in intelligence (which is impossible to live up to), or as only doubtfully

capable of doing things which are easily within the capacity
of a child of twelve. The latter attitude is quite unintentional
and best ignored. With regard to the former, remember he is
a first-class teacher and enjoys explaining things – do not mind
asking about anything you do not understand.

4. When you get instructions about a job, you will usually
find at the end, or when you start work on it, that although
you know pretty clearly what it is all about, you have only a
hazy idea what you yourself are supposed to be doing. In these
circumstances, reiterate, 'Yes, but what exactly do you want
me to do?' until you get a satisfactory answer.

5. In general, he will expect you not so much to do what he
tells you to do, as to do what he meant to tell you to do, or
what he would have told you to do if he had thought it out
more carefully. Therefore, never go on with a job if it seems
unlikely that the result will be worth the labour, or if you think
there is a better way of tackling the problem, but refer the
matter back to him with your own suggestions.

6. Never mind admitting having made a mistake. He is well
accustomed to the fact that most people are fools by compari-
son with himself, and takes their lapses with unruffled good
humour.

7. Do not think the occasional 'Nonsense', or 'That's
rubbish', etc. are criticisms of your work. They are merely
conversational expressions between equals, and unless you are
convinced you are wrong you should stick to your opinion.
On the other hand, I am quite unable to account for the
occasional really devastating criticisms. In general, they
appear to be unjustified, and I believe they are not deliberate.
I think the proper reply is, 'Do you realize what you are saying, and do you really mean it?', but I have never got my
breath back in time to say it.

8. Do not mistake impatience for ill-humour, and do not
take too much notice of the impatience. Professor Bernal's
estimate of the time required to do a job is usually between a
third and a half the time actually required. (This applies to
his own work as well as yours.) Do not worry, therefore, if you
take much longer than he thought would be necessary over
any job – you will find that he will not be at all upset when

you say it is not finished, but will wait quite patiently for the result.

9. These notes – to point out some of the snags you may encounter. There is another side to the picture, but that needs no introduction.

The last reference arose from the fact that Bernal was a great lover. His sexual appetite was reputed to be extraordinary. His foreign hosts, especially the Russians, were well aware of this, and usually made some appropriate arrangements for him. At Cambridge, in the 1920s, he told Charles Snow that he proposed to do some historical research to see how many great scientists had been as fond of women as he was. He reported he had found nothing of significance: unlike him, most were 'depressingly normal'.[222] He was well endowed physically ('I'm told he has fascinating extremities,' the wife of a distinguished scientist said to her friend when they were discussing his sexual prowess), and with his many experiences, and specialist insights based on wide reading, his performances in bed earned him a rapturous reputation. There was even 'a club' of women who had slept with him. When a new body appeared on his staff, bets would be taken as to how soon she would be eligible to join 'the club'. There are some delightful stories of the scrapes Bernal got into in his erotic pursuits: for instance, when on one occasion he was chased up the street by a furious naval officer with a revolver after being caught *in flagrante*. But were his continuing involvements with women 'erotic' or 'amorous'? Pirie insists on the latter. He does not accept that Bernal was concerned primarily with copulation. He was interested in women as individuals, and went to great lengths to interest them in himself. On one occasion Pirie was at the wheel driving back to Cambridge, with Bernal and a girl in the back. 'He took no notice of me and began to court her vigorously, telling lies about himself, until he had won her.'

He gave much pleasure to very many women, and remained on good terms with them even when they parted. He had one legal wife, Eileen, and two other women – Margaret Gardiner and Margot Heinemann – with whom he set up a household.

All three would appear together with him at functions of common interest, seemingly without personal strain.

What was more significant was whether individuals, such as myself, could join 'a club' of another kind, that is one of personal friends. He was shy, and most people were intimidated not so much by him as by his reputation. When first I got to know him ordinary discussion was difficult. We were two shy birds looking at each other, not knowing how the tension could be eased, until I discovered that all I needed to do was to ask a purely scientific question, at which his shyness would disappear, and I would be plunged into a river flowing with originality. In this way, over a number of years beginning some time in 1950, we began to develop a personal relationship. I could begin to separate his reputation from him as a person. This was fostered – and it was essential – by my friendly relations with Anita Rimel, Bernal's most efficient and understanding secretary/assistant.

His was the most varied personality. As a child, aged about nine, he was told to listen to the birds singing. He did, and commented they did not sing, but twittered. Years later, when at Cambridge as an assistant director of research under Rutherford, this same independence was apparent. J. G. Crowther recalled that once, when he was seeing Rutherford, Bernal came in and was rebuked heavily because something was not as clear as the director wanted it. 'Bernal stood by, hanging his head, but still unable to forget the complications. It was a clash of temperaments and ways of looking at things.'[223] Others were puzzled by this approach. Sir Frederick Warner, who first met him in 1933 in a group concerned with the study of the philosophy of Marxism/Leninism, remembers him as 'obviously very intelligent and brainy, but very highbrow'.[224] Peter Pauling had no doubts that Bernal really was a genius. Once he told his father, the Nobel laureate Linus Pauling, that he thought one of Bernal's sons had suffered more by being his father's son than he (Peter) had suffered from being his father's son. Linus Pauling had replied, 'Jesus Christ, I would have suffered, too, if I had been Bernal's son.' Peter Pauling told this to Bernal, who loved it, and thought it was 'a very funny story'.[225]

Marcus Brumwell, who was introduced to Bernal by Herbert
Read, came to know him intimately for over thirty years. He
was delighted, particularly, by the way in which Bernal was
able to link the arts, especially the visual arts, and science.
Brumwell would take him to art shows, and would be astonished by his wide knowledge. In Barbara Hepworth's studio
in St Ives, Brumwell would see him 'write the equation of part
of a sculpture on that part, using delible pencil, of course.
Barbara has told me how they both used to clear space on the
floor – very difficult in her studio, and draw things for each
other, both excitedly understanding each other's ideas'. She
made a series of quasi-mathematical drawings in the early
1940s, one of which Brumwell has, and which Bernal defined
as being 'the locus of the ultimate intersections of consecutive
curves in a system of curves'. Bernal told Brumwell that although to the eye the base of the Parthenon looked perfectly
flat, it was some centimetres higher in the middle than at the
ends, which was why it looked so level. Brumwell mentioned
this to Barbara Hepworth, and she said, 'Why, of course,
what would you expect? Put a flat edge on any of my horizon-
tal flat carvings, and you will always find, and at once, it isn't
flat, it just looks flat.' Bernal took Harold Spencer-Jones, then
Astronomer Royal, on his first visit to a show of contemporary
art, and was complimented 'on what a marvellous guide you
are to your naive astronomical friend'.

On another occasion, he took the artist Ben Nicholson to
C. D. Darlington's laboratory, at the John Innes Horticultural
Institute, so that Nicholson could 'look at vegetable cells, or
genes, or chromosomes through the microscope. Des wanted
the artist to see how an observant and imaginative and accurate scientist's eye, such as Darlington's, can see things which
most people would not realize were in front of their eyes, until
it was pointed out to them. Ben, very unscientific, was fascinated, and clearly understood what Darlington showed him.'[226]

On the evening of 12 November 1950, Bernal gave a party
in his flat, on the top floor above the laboratories in Torrington
Square, for some of those who had been at the aborted
Sheffield Peace Congress. Among them was Picasso. On the
way upstairs, Bernal insisted that he look at some crystals.

H

Picasso asked, 'If I put one of my paintings under your transformer would it come out like a crystal?' Not a very profound
question, but in the gaiety of the atmosphere somebody asked
Picasso to draw a souvenir. He rejected paper and said, 'There
is much more room on the wall.' And on an area 7 ft by 4 ft
6 in. above some bookshelves, using a multi-colour grease
pencil, 'he began with a swish of line that immediately became
a real face, but had devil's horns, closed blind eyes and a shut
little mouth. Then he stepped back and shook his head,
pounced on the wall and touched the horns into a laurel
weath, opened the devil's eyes, and widened his mouth till he
looked like an anxious god', wrote Lena Jeger, a Labour MP
who was at the party. Picasso stood back and said, '*Il a l'air
solitaire*'. He began to draw a girl, who 'arrived on the wall,
firmly and suddenly. Professor Bernal ungratefully thinks she
is a little insipid compared with the god-devil.' Then someone
asked, 'What has this to do with peace?' Picasso gave them
wings.*[227]

Of course, Bernal had his critics, and these included a few
who worked closely with him in his different interests. Norah
Wooster, who was his first research student at Cambridge in
1929, worked with him for three years, but says she was never
'intelligent enough' to make use of his elusive discussions of her
problems. The fact that he was everlastingly away from the
laboratory pursuing his political activities, sympathetic though
she and her husband were to these, detracted from his value
as a director of studies. Nora's research was carried out on the
prototype Bernal goniometer manufactured by W. G. Pye.
Typical of his genius and his shortcomings, the instrument
was hideously difficult to adjust, and keep in adjustment,
though when redesigned by Peter Wooster in later years, and
manufactured by Unicam, it achieved worldwide success as
their S25.

A more serious criticism of Bernal, however, made by the
Woosters, was his unreliability. They feel particularly bitter,
even today, about a research grant for Peter which Bernal had

---

*When the house was pulled down, the unique mural was cut out and is now
on display at the Institute for Contemporary Arts in the Mall in London.

promised to press for, but never even mentioned at the Faculty Board meeting. Nora was so upset that she wrote him what she described as 'a biting letter', for which she is sure she was never forgiven.[228] More surprising was his inability to support his far-reaching plan for the use of crystallography in the war effort. A high-powered executive from the government came to Cambridge to discuss this, and having heard Bernal's exposition said, 'This sounds like jobs for the boys.' Bernal made no comment, and the plan was never again heard of. That he did not put up a fight is a matter of interpretation. J. G. Crowther pointed out that he was not courageous enough in dealing with people.[229] Nora Wooster says Bernal excused himself by saying he always became acutely aware of the force of the arguments on the other side. I am persuaded there was another factor. One might detect a tendency in his scientific work to accord a beautiful idea as much importance as the actual facts. He was selective about the facts, and stubborn facts for a while could be evaded by ignoring them. So, sometimes, might personal difficulties with students or colleagues.

However, Peter Wooster thought very highly of Bernal as a scientist. 'His inspiration was quite marvellous, and he produced a great many ideas, both theoretical and practical.' There are no doubts about Bernal's stimulating brilliance. The personal experience of F. H. C. Crick, not the easiest of men, is relevant. Shortly after the war, he sought a place in Bernal's laboratory. He was upset to be told there were applications from all over the world, and why should he be admitted? When he met Bernal, he found him most interesting and original. Crowther wrote, 'Many of Bernal's ideas were right, but many were also wrong. For example, he concluded that exact measurement of details in the X-ray analysis of biological molecules was not important; Crick came to the opposite conclusion. He found Bernal personally very considerate, which changed his previous belief that geniuses always behaved badly.'[230] W. H. Taylor, brought from Manchester to work with Bernal at the Cavendish, described him as 'spraying out ideas', but he left it to others to pick them up and work them out. He liked to float around, throw out brilliant ideas, but he did not like to be cornered. That impressionist approach infuriated Rutherford who demanded 'elegant experiment and irrefutable logic'. Bernal found such an approach, based on 'heavy insistence on the obvious', limited. A result was that Bernal's laboratory did not have the high-level backing to obtain the resources for development it needed.[231] For Bernal it was the intellect that mattered. Perhaps this was why he seemed to have less than ordinary sense about everyday things. Sir Charles Goodeve recalled that, during the war as Controller of Research at the Admiralty, he invited Bernal to accompany him to a viewing of *Hajile* (Elijah who went up like the tail of a rocket), a proposal by Nevile Shute Norway. At midday, Goodeve went to the door of the United Services Club to pick up Bernal. He found the doorman in violent discussion with a most shabbily dressed individual who was insisting that Goodeve was waiting for him. 'He looked such a tramp,' Goodeve said, 'that I could not speak to him. He let me down badly.' Yet, Goodeve recalled how at a Faraday Society meeting in the 1950s, held in the Royal Institution, two foreign scientists (probably a German and a Dutchman), became very angry with each other, and were almost exchanging blows, when Bernal, as chairman, rushed out to separate them, then went to the blackboard and demonstrated how each was right. 'He restored order and sanity, gave a brilliant, impressive performance.'[232]

In spring 1963, J. Sutton, professor of geology at Imperial College, in a lecture at Birkbeck mentioned some very old beach deposits present in north-west Scotland. Bernal was at the lecture, and at dinner afterwards asked Sutton if he had tried to calculate the maximum fetch (that is, the extent of open water to which these deposits might have been exposed). Following this, Bernal spoke about his own interest in the subject which was related to his work on possible invasion beaches. The conversation has remained in Sutton's mind because 'I was so struck by this example of his great breadth of interest in scientific subjects of all kinds, and the thoroughness with which he had gone into this branch of geology. Incidentally, the very fact that he had found time to come to a lecture organized by the Geology Department was, in itself, a comment on how widely he was prepared to range.'[233]

Crowther has no doubts that in public affairs Bernal's 'weaknesses were catastrophic. In ordinary social and political management, he was less than normally intelligent.' Crowther was involved with him very closely over a number of years in the peace movement and in the World Federation of Scientific Workers. Bernal was a very good chairman, but an impossible public figure. He never developed the qualities of a political Marxist like Lenin or Mao, who could handle people and Marxism harmoniously. Crowther thought that Bernal tended to ignore things he did not like, consequently was able to feel at home in incompatible situations.[234]

Hyman Levy thought that Bernal's peace efforts were a mistake. Julian Huxley remembered how, at the Wroclaw Congress of Intellectuals for Peace in 1948, which disillusioned many Western left-wingers because of the authoritarian political attitude of the Russian participants, as expressed in particular by Alexander Fadeyev, Bernal 'was surprised at the turn of events, but tried to restore our spirits by reassuring us that this was a harmless letting-off of fireworks, and that we would soon really discuss peace'.[235, 236]

Bernal's prime loyalty was to the Russians. When the political differences between them and the Chinese could no longer be hidden, these were made apparent in such bodies as the World Federation of Scientific Workers. At the Budapest meeting in 1965, Chu Pei Yuan abused the Russians. The WFSW president, Cecil Powell, closed the meeting, after 'leaning over backwards to accommodate the Chinese'.[237] The points raised by the Chinese were an accumulation of resentments that had begun to emerge in the 50s. But, according to Crowther, Bernal did not understand. In fact, for many years 'Bernal' was 'a dirty word' in China. This arose, in part, from what the Woosters described as his 'almost sycophantic attitude to the Russians'. It was that which prevented him from producing the *opinio conciliatrix*, for which he was well known and for which Joseph Needham so much admired him.

Stephen Spender kept a journal of a meeting of the Société Européenne de Culture (ECA) in Venice in March 1956. During a discussion on 'littérature engagée', Bernal said that although they were living at a time when life was being transformed by scientific achievement, writers were not revealing any awareness of that future. 'He said there had never been such a gap – not even in the 1890s – between the littleness of literature and the greatness of man's power and knowledge.'[238] Spender felt the force of that reproach, but he pointed out they were discussing 'in terms of knowledge what would only be real if discussed in terms of imagination'. After the meeting, Bernal said to him, 'You have me there.'

Again, Bernal, in reply to Ignazio Silone, said 'there was something in' the accusation of germ warfare conducted in Korea by the Americans. Spender commented he thought in meetings of this kind the issue became 'very confused if delegates from the West, without declaring themselves to be so, were communists.' Campagnolo, the head of the ECA, became greatly annoyed, and declared no one was a delegate representing anything. Each participant was simply a member of the ECA. Spender countered that 'it would be nice to invite a few people from countries behind the Iron Curtain who were anti-Communists'. He noted in his journal, 'Bernal did not reply but covered his face with his hands'.

At the showing, during the meeting, of an Italian anti-fascist film directed by Pasolini, Spender 'was curious to see how Bernal, sitting on my left, was reacting. So while an anti-fascist, who had been shot several times in the back, was being thrown by the fascists into the flames of his motorcycle . . . I stole a few glances at my colleague. His mouth hung open, he was breathing heavily and perspiring. From time to time he passed his hand over his forehead, at moments he shut his eyes unable to bear the sight of the pain on the screen.' Spender added, 'This, I thought, from a man who is so intent on the vision of socialist construction that he considers the death of thousands of people, slave labour, etc., as irrelevant.' Later, Spender asked Bernal how it was that Rakosi, the Hungarian, could rehabilitate Rajk, and remain in power? Bernal did not reply. 'Not answering is, in fact, part of Bernal's repertoire. . . . On the whole he simply ignores all subjective questions, only answering objective ones about things such as the world's population, education and science and the like.'

But, finally, Spender did succeed in involving Bernal in a

pointed discussion. Bernal said about Stalin, 'We seem to have made some very serious mistakes. I don't know how it happened, but it is bad.' Of the two systems in the world, he preferred the Communist. 'You have to think of the utter unnecessary misery and waste and lack of opportunity that exists in the world as it is at present,' Spender reports him as saying. 'What people fail to realize is that things don't have to be as they are.'

Spender was an ex-member of the Communist Party. This should be remembered when reading his strictures on Bernal. It coloured, also, the attitude of Silone, another ex-Communist, to Bernal during that meeting. Silone remembered 'an astonishing remark' by Bernal, whom he quoted as saying, 'In capitalist countries, culture suffers from the gulf that separates the common people from the higher forms of art – James Joyce, for instance, being read and understood only by a handful of initiates, while the masses are content with comic strips. On the other hand, I have seen for myself how successfully the gulf has been bridged in the socialist society of Russia, where kolkhoz workers, students, scullery hands, poets, scientists all read the same books, enjoy the same films and paintings – in short, share the same aesthetic values.' Silone asked the Soviet participants to explain how that was achieved. The novelist, Fedin, replied that in Russia they, too, have 'a division of cultures'. Further, 'we produce a great many books and films which have no artistic value and are put out solely for mass consumption'. There was an embarrassed silence. Silone concluded that the new relationship between the Russian people and art was a figment of Bernal's imagination. After another unpleasant exchange, Silone wrote, Bernal 'looked at me contemptuously with scorn in his eyes of the kind which the true believer reserves for the infidel'.[239]

Both Spender and Silone were typical of the left-wing intellectuals who stood against fascism in the 1920s and 30s. Their progress was on similar lines: membership of the Communist Party, followed by disillusionment, then embracing of a moderate socialism, becoming very personal and almost apolitical. They did not understand that the Soviet Union was really a world Bernal had invented when young, long before the 1917 revolution: it remained always for him his Utopia, thus it presented a reality of a special kind: the hardships, barely seen as possible injustices, were regarded as a price necessary to pay for an inevitable future of wellbeing.

Bernal spent three months in China in the autumn of 1954. He visited seven of the eleven major universities and some fourteen technical colleges, in most of which he gave lectures. Kathleen Lonsdale told a delightful story of how during her visit in 1955, some of her Chinese colleagues in Manchuria asked her, 'How far behind the West are we in our technology?' 'About twenty years,' she replied. The Chinese laughed heartily, and said, 'Splendid, we've caught up ten years in one year. Professor Bernal was here last year, and he told us we were thirty years behind!' He went to China again in October 1959 for the tenth anniversary celebrations. He arrived in Peking on 30 September feeling very tired. The following National Day was very hot, and he stood for hours in the crowds watching firework displays. A message was passed to him that Khrushchev wanted to see him. Bernal met him as the Russian leader was taking his leave of Chairman Mao. They exchanged a few words, and arranged to meet the next day. Bernal was then greeted by Mao, who asked about the book *Science in History*, and by Chou En-Lai. On 2 October he met Ho Chi Minh and Khrushchev. He heard, also, a choir consisting of 230 generals, all males, and one female general. He was astounded by the sight and sound. This was not surprising as he had no ear for music. I remember attending a concert with him in Budapest. The soprano had an excellent voice. He whispered to me, 'If she sings any louder I'll have to leave. I'm really in pain.' I was puzzled as to why music played no part in his imaginative life. He did not seem to have any aural difficulties, but music provided no splendour, no alternative world for him. Sir John Kendrew told me that in Cairo in 1941, he introduced Bernal, who was on a visit with Zuckerman to look at bomb damage, to the journalist, Bertha Gaster. She showed him around, and looked after him. He questioned the age of a mosque, and added, 'I know about everything, except sport and music.'[240] Soon after he had joined the Communist Party in 1923, he told Pirie that he was

studying football and cricket because he had Party instructions
that he must be able to converse with workers about the things
that interested them.

Kendrew, then twenty-four, was uncertain about what to
do after the war. He was a Cambridge graduate in chemistry,
and had taken a course which included some biochemistry.
He asked Bernal for advice. Bernal said, 'It's no use my trying
to get you into Birkbeck. As a Communist I find it very difficult
to get money.' He urged him to see Bragg at Cambridge, and
Bragg introduced him to Perutz. But, before that, in 1944,
Kendrew met Bernal in Ceylon at Mountbatten's headquarters
in Kandy. Mountbatten was Commander-in-Chief, South-
East Asia, and Kendrew was the scientific adviser to Mountbatten's Allied Air Commander-in-Chief. The Command had
a particular problem, on which Bernal was consulted. They
had run out of fragmentation bombs temporarily. What would
happen if they used depth charges, which gave a bigger bang?
Bernal worked out the impact effect with a slide rule. At a
trial, they went into a ditch nearby to observe, Bernal assuring
them they were far enough away. However, the explosion did
affect them. Bernal said, 'I think I must have got the decimal
point wrong.'[240]

Bernal was raised on the Holy Scriptures. He turned early
to Marxism, which he embraced with religious ardour. Pirie
believes that if Bernal had lived longer he would have returned
to Catholicism: he was still religious at Cambridge at the age
of twenty. (When Pirie told me this I asked him why he himself had not become a Communist? He replied, 'Because I'm
an atheist. I could not take on a religion.') Pirie recalled how
on a visit to Leningrad in 1931, on the second day the group
visited a cathedral reported to have religious services still
going on. Most of them just looked in to confirm that. John
Pilley and Bernal stayed on, apparently entranced by the
ritual. Bernal returned alone at midnight filled with 'a religious
ecstasy', inspired by what he had seen of religious revival in
the Soviet Union.[241]

Bernal did come to understand that the early Soviet ideas
on the planning of science, which so excited him in the
twenties, had to be reintroduced into the Soviet scene through

his writings and the works of others. The great originality which was released by the revolution was damped down under Stalin. In the natural sciences, on the occasion of his first visit in 1931, Bernal found that in spite of a well-developed morphological crystal physics, the most recent branch of X-ray crystallography did not exist. During his 1932 visit, he gave some lectures on this. He was, with N. V. Belov, the co-author and unofficial director of the first Soviet interpretations of the structure of certain complex crystals. But it was not until after 1945 that there was a real improvement in Soviet structural crystallography. However, he was sobered by the fact that when he looked out of a window in the skyscraper building which housed science there were shacks, still lived in, just next door. He was saddened visibly by the events of August 1968 when the Czechoslovak Academy of Sciences was closed by the military forces of the Warsaw Pact. The Russian handling of Dubček disturbed him more than the events of 1956 in Hungary, about which he had made representations to the Soviet authorities.

Was there in Bernal's last years the beginnings of an insightful disillusion? It is not possible to say, for he could not communicate physically, and his immediate interpreters, through whom alone his thoughts could be heard, were softcore supporters of the Kremlin's way of life. Is Pirie's comment valid: that is, that Bernal's scientific faith was basically a transposition of his Catholic faith, so that he remained always 'an anonymous Catholic'? It is true that religious feelings cannot be wished away, and although science makes dogmatic statements difficult to accept, faith invested remains always.

Early on the morning of 22 July 1963, Stanley Lenton, the chief technician in Bernal's department, was preparing to drive Bernal's new car to meet him at Victoria, London, air terminal at about 8 a.m. off a plane due to arrive at the airport from New York at 6.30. In the event, Lenton did not pick him up until 1.30 p.m. The plane had been delayed in New York, where Bernal had been obliged to sit in the aircraft on the tarmac for several hours. Moreover, the air conditioning was not working, and there was a heat wave. 'When I met him,' Lenton told me, 'he was not with it. He looked extremely tired. In addition, he had sat between two very fat people, whose flesh overflowed on to him. He was done in, and I had to guide him by the hand to the car. I took him to Birkbeck, where he had a cup of coffee and a sandwich, and then went into an Academic Board meeting until about 5 o'clock.' Harry Carlisle, who was at that meeting, recalls, 'He was very tired, and he looked it. I could see him nodding off from time to time. About half-way through, he asked me to take over. That night he had his first stroke.'

Bernal had insisted on going to the meeting because he was at that time most punctilious about fulfilling his college responsibilities. The challenge, led by John Lockwood, Master of Birkbeck, to show why crystallography should continue in the college, was at its most ferocious. A meeting of the Professoriate Committee on 8 November 1962 considered the report of a special committee appointed by the Professoriate on the future of crystallography at the college. Bernal argued, with the support of strong letters from Kathleen Lonsdale and J. Monteith Robertson, that if nothing was done to establish the future of crystallography at the college the staff would go, and the study itself would become vestigial. The committee recommended that a Chair of Crystallography should be established within the Department of Physics, and should continue there until the end of the current quinquennium 1962–1967, and to that the Academic Board gave assent. This was a victory for Bernal, and yet it was not. Certainly, those close to him at the time recognized that 'the victory' was won at great mental and physical cost.

The battle not only for survival, but also for development, consumed a great amount of time and energy. Bernal's colleagues were loyal and gave him unstinting support. A letter signed by C. J. Bullen, C. H. Carlisle, J. W. Jeffery, S. Lenton, and A. L. Mackay, dated 16 January 1963, revealed the degrading conditions under which they continued to do research and teaching. Their overriding complaint was 'the filth and squalor of the buildings, 21–22 Torrington Square'. Their second complaint was the overcrowding. The houses were built about 1825. No redecorating had been done since 1955. 'The dirt is such that any idea of carpets, pictures, or normal furniture, such as is to be found in all other departments, is ridiculous. Clothing very rapidly becomes dirty, and any papers or books cannot be left out for more than a short period without becoming soiled.' There were only two part-time cleaners to deal with forty rooms. 'The toilet on the third floor does not work, and is in an appalling state. There are frequent floods, through the floors and roof, both due to human agency and to the elements.' The chemistry department had their store of inflammable liquids under the wooden stairs, providing an unjustifiable fire risk. 'The dirt hinders research seriously in that it is impossible to do proper optical and electron microscopy without contamination. Micro-chemical work of all kinds is rendered impracticable.'

There is no doubt that the in-fighting and bickering of this internal battle added to the stresses which resulted in Bernal's first illness. It was in the early days of the Aldermaston marches (those remarkably vivid expressions of British anti-nuclear weapons feelings) that Bernal began to complain his feet were troubling him. The in-comment among his friends was that he was suffering from 'Pobble's disease'. (Edward Lear wrote, 'It's a fact the whole world knows, that Pobbles are happier without their toes.') Pirie had begun to observe that Bernal was becoming limp and heavy. On one march, he was hit accidentally in the spine by the pole of a banner, so badly that he was obliged to sit down for a time at the roadside to recover. He was out of circulation for two to three months after his first stroke, but a year later was cleared for driving.

I have a tragic memory of going to see him in Torrington Square, where he lay on a couch in a room on the ground floor. I began to talk to him about a number of things, but he was not responding. I said, 'You're very gloomy, aren't you?' He looked hard at me. 'Well, I am gloomy. I'm physically imprisoned by this useless body now, and my brain is still as active as ever, and I can't do the things I want to do.' On another occasion he said, 'Do you understand that death is only inevitable in practice, but not in principle. We must accept death because we have inherited bodies for which death is the normal end, but it is really an inherited resultant of biochemical facts and processes.' Then he paused, and added,

'However, life does not die. In a society there is immortality through continuity, but this cannot apply to the individual.'

Bernal's dying was six years long, a gradual descent from fullness to inactivity which tortured those who cherished him, as they saw him falling away in a general vascular degeneration. The hopes that followed his first stroke began to vanish after 1965, with his second, which left him paralysed down one side, and his speech began to fade. In the summer of that year, he and Margot Heinemann had a holiday at the Brumwell home at Feock in Cornwall. Whilst there, he dictated notes for an autobiography to the age of thirty-five. Thereafter, he appeared less frequently in public places in his wheelchair. He was incapable of self-movement and had to be lifted for everything. In May 1968, when he could no longer put pen to paper, Brumwell gave him an electric typewriter, which Bernal used to thank him for giving him his 'first link with the outside world'. In his few remaining years, he gradually became a cabbage, unable to communicate except through his devoted Anita Rimel: her guess was his statement. As she wrote to me in March 1970, 'It is difficult to get the kind of reply from Desmond now that one would previously have done. Anything requiring deep or prolonged thought soon distresses him and we have to break off.' He was looked after by his wife Eileen at their house in Albert Street in Camden Town, but he would be moved occasionally to be cared for by Margot Heinemann in Southwood Lane, Highgate. By the autumn of 1969 he had become so frail that it was not possible to move him further than a few feet from his bed into an armchair. How sad it was for those around him never to be able to know what his remarkable brain was producing in his physical wreckage. 'He always hoped that someone would dissect his brain to find out why he was so clever,' his doctor, Hugh Faulkner, told me.

His end came on 15 September 1971. He passed away peacefully, without pain and without knowledge of his approaching death. Perhaps he died willingly, mindful of Leonardo da Vinci's comment, which he knew well, 'May I be deprived of movement if I ever weary of being useful'. Certainly, those who loved him could not have wanted him to linger on in such wretchedness. Only colour television seemed to give him any pleasure. His will has a codicil dated 28 June 1971 which carries the words, 'The Testator being able to read but unable to write his name this will was signed by him with his mark in our presence and attested by us in the presence of him and of each other.' His beneficiaries were the immediate members of his family, and the National Hospital for Nervous Diseases, to whom he left his body 'for such anatomical examination as may be thought desirable'. The cadaver ended up at University Hospital Medical School, as the National Hospital does not have a department of anatomy recognized by the Anatomy Acts. On 18 July 1973, his remains were buried finally in the Battersea Cemetery, Lower Morden Lane, Morden, Surrey. There is no individual grave, but the location on the lawn is Section Y, Grave Space No. 35.

His family tree at his death was as follows:

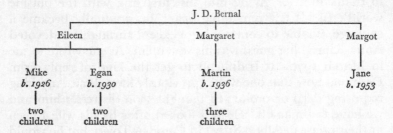

Tributes to him arrived from all over the world: a moving obituary in *The Times*, unsigned but written by Dorothy Hodgkin, expressed the general sense of loss. She was one of the speakers at a memorial meeting at the Mary Ward Hall in Tavistock Place, London, on 8 December 1971, at which the other speakers were Ivor Montagu, Brumwell, Romesh Chandra, general secretary of the World Council of Peace, John Gollan, general secretary of the CPGB, Burhop, and R. Arnott, European Secretary of UNA Youth. They represented his socio-political links, and the incredible amount of work he got through during his seven years, 1958–1965, as president of the World Peace Council. Montagu has 'vivid memories of Desmond arguing in a plane above Germany about the significance of the neolithic sites below; listening

rapt – without earphone translation – to the speech in Latin
of a Hungarian bishop; so exhausted after a conference he
could hardly drag one foot after another, but insisting on join-
ing the rest at a midnight ballet, or rising at the crack of dawn
rather than miss a worthwhile film or a view of the Picassos at
the Pushkin'.[242] On 24 January 1972, there was a memorial
meeting organized by Birkbeck College. Speakers included
Snow, Kendrew, Blackett, and Zuckerman. The last-named
caused a stir amongst those very close to Bernal by 'damning
him with faint praise', as one intimate put it.

Bernal's continuing influence is expressed in The Bernal
Lecture on some aspect of the social function of science given
triennially at the Royal Society, for which he provided an
endowment of £2000 in 1969; in the annual Birkbeck College
lecture, again on some aspect of the social impact of science;
and in a series of occasional lectures organized by the J. D.
Bernal Peace Library, whose books are housed in the Marx
Memorial Library at Clerkenwell Green, London, of which
he was president from 1952 to 1971. There are, also, Bernal
Memorial scholarships for research on some aspect of peace
established by national committees in a number of socialist
countries in Europe.

Bernal was a man whose achievements have an all-embracing freshness. The future was always with him. It presented
itself in many forms: the embrace of a woman; the urgent
entry into a problem; the temperature of the morning; a visit
to an art gallery; a scientific paper to be written or delivered;
a telegram from a world political leader; an appeal for a
signature against an injustice. And these different forms, which
reflected faithfully his passionate times, were all linked into
one pattern of understanding. He knew that this wide knowledge made life more complicated, but that was essentially
what being a human meant – to think rationally, and to define
and solve problems. His future was a rationally planned
economy, that was why he was a socialist. He went into death
having changed the framework of our times by opening paths
which for his colleagues had not existed, leading to avenues
still in process of development. It is due to him that we understand, to rephrase Aneurin Bevan, that the language of science

is priorities, that science is not neutral in that it is a key instrument in the hands of a ruling group, that the scientific community is not just a small elite but millions of scientific *workers*, that for scientists politics can no longer be regarded as an evil which they must shun, and that the new world of peace and love is within our hands for we have the means to realize it if we have the will to do so.

References

1 *Beginnings*

† This sign indicates quotations from Bernal, J. D. 'How I became a scientist' (sent to Boris Polevoi, USSR, 1954, for inclusion in a series entitled *Real Men of the Western World*).
‡ This sign indicates quotations from Kern, Elga (ed.), *Wegweiser in der Zeitwender*, Munchen/Basel, 1955, to which Bernal, J. D. contributed an autobiographical essay, 'Verantwortung und Verpflichtung der Wissenschaft', pp. 140–68.

1 Silone, Ignazio, *Emergency Exit*, London, 1969, p. 118.
2 Cellini, Benvenuto, *Memoirs*, London, 1906, p. 7.
3 Lynd, Robert, *Home Life in Ireland*, London, 1909, p. 105.
4 Lynd, p. 85.
5 Lynd, p. 255.
6 Snow, C. P., in Goldsmith, M., and Mackay, A. L. (ed.), *The Science of Science*, London, 1964, p. 20.
7 Bernal, J. D., *The Freedom of Necessity*, London, 1949, p. 170.
8 Wells, H. G., *Experiment in Autobiography*, London, 1934, p. 646.

2 *Development*

9 Shakespeare, *King Henry IV, Part 2*, 111, (i).
10 'Old Chrysanthemum', *New Statesman*, 6 March 1954.
11 Bernal, J. D., in comments to Kingsley Martin on proofs of article quoted in reference 10.
12 Snow, C. P., in Goldsmith, M., and Mackay, A. L. (ed.), *The Science of Science*, London, 1964, p. 21.
13 Isherwood, Christopher, *Lions and Shadows*, London, 1938, p. 73 f.

14 From 'As it seemed to us', *The New Yorker*, 41, 3 April 1965, p. 180.
15 *The Times* diary, London, 17 September 1971.
16 Montagu, Ivor, *The Youngest Son*, London, 1970, p. 184.
17 Snow, p. 21.
18 Homberger, Eric, *The Art of the Real*, London, 1977, p. 10.
19 Montagu, p. 196.
20 Bernal, J. D., 'The importance of symmetry in the solids and liquids', *Acta Physica*, Hungarian Academy of Sciences, VIII 3, 1958, pp. 269–76.
21 Ewald, P. P. (ed.), *Fifty Years of X-Ray Diffraction*, Utrecht, 1962, p. 375.
22 Noyes, Alfred, *Wizards*, in *Benn's Augustan Book of Modern Poets* (Noyes), London, 1931.
23 Bernal, J. D., 'William Thomas Astbury', *Royal Society Biographical Memoirs*, Vol. 9, Nov. 1963, p. 2.
24 Snow, p. 9.
25 Caroe, G. M., *William Henry Bragg, 1862–1952*, London, 1978, p. 176.
26 Ewald, p. 524.
27 Ewald, p. 524.
28 Caroe, p. 176.
29 Bernal, J. D., 'William Thomas Astbury'.
30 Caroe, p. 176.
31 Ewald, p. 523.
32 Ewald, p. 523.
33 Ewald, p. 525.
34 Snow, p. 24.

3 *Future Perfect*

35 Day Lewis, C., *Transitional Poem*, London 1928.
36 Wood, Neal, *Communism and British Intellectuals*, London, 1959, see particularly chapter V, 'Utopians of Science'.

4 *Soviet Challenge*

37 Strachey, John, *The Coming Struggle for Power*, London, 1932, p. 357.
38 Bernal, J. D., *The Freedom of Necessity*, London, 1949, p. 336.
39 Bukharin, N. I. and Preobrazhensky, E. A., *The ABC of Communism*, Moscow, 1921, London, 1924, and 1969.

40 From the Foreword to *Science at the Cross Roads*, London, 1924.
41 Needham, Dr Joseph, Foreword to *Science at the Cross Roads*, London, 1971, p. viii.
42 Bernal, p. 337.
43 Bernal, p. 338.
44 Bernal, p. 338.
45 Crowther, J. G., *Fifty Years with Science*, London, 1970, p. 78.
46 Crowther, p. 79.
47 Guest, Carmel Haden (ed.), *David Guest, a scientist fights for freedom (1911–1938)*, London, 1939, pp. 151, 512.
48 Crowther, p. 79.
49 Holmes, C., *Soviet Studies*, July, 1972, pp. 86–90.
50 Crowther, p. 86 f.
51 Cross and Hodge, *The Long Weekend*, London, p. 248.
52 Keynes, J. M., 'Democracy and efficiency', *New Statesman*, Vol. XVII, 28 January 1939, p. 122.
53 Snow, C. P. in Raymond, John (ed.), *The Baldwin Age*, London, 1960, p. 248.
54 Bernal, J. D. (as B.Sc.), 'British scientists and the world crisis', *Labour Monthly*, 1932, p. 702 f.
55 Gardiner, Margaret, 'Moscow winter 1934', *New Left Review*, 98, July–August 1976, p. 43 f.

5 Commitment Decade

56 Auden, W. H., 'The Witnesses' in *Collected Shorter Poems 1927–1957*, London, p. 63.
57 Snow, C. P., in private communication to G. P. Werskey.
58 Stevenson, John, *Social Conditions in Britain Between the Wars*, Harmondsworth, 1977, p. 225.
59 Varga, E., *The Great Crisis and Its Political Consequences*, London, 1934, p. 170.
60 Bernal, J. D., *Cambridge Left*, Winter 1933.
61 Bernal, J. D., *The Freedom of Necessity*, London, 1949, p. 348.
62 Harrow, Roy, *John Maynard Keynes*, Penguin.
63 Wood, Neal, *Communism and British Intellectuals*, London, 1959, p. 52.
64 Saville, John, 'May Day in 1937', in *Essays in Labour History 1918–1939* (ed. Briggs, Asa, and Saville, John), London, 1977.
65 *Britain Without Capitalists*, London, 1936, p. 407 f.
66 Fremlin, J. and R., Statement to author, January 1978 in Birmingham.

244 REFERENCES

67 Hogben, Lancelot, *Dangerous Thoughts*, London, 1939, p. 197.

6 *Blast and Counterblast*

68 Spender, Stephen, *The Still Centre*, London, 1935.
69 Bernal, J. D., Letter to Marcus Brumwell, January 1960.
70 Ashby, Eric, 'Science and anti-science', *Proc. Roy. Soc. London, B*, 178 (1971) 29–42.
71 Zuckerman, Solly, *From Apes to Warlords 1904–46*, London, 1978, p. 395.
72 *Scientific Worker*, October 1935, 79–80.
73 Werskey, G., 'Making socialists of scientists', *Radical Science Journal*. 1975, p. 61.
74 Wootton, Barbara, *A World I Never Made*, London, 1967, p. 58.
75 Bernal, J. D., *The Social Function of Science*, London, 1939, p. 412.
76 Hogben, Lancelot, *Dangerous Thoughts*, London, 1939, p. 24.
77 Baker, John R., 'Counterblast to Bernalism', *New Statesman*, 29 July 1939, pp. 174, 175.
78 Bernal, J. D., *New Statesman*, 5 August 1939, pp. 210, 211.
79 Bernal, J. D., *The Freedom of Necessity*, London, 1949, p. 125.
80 Baker, John R., *New Statesman*, 2 March 1940, p. 276.
81 Baker, John R., *The Scientific Life*, London, 1942, p. 7.
82 Polanyi, Michael, *The Logic of Liberty*, London, 1945, p. 69.
83 Meynell, Francis, *My Lives*, London, 1974, p. 203.
84 Thomas, Hugh, *John Strachey*, London, 1973, p. 127.
85 Waddington, C. H., *Behind Appearances*, Edinburgh, 1969, p. 58.
86 Waddington, p. 55.

7 *Days of Fulfilment*

87 Brecht, Bertolt, *Last Poems, 1953–1956*, edited by John Willett and Ralph Mannheim, London, 1976.
88 Bernal, J. D., *The Social Function of Science*, London, 1939, p. 165.
89 'X-ray', *The Communist*, Vol. 1, Nos. 3, 4, 5, April–June, 1927.
90 Burhop, E. H. S., in Goldsmith, M., and Mackay, A. L. (ed.), *The Science of Science*, London, 1964, p. 33.
91 Fremlin, J. H., Private communication, January 1978.
92 Zuckerman, S., *From Apes to Warlords, 1904–46*, London, 1978, p. 103.

93   Zuckerman, p. 113.
94   Snow, C. P., in Goldsmith and Mackay, p. 27.
95   Zuckerman, p. 131.
96   Zuckerman, p. 135.
97   'Quantitative study of total effects of air raids (Hull and Birmingham Survey).' Ministry of Home Security Research and Experiment Department. 2770. (8.4.1942).
98   Zuckerman, p. 143.
99   Clark, Ronald W., *Tizard*, London, 1965, p. 308.
100 Crowther, J. G. *et al.* (ed.), *Science and World Order*, Harmondsworth, 1942, p. 9.
101 Crowther, p. 30.
102 Crowther, pp. 31, 34, 35, 36, 37, 71.
103 *Nature*, 3800, pp. 150, 263
104 Jackson, W. C. F., *Overlord, Normandy*, London, 1944, p. 13.
105 Zuckerman, p. 88.
106 Jones, R. V., *Command and Complementarity*, Birkbeck College, 1973, p. 3.
107 Zuckerman, p. 158.
108 Zuckerman, p. 153.
109 Zuckerman, p. 157.
110 Fergusson, Bernard, *The Watery Maze*, London, 1961, p. 285.
111 Fergusson, p. 285.
112 Fergusson, p. 285.
113 Fergusson, p. 285.
114 Zuckerman, p. 26.
115 Snow, p. 28.
116 Hussey, Tom, letter to author dated 8 April 1979.
117 Jackson, p. 174.
118 Fergusson, p. 303.
119 Fergusson, p. 345
120 Lampe, David, *Pyke*, London, 1959, p. 128.
121 Lampe, p. 126.
122 Zuckerman, p. 158.
123 Lampe, p. 137.
124 Goodeve, Sir Charles, statement to author, April 1978 in London.
125 Lampe, p. 129.
126 Perutz, M., *Science News IX*, Harmondsworth, 1948, p. 141.
127 Zuckerman, p. 159.
128 Lampe, p. 146.
129 Lampe, p. 147.

130   Zuckerman, p. 161.
131   Zuckerman, p. 162.
132   Zuckerman, p. 164.
133   Zuckerman, p. 164.
134   Zuckerman, p. 266.
135   Snow, pp. 27, 28.

8 *Science Internationale*

136   Ehrenburg, I., *Post-war Years 1945–54*, London, 1966, p. 182.
137   Bernal, J. D., *Pilot Papers*, Vol. 1, No. 2, July 1946, p. 35.
138   Bernal, J. D., *In Memory of Paul Langevin*, London, 1947, p. 18.
139   WFSW, Summary report of the First Assembly, W72/49, p. 5.
140   FAS, *Public Interest Report*, Vol. 29, No. 9, November 1976, p. 1.
141   Goldsmith, Maurice, *Frédéric Joliot-Curie*, London, 1976, p. 177.
142   WSFW Report of the 11th Meeting of the Executive Council, W162/52 (report) p. 3.
143   Ehrenburg, p. 215.
144   Bernal, J. D., *World Without War*, London, 1958, p. 2.
145   Bernal, p. 284.
146   Bernal, J. D., *Science for a Developing World*, Prague, 1962, p. 131.
147   Bernal, J. D., *Scientific World*, 1966, No. 3, pp. 5–8.

9 *Science in Policy*

148   Farrington, Benjamin, *Francis Bacon*, London, 1951, p. 13.
149   Bernal, J. D., Trueman Wood Lecture, Royal Society of Arts, 16 May 1945.
150   Bernal, J. D., *The Builder*, 16 November 1945, p. 402.
151   Bernal, p. 402.
152   Werskey, Gary, 'Making socialists of scientists', *Radical Science Journal*, No. 2/3, 1975.
153   Goldsmith, Maurice, *Frédéric Joliot-Curie*, London, 1976, p. 64 f.

10 *Pursuit of the Possible*

154   Einstein, A., and Infeld, L., *The Evolution of Physics*, London, 1937.

155   Crowther, J. G., *Fifty Years with Science*, London, 1970, p. 110.

156   Olby, Robert, *Path to the Double Helix*, London, 1974, p. 251.

157   Olby, p. 252.

158   Weaver, W., 'Molecular biology: origin of the term', *Science*, 1970, pp. 170, 581–2.

159   Kohler, Robert E., 'The management of science: the experience of Warren Weaver and the Rockefeller Foundation Programme in molecular biology', *Minerva*, XIV, Autumn 1976, pp. 3, 279–306.

160   Astbury, W. H., 'Adventures in molecular biology', Harvey Soc. Series 46.

161   Woodger, H. H., in letter to J. Needham dated 16 June 1932, Needham Archives, Cambridge.

162   Bernal, J. D., *The Origin of Life*, London, 1963, p. ix.

163   Bernal, p. ix.

164   Bernal, J. D., 'Theoretical and mathematical biology', p. 97.

165   Bernal, J. D., 'The place of X-ray crystallography in the development of modern science', *Radiology*, 15, 1–12.

166   Snow, C. P., in Goldsmith, M., and Mackay, A. L. (ed.), *The Science of Science*, London, 1964, p. 19.

167   Bernal, J. D., Goldschmidt Memorial Lecture, London, 1948, p. 2.

168   Bernal, J. D., *Nature*, 133, 1934, p. 794.

169   Hodgkin, D. C. and Riley, D. P., 'Some ancient history of protein X-ray analysis' in Rich, A. and Davidson, N. (eds), *Structural Chemistry and Molecular Biology*, London, 1968, pp. 15–28.

170   Bernal, J. D., *The Origin of Life*, p. xi.

171   Bernal, J. D., 31st Guthrie Lecture, 1947.

172   Bernal, J. D., *The Physical Basis of Life*, London, 1951, p. 5.

173   Bernal, *The Physical Basis of Life*, p. 6.

174   Pirie, N. W., *New Biology*, 12, 1952, p. 106.

175   Bernal, J. D., *Science and Industry in the Nineteenth Century*, London, 1953, p. viii.

176   Ehrenburg, I., *Post-War Years, 1945–54*, London, 1966, p. 214.

177   Bernal, J. D., and Fowler, R. H., 'A theory of water and ions solution, with particular reference to hydrogen and hydroxyl

ions', *Journal of Chemical Physics*, Vol. 1, No. 8, August 1933, pp. 515–48.

178   Bernal, J. D., RI Lecture, 31 October 1958: *Proc. Roy. Instn.* 37, No. 118 (1959), p. 393.

179   Carlisle, H. E., Statement to author, February 1977, in London.

180   Bernal, J. D., and Fankuchen, I., *J. Gen. Physiol.* 25, 1941, pp. 111, 163.

181   Olby, p. 259.

182   Bernal, J. D., American Institute of Physics Archives.

183   Bernal, J. D., American Institute of Physics Archives.

184   Bernal, J. D., *Nature*, 203, 4948, 1964, 916–17.

185   Perutz, M., Statement to author, 17 July 1948, in Cambridge.

186   Perutz, M., *ibid*.

187   Perutz, M., 'The structure of large molecules', 1955, in Homberger, Eric *et al.*, *The Cambridge Mind*, London, 1970, p. 198.

188   Hodgkin, D. C., Unpublished paper, 'Crystallographic measurements and the structure of protein molecules as they are', 1978, p. 17.

189   Perutz, M., 'The structure of large molecules', p. 199.

190   Bernal, J. D., *Labour Monthly*, July 1968, p. 325.

191   Olby, p. 263.

192   Bernal, *Science and Industry in the Nineteenth Century*, p. 199.

193   Bernal, *Labour Monthly*, July 1968, p. 325.

194   Bernal, *Labour Monthly*, July 1968, p. 325.

195   Birbeck College, P. Dep. Cmt. Min. 7. (1960), pp. 7–12.

11   Sordid Affairs

196   Heinemann, Margot, *The Adventurers*, London, 1960.

197   British Association for the Advancement of Science (BAAS), Notes of Council meeting, 4 November 1949.

198   Crowther, J. G., Statement to author, March 1977, in London.

199   Lecourt, Dominique, *Proletarian Science*, London 1977, p. 40.

200   Lecourt, p. 54.

201   Popovsky, Mark, *New Scientist*.

202   Ashby, Eric, *Scientist in Russia*, Harmondsworth 1947, p. 106.

203   Bernal, J. D., *The Modern Quarterly*, 4, 1949, pp. 203–17.

204   Medvedev, Z., *Nature*, 286, 28 July 1977, p. 285.

205   Medvedev, *Nature*, p. 285.

12 *Science in History*

206 Donne, J., *Second Elegy*.
207 Ravetz, J. R., *Technology and Culture*, 3, 1972, p. 664.
208 *Voprosy Istorii Estestvoznaniya i Tekniki*, No. 6 (1958), pp. 72–150. This includes, also Bernal's closing words answering criticisms.
209 Medvedev, Zhores A., *The Rise and Fall of T. D. Lysenko*, New York, 1969, p. 135.
210 Bernal, J. D., *Modern Quarterly*, 8, 1953, p. 137.
211 Bernal, p. 137.

13 *Speculation and Holism*

212 Szent-Gyorgyi, Albert, *Bio-energetics*, London, 1957.
213 Good, I. J. (ed.), *The Scientist Speculates*, London 1962.
214 Bernal, J. D., in *The Scientist Speculates*, pp. 11–28. Subsequent quotations are from the same source.
215 Hodgson, J. L., *The Great God Waste*,
216 *Proc. R.S.A.*, Vol. 282, 1964, pp. 1–154. Subsequent quotations are from the same source.
217 Bernal, J. D., *The Social Function of Science*, London, 1939, p. 116.
218 Bernal, J. D., 'The transformation of scientific information: a user's analysis', International Conference on Scientific Information, Washington, 1958. *Proceedings*, 1959, I, 67–75. Washington, NAS–NRC.
219 Coblans, H., in Goldsmith, M., and Mackay, A. L. (ed.), *The Science of Science*, London, 1964, p. 101.

14 *Endings*

220 Scarfe, F., in Skelton, Robin (ed.), *Poetry of the Thirties*, Harmondsworth 1964, p. 84.
221 Swann, Brenda, in a talk with the author, 11 February 1977, in London.
222 Snow, C. P., *Public Affairs*, London 1971, pp. 188.
223 Crowther, J. G., *Fifty Years with Science*, London, 1970, p. 110.
224 Warner, Sir Frederick, in a talk with the author on 21 March 1977, in London.
225 Pauling, Peter, *New Scientist*, 31 May 1973, p. 558.
226 Brumwell, Marcus, in talks with the author over a number of years.

227 Jeger, Lena, 'The Professor's Picasso', in *Manchester Guardian*, 19 July 1960.

228 Wooster, Norah, in a talk with the author on 25 February 1977, in Cambridge.

229 Crowther, J. G., *The Cavendish Laboratory 1874–1974*, London, 1974, p. 312.

230 Crowther, *The Cavendish Laboratory*, p. 312.

231 Crowther, *The Cavendish Laboratory*, p. 282.

232 Goodeve, Sir Charles, in a talk with the author on 25 April 1978, in London.

233 Sutton, J., letter to the author dated 13 July 1978.

234 Crowther, J. G., in a talk with the author 4 March 1977, in London.

235 Huxley, Julian, *Memories II*, London, 1973, p. 63.

236 Goldsmith, Maurice, *Frédéric Joliot-Curie*, London, 1976, p. 185.

237 Powell, Cecil, in a talk with the author in 1965.

238 Spender, S., *The Thirties and After*, Harmondsworth 1978, p. 177.

239 Silone, Ignazio, *Emergency Exit*, London, 1969, pp. 189–90.

240 Kendrew, Sir John, in talks with the author in November 1977 and September 1978, in London and Athens.

241 Pirie, N. W., in a talk with the author in June 1978, in London.

242 I.M., 'Prof. J. D. Bernal', *The Times*, London, 13 October 1971.

Index